The Color of Hunger

The Color of Hunger

Race and Hunger in National and International Perspective

Edited by
DAVID L. L. SHIELDS

ROWMAN & LITTLEFIELD PUBLISHERS, INC.

ROWMAN & LITTLEFIELD PUBLISHERS, INC.

Published in the United States of America
by Rowman & Littlefield Publishers, Inc.
4720 Boston Way, Lanham, Maryland 20706

3 Henrietta Street
London WC2E 8LU, England

British Cataloging in Publication Information Available

Library of Congress Cataloging-in-Publication Data

The color of hunger : race and hunger in national and international perspective / David L.L. Shields, editor.
p. cm.
Includes index.
1. Food supply—Social aspects—Congresses. 2. Hunger—Social aspects—Congresses. 3. Racism—Congresses. 4. Poverty—Congresses. 5. Minorities—Congresses. I. Shields, David Lyle,
HD9000.6.C594 1995 363.8—dc20 94–46882 CIP

ISBN 0–8476–8004–5 (cloth : alk. paper)
ISBN 0–8476–8005–3 (pbk. : alk. paper)

Printed in the United States of America

™ The paper used in this publication meets the minimum requirements of American National Standard for Information Sciences—Permanence of Paper for Printed Library Materials, ANSI Z39.48–1964.

Contents

Preface vii

1. **What Color is Hunger?** 1
David L. L. Shields

2. **The Face of Hunger in America** 15
Michele Tingling-Clemmons

3. **Stereotypes of Africa in U.S. Hunger Appeals** 25
Mutombo Mpanya

4. **Race and Poverty in the Psychology of Prejudice** 35
David L. L. Shields

5. **Racism in Foreign Policy and Development Programs** 55
Percy Hintzen

6. **Multilateralism, Racism, and the Culture of Altruism** 71
Nazir Ahmad

7. **Getting at Hunger's Roots: The Legacy of Colonialism and Racism** 87
Kevin Danaher

8. **Indians, Land, and Poverty in Guatemala** 105
Beatriz Manz

9. **Sweetness and Death: The Legacy of Hunger in Northeast Brazil** 121
Nancy Scheper-Hughes

10. **Hunger Amidst Plenty: A South African Perspective** 145
Tshenuwani Simon Farisani

11. **Overcoming International Apartheid** 159
Dessima Williams

Index 173

About the Contributors 177

Preface

Some diseases strike certain racial/ethnic groups with greater frequency than others—sickle cell anemia, for example. Like these, hunger is not equally distributed among the racial families of the earth. Unlike racially tethered diseases, however, hunger is largely a political decision. The politics of race determine, in part, the victims of hunger. That is the thesis of this book.

From the outset, it is important to emphasize that neither the concept of race nor hunger is unambiguous. Nineteenth-century anthropologists were fond of discussing race, and racist assumptions often undergirded their theorizing. But contemporary social science has a much more tenuous relationship with the concept of race. For example, the *New Columbia Encyclopedia,* under *race,* says: "Even to classify humans on the basis of physiological traits is difficult, for the coexistence of races since earliest times through conquests, invasions, migrations, and mass deportations has produced a heterogeneous world population." While most contemporary anthropologists agree on the existence of distinct racial groups, the actual application of racial categorization is difficult, if not impossible.

Similarly, the concept of hunger is unavoidably imprecise. How deprived of nutrients (and which ones) must a person be to be classified as hungry? Estimates of the number of hungry in the world vary widely—from about 250 million to well over a billion—partly as a result of differing conceptualizations of hunger. How one chooses to define hunger is partially political, with those wanting to critique the status quo using relatively generous approaches that lead to high estimates of their numbers, while those with a conservative ideology adopt a more stringent approach. It is simply indisputable, however, that hunger exists on a catastrophic scale and that severe hunger is one of the world's main causes of premature death.

Hunger and race are both political terms. How one perceives their connection is also rooted to some extent in political ideology. Is the linkage between hunger and race due exclusively to the mediating role of social class? Some would argue so, though that is not the position adopted by most of the contributors to this volume. Most would agree with the statement by sociologist John Ogbu, "Where racial stratification coexists with class stratification, as in the U.S., there is compelling evidence that the racial stratification is more basic to social structure."[1] Still, even within the current work, different authors accent the role of class and race differently when analyzing hunger and its roots. Kevin Danaher, for example, emphasizes the role of class more than Percy Hintzen. Despite their diverse viewpoints, all would agree that race is neither irrelevant, on the one hand, nor all-defining, on the other.

Several of the chapters that appear in this book were first presented at a conference on "The Color of Hunger" on 25 April 1992, in Berkeley, California. The conference brought together researchers, activists, and public policy advocates to discuss the links between race and hunger. The conference presenters reflected a rich diversity in background, perspective, training, and—yes—racial/ethnic identity. Some of this diversity is preserved in this book, which encompasses a wide range of styles, methods, objectives, and viewpoints.

Although no amount of advance planning could have created such a fitting set of circumstances, the conference itself was sandwiched between poignant historical events that symbolized on the broader public stage what the conference was all about. Just four days prior, less than ten miles from the conference site, the first official state execution in twenty-five years occurred in California. Personally, I am opposed to the death penalty whether it is carried out quickly in the state's gas chamber against convicted felons or slowly in the state's ghettos against people guilty only of being poor. Premature death that culminates from many years of day-in and day-out inadequate nutrition is clearly cruel and unusual punishment, even if you believe the mythologies that blame the poor for their poverty. And it is no accident that both death row and poverty street are the nation's most effective affirmative action recruiters—"minority" candidates are certainly given easier admittance.

The days following the conference gave rise to two striking images that similarly underscored the importance of the conference theme. The first was largely a back-page story, despite its symbolic value. The second commanded banner headlines across the country.

- **Image 1**. A buried headline from Wednesday, 29 April, read, "Biggest Fund-Raiser Ever Nets $9 Million for GOP." The accompanying picture included then-President George Bush and several other people—mostly white, mostly men, all wealthy. Dinner that night cost a minimum of $1,500 per person, and among the crowd of about 4,000 were at most a small handful of people of color, though, as it turned out, the single largest donor was a Japanese businessman with a shady past clearly trying to buy political influence.

- **Image 2**. Fires everywhere. Riots. Looting. Anger unleashed. The day after Bush's elegant banquet for the powerful, the wealthy, and the mostly white came startling images from the flip-side of the American reality. In small Simi Valley, California, the Rodney King verdict was announced. Four Los Angeles police officers were acquitted of using excessive force against motorist Rodney King, despite the widely televised videotape of the vicious beating. Within hours of the jury's announcement, Los Angeles was in a state of emergency; violence, outrage, destruction, hatred, and revenge quickly swept across the country in a furious storm of protest.

The death toll from the rioting/revolting exceeded that which resulted from the Watts riots that occurred in Los Angeles in 1965, as did property damage. After the Watts riots, many studies were conducted that identified poverty and lack of opportunity as major precipitating factors to the racially charged rebellions. Twenty-seven years later, conditions were only worse, and South Central Los Angeles, as well as hundreds of similar communities throughout the country, was a tinderbox of anger ready to be set ablaze. People of color revolted against Rodney King justice, demanding that the justice of a different King—Martin Luther King, Jr.—be revitalized.

To comprehend the wrath and destruction that followed the King verdict, it is necessary to remember that the rebellion followed decades of maldistribution of resources: the mostly white rich have gotten steadily richer, while the dark inner cities have grown comparatively poorer. For example, from 1965 (the year of the Watts riots) to 1992 (when the Rodney King uprisings occurred), income for the wealthiest 1 percent of Americans rose by over 300 percent in constant dollars. By contrast, the average income of a black male rose by a stagnant 12 percent. The Center on Budget and Policy Priorities recently reported that "the gaps between both rich and poor families and between rich and middle class families are now wider than at any point since the Census Bureau began collecting these data in 1947."[2]

Politicians line up to express their support for the poor and to disavow racism, but both conservatives and liberals have found avenues away from responsibility for poverty and hunger. Conservative politicians escape responsibility by the now familiar refrains that blame the victims. The hungry are to blame because they are either too lazy, too dependent, or too lacking in appropriate values. On the other hand, more liberal politicians say that the tables of the hungry are bare because the cupboards of the federal budget are bare. Ironically, whether the federal coffers are empty seems to be a function of who is reaching in. During the recent recession, senators and representatives gave themselves a raise, and while we are being told that there is no money to be found, senators and representatives will receive more in retirement than most people earn over a lifetime. When the table is set from the cupboards of the federal budget, there are either a few scraps of meatloaf or a full-course lobster banquet, depending on who is coming to dinner.

I mentioned at the outset that "The Color of Hunger" conference roughly coincided with the first state execution in California in twenty-five years.

Death row, like the ghetto street, is disproportionately populated by people of color. But the fact that Robert Alton Harris, the man executed, was European American also reminds us that stereotypes are never reality. While poverty afflicts people of color disproportionately, the majority of the U.S. poor are white. Hunger, and the possibility of hunger, is a problem for all people, regardless of their racial/ethnic identity.

This book incorporates papers from "The Color of Hunger" conference, as well as a number of chapters that were added later. It opens with a chapter that summarizes the main contention of the book—that race and hunger are linked. It briefly discusses the connections between race and hunger, both domestically and internationally.

The second chapter presents a personal narrative about hunger and poverty among people of color in the United States, especially as they relate to the African American community. Michele Tingling-Clemmons offers an analysis of hunger in the United States that relies primarily on class analysis. But Tingling-Clemmons is clear that race makes an independent, though indirect, contribution to hunger. Deliberately or otherwise, the wealthy and powerful manipulate racial stereotypes to divide the poor against themselves and sever them from the dominant middle class. The success of this strategy enables a trickle-up economy as social programs, tax codes, and legislative priorities are all shaped for the aggrandizement of the power brokers.

Chapter 3 probes the use of racial and geographic stereotypes that U.S. hunger relief organizations use in their fund-raising appeals to the general public. In recent years, these organizations have made a significant effort to help the victims of famine in Africa. However, according to data collected by Mutombo Mpanya, the images they use and the messages they send tend to undermine the dignity of African peoples in the eyes of the American community, as well as in the eyes of the African recipients themselves.

To one extent or another, all the chapters of the book implicate stereotyping and prejudice as one cause—direct or indirect—of hunger. In chapter 4, I provide a psychological analysis of the link between racial prejudice and hunger. I maintain that the causes of hunger are primarily social-structural, but that it is important to understand the psychological underpinnings of those social-structural arrangements.

When world hunger is discussed in public forums, one often hears reference to U.S. development assistance programs. Do these help? In chapter 5, Percy Hintzen maintains that the development assistance programs of the United States, like its foreign policy more generally, are saturated with assumptions of white supremacy. People of color are disproportionately hungry in the world in part because of, rather than in spite of, food aid and development assistance from Europe and the United States.

In chapter 6, international agencies—development agencies and the international media, in particular—are the focus of analysis. At first glance, many international agencies seem to be models of multiculturalism and interracial cooperation. Most organizations within the United Nations, for example, have people of color in top leadership positions. Does this mean that there is no racism in these organizations? Not so, maintains Nazir Ahmad, himself once an employee of the World Bank. He suggests that subtle racism pervades these organizations, influencing their goals, methods, and world views. Rooted in white, Western experience, these perspectives work to the ultimate detriment of the hungry in the Third World.

Kevin Danaher, in chapter 7, presents an historical summary of the linkage between hunger and race in the contemporary world. Analyzing the evolution of colonialism, Danaher indicates how racial ideology greased the wheels of imperialism and its accompanying economic exploitation. During the decades and centuries of colonialism, the indigenous food production systems of much of Asia, Africa, and Latin America were systematically dismantled so that agriculture could be redirected to benefit the colonial centers of power. The legacy left by that era is a world where the color of hunger is everything but white.

Chapters 8-10 offer case studies of hunger and race in different national contexts. Beatriz Manz, an anthropologist who grew up in Chile, probes the intersections of race, culture, land policy, and politics in Guatemala where malnourishment among the Maya is prevalent. Further South, the Northeast of Brazil is the locus of Nancy Scheper-Hughes's probing and moving anthropological study of how the connection between race and hunger is entangled with the evolution of sugar production. Finally, T. Simon Farisani, a black South African, reflects on the legacies of apartheid in his native land, now that the seeds of a new, democratic society have been planted.

The book closes with a chapter by Dessima Williams, who urges all to enter the fight against global apartheid. Drawing lessons from Grenada, she ends the book on a note of hopefulness tempered by realism. She reminds us that history is open-ended; eradicating hunger is neither impossible nor guaranteed.

Let me conclude by offering thanks to the sponsors of "The Color of Hunger" conference, who made not only the conference but also this book possible: The Unitas Economic Justice Program, the Institute for Food and Development Policy, Oxfam America, Global Exchange, the California Rural Legal Assistance Foundation, the Center for Independent Living, the Overseas Development Network, the Berkeley Emergency Food Project, the University Religious Council, Cody's Books, the Blue Nile Restaurant, the Jobs for Homeless Consortium, Bread for the World, and the following organizations associated with the University of California at Berkeley: The Graduate Assembly, the CalCorps Program, STARCH, the American Indian Graduate

Student Association, the Coalition for Justice in Public Health, and the Association of Latin American and Spanish Undergraduates. Several individuals also deserve special recognition and thanks for their invaluable contributions to the conference and this volume: Sarah Bailey, Brenda Jo Light Bredemeier, Deborah Chu-Lan Lee, William Ng, and Sandra Nova.

Notes

1. J. U. Ogbu, "Class Stratification, Racial Stratification, and Schooling," in L. Weis (ed.), *Class, race, and gender in American education* (Albany: State University of New York Press, 1988): 163-182.

2. "Gap Between Rich and Poor Widest Ever Recorded," press release dated 30 July 1987, Center on Budget and Policy Priorities, Washington, D.C. The same trend toward an increasing gap between the wealthy and the nonwealthy has continued. See, for example, the 1991 report by the Center on Budget and Policy Priorities, "Selective Prosperity: Increasing Income Disparities Since 1977."

CHAPTER 1

What Color is Hunger?

David L. L. Shields

Imagine, for a moment, that unknown terrorists have detonated a crude atomic device in a large urban area. One hundred and fifty thousand people are instantly incinerated, about the same number that died in the bombing of Hiroshima. Moreover, immediate death is only the tip of the tragic iceberg; hundreds of thousands more are left with various debilitating injuries and diseases. Then, just three days later, a second atomic device is detonated spreading a similar level of death and destruction to another city. And then, after three more days, yet another bomb explodes.

Let us take our thought experiment one step further. Imagine, now, how the world would respond to such an unparalleled crisis. Picture the massive human and economic resources that would be marshaled. A monumental, highly coordinated, and unanimously supported effort would be galvanized, aimed at achieving one goal—finding and eliminating the terrorists. World attention would be riveted to the crisis; a massive public outcry would demand effective action and would settle for nothing less than an end to the threat. Politicians the world over would talk of little else.

The above scenario, of course, is fiction. Well, partly. It is fiction only with respect to the instrument of death and the quality of the response. In reality, hunger is the weapon, and it claims the lives of more people every three to four days than died in the bombing of Hiroshima. But the response to this massive crisis is shocking in its near nonexistence, leading some to refer to hunger as the "silent emergency." Despite its unparalleled infliction of misery, suffering, and death, hunger is calmly and dispassionately accepted within the citadels and cathedrals of power as simply part of the present world order.

It may be no exaggeration to say that the "Third World war" has started. It is against the Third World, a world populated predominately by people of color. The war has little to do with territorial conquest, but everything to do with control of resources—food among them. The victims, almost entirely civilians, are dying from hunger and disease rather than bombs.

The Causes of Hunger

Food is a basic human right. This is not just an ethical statement; it is codified in law and in international agreements. In fact, few human rights have been endorsed with such frequency and with so little dissent. Despite this striking consensus, hunger continues to claim more lives than AIDS, heart disease, cancer, car accidents, and drug overdose combined. Every year roughly 15 million children under the age of five die agonized, hunger-related deaths.[1]

Two ironies, unnerving in their implications, accompany the tragic statistics on hunger. The first is that, despite its unparalleled seriousness, hunger receives relatively little notice. Apart from an occasional story about an unusually large concentration of hunger in the form of a massive famine, little attention is given to the topic. Even famine stories, to gain column inches or TV sound bites, must exceed previous famine reports in the magnitude of calamity inflicted. Hunger is, indeed, a silent emergency. And this oddity is made yet more startling in light of the second, namely, that death due to hunger-related causes is totally unnecessary. Hunger—even starvation—occurs in a world with excess food. Unlike so many other causes of suffering and premature death, hunger does not require additional research to discover an antidote. We know the cure; we have the cure. We simply don't make it available. But why?

There are literally hundreds of books and articles dealing with hunger and its causes. Hunger is attributed to demographic trends, climatic variations, intrafamilial distributions of power and income, storage and transportation inadequacies, technological shortcomings of all manner, macroeconomic issues, and so on. The hunger literature is replete also with discussions of the relationship between hunger and other global problems, such as sexism, the environmental crisis, and a lack of accountable democratic structures. All of these analyses are quite useful and have something important to contribute to our understanding of hunger. Many of these themes are discussed in this book. But conspicuously absent from previous analyses of hunger is any explicit discussion of the link between hunger and race or racism. This is surprising, since connections are obvious.

Race and Hunger in the United States

There is little doubt that people of color are represented disproportionately among the hungry in the United States. Most everyone recognizes this fact. For example, an article in the *Western Journal of Medicine* reports that "the lower life expectancies for many ethnic minority groups and subgroups stem largely from their disproportionately higher rates of poverty, malnutrition, and poor health care."[2] Similarly, *Washington Post* staff writer Charles Trueheart, in reporting on the strange concept of "excess death" (a concept that refers, for example, to the 75,000 black Americans who die each year above the rate that would be expected if all things were otherwise equal), suggests that malnutrition is a significant contributor to the elevated death rates of minorities.[3]

Back in 1980, the Presidential Commission on World Hunger reported that hunger in the United States was considerably elevated among Native Americans and migrant and seasonal farm workers, most of whom are Hispanic.[4] Indeed, hunger among U.S. Indians is shockingly high and reflects a long and shameful history of the deliberate use of food as a weapon. Hunger was a primary contributor, for example, to the genocidal reduction of the native California Indian population, from about 150,000 to 20,000 in a matter of just three decades in the mid-1800s.[5] Today, even when the caloric intake of Indians is sufficiently high, other forms of chronic malnutrition contribute substantially to lower life expectancies and higher infant mortality rates—lasting tributes to the total disruption of the cultural and spiritual links that once tied these indigenous peoples to their primary food sources.

The irony of hunger among migrant farmworkers is brought home in a report by the advocacy group *Public Voice for Food and Health* which points out that despite their critical role in preparing and harvesting the nation's crops, these workers remain among the most impoverished and poorly nourished populations in the country. According to the data gathered, migrant farm workers, who have relatively low participation rates in such benefit programs as food stamps, despite their elgibility, suffer inordinately from malnutrition-linked health disorders.[6]

Though most everyone acknowledges a connection between hunger and race in the United States, supporting statistics are hard to come by. One study published in the *American Journal of Clinical Nutrition* reports that African Americans exhibit a higher prevalence of "clinical signs of nutrient deficiency" than European Americans,[7] but the correlation between "nutrient deficiencies" and undernutrition is less than perfect. Another study indicates that children of recent immigrants are particularly at risk for malnutrition, and a column in the influential British journal the *Economist* reports that black children in the United States suffer the effects of malnutrition at twice the rate of white children.[8] Andrew Hacker, author of *Two Nations: Black and White, Separate, Hostile, Unequal,* quotes a government report indicating that African Americans are two-and-a-half times more likely than European Americans to die of "nutritional deficiencies."[9] Finally, the Pediatric Nutrition Surveillance System (PNSS), established by the Centers for Disease Control, has reported that, among new clients of public programs designed to assist at-risk families, several ethnic groups—but especially Asian/Pacific Islanders—exhibited higher than expected rates of stunted growth and underweight among children less than five years of age.[10] Despite occasional reports such as these, no careful, systematic data is available on a nationwide basis regarding the prevalence of hunger among different racial/ethnic groups.

Hunger and Poverty

Since food flows to wherever there is money to purchase it, poverty provides one (admittedly imperfect) gauge of risk of hunger. With regard to poverty, there is broad consensus. Poverty afflicts people of color in greater proportion than European Americans. In the United States, about one of every nine white Americans is poor, but among African Americans and American Indians, one in three lives in poverty; one of every four Latino or Hispanic Americans is poor. Amplifying on the implications of these numbers, Steven Wineman writes:

> The most profound indignities in American life continue to be reserved for people of color. In vastly disproportionate numbers, people of color are more likely than any segment of white America to be poor, to be on welfare or suffer unemployment or hold the most menial jobs, to be in single parent families, and to suffer ill health. ...There is a clear relationship between poverty, to which people of color are disproportionately subject, and poor health...The life expectancy of Blacks is six years shorter than whites, and in 1977 the infant mortality rate among Blacks was 23.6 per 1,000 live births, compared to 12.3 per 1,000 live births among whites. Most government statistics give no information about Asians and Native Peoples and do not distinguish between different groups of "Hispanic origin"—which itself reflects and reinforces the denial of cultural diversity in our society.[11]

Yes, poverty is distributed unevenly, but some would argue that our welfare system keeps people from abject poverty and the food stamp program (and other nutritional support programs) keeps poor people from the necessity of living with hunger. Furthermore, the argument continues, African Americans and other racial minorities receive disproportionate benefit from federal assistance programs at public expense. Therefore, the argument concludes, no one should complain, no one must suffer extreme poverty, and certainly no one need go hungry, least of all the primary beneficiaries of a benevolent state—the racial/ethnic minorities of the United States.

This line of argument can be heard in the long-running welfare reform debate. It is largely a debate about race, though few admit this obvious reality. Welfare programs are stereotyped as "black" programs, and racial attitudes influence opinions about what should be done to fix an obviously ineffective system. But are welfare and other means-tested programs (i.e., programs requiring a low income to quality) primarily benefiting minorities? Contrary to stereotypes, the majority of welfare and food stamp households are white, and the number of persons in each household is relatively low.

Table 1 presents some of the basic numbers. Scanning the table, it is difficult to detect any clear pattern of discrimination or favoritism. Some may point out that African Americans comprise 32 percent of the recipients of cash assistance and 33 percent of the food stamp recipients, despite the fact that they make up only about 13 percent of the population. But these disparities simply reflect the higher concentration of African Americans in the poverty population. In reality, the chart, while accurate, may present an exaggerated view of the benefits distributed to people of color.

Table 1: 1991 Distribution of Poverty Population and Government Assistance

	% of Poverty Population	% of Means-Tested Cash Assistance Recipients	% of Food Stamp Recipients
European Americans	49.7	48	46
African Americans	28.7	32	33
Hispanic Americans	17.8	15	17
American Indians	01.3	01	01

Source: U.S. Census Bureau

First of all, included in the chart are only those assistance programs that are most often the subject of partisan debate—precisely those programs that are most used by racial minorities. As Marcus Alexis, a Northwestern University economist, points out, "'welfare' is the new code word that's being substituted for Willie Horton...Inner-city Blacks are viewed as chronically poor, heavily subsidized, irresponsible, high-cost individuals."[12] But these programs are by no means the totality of what the government doles out to individuals. The largest "welfare" program is Social Security, the recipients of which are 88 percent white. In fact, since blacks have a life expectancy almost a decade shorter than whites, African American workers spend decades paying into a system from which their white counterparts benefit for a significantly greater number of years.[13] Medicare is another large benefit program. Again, African Americans receive less benefit. Recent studies have revealed that blacks are less likely than whites to receive preventative care and costly operations.[14] Curiously, however, there are no complaints about a social security or medicare nobility paralleling the Reagan-era charges of "welfare queens."

Similar biases are present in numerous other government programs. Take, for example, disability benefits. The average African American beneficiary receives a little less than $6,800 and the average Hispanic slightly over $6,600. Compare those figures to the average for white recipients: $7,900.[15] Take aid to farmers. According to an analysis of records from 1980 to 1992, struggling black farmers receive an average of $21,000 less than white borrowers from the Farmers Home Administration loan program, a program intended to help save family farms.[16]

The reality is that while people of color are in greater need of economic assistance, they get less. Despite popular beliefs to the contrary, this is even true of the programs designed specifically to help those in poverty. The percentages in Table 1 refer only to numbers of participants, not to average benefits. The average black recipient of Aid to Families with Dependent Children, the main "welfare" program, receives more than $200 per year less than the average white recipient.[17] When all government transfer programs are combined, African Americans receive about 74 percent and Hispanics receive about 71 percent of what European Americans receive per capita.[18] Unfortunately, similar statistics are unavailable for other racial/ethnic minorities. Complicating the picture further, studies have indicated that eligible members of minority communities are less likely than majority group members to apply for assistance through programs such as food stamps,[19] and clients often perceive race discrimination at the local level.[20]

Poverty Is Not the Whole Story

If poverty is distributed differentially among different racial/ethnic groups, it is almost axiomatic that hunger also is not evenly distributed. But it is also important not to assume that the road from poverty data to conclusions about hunger is a straight one. Other factors enter the equation. Some people (and countries) can be quite poor in economic terms and still maintain adequate diets. Similarly, some people can have adequate financial resources but suffer hunger nonetheless, as a result of other factors that are more social, religious, or political in nature.

Food is not simply a nutrient resource; it has cultural significance. Mary Douglas makes this point in an edited volume that views hunger as a social problem more than a nutritional one.[21] In an opening chapter, she complains that students of nutrition too often perceive of hunger as a technical problem, "in the same terms as getting fodder into cattle troughs" (p. 2). The book, *Food in the Social Order*, presents field studies of three communities—the Oglala Sioux of the northern plains, black and white rural residents of North Carolina, and Italian Americans in a Philadelphia suburb. The finely nuanced essays portray how food is used symbolically in each population to reinforce ethnic identity and community norms. One implication is that hunger not only robs the physical body of nutrients, but also eats away at one's vital sources of communal wisdom and cultural heritage.

Different population groups derive their nutrients from different food sources, even if they live within the same general locale and have similar financial capabilities. The availability, price, and nutritional content of specific foods may differentially impact two racial/ethnic groups with identical socioeconomic status. There is an ecology to food consumption that situates it not only within economics, but also within cultural practices, familial patterns, and individual preferences.[22] This is one reason that Western relief workers are sometimes surprised to see food "squandered," even amidst severe hunger. The competition between individual nutritional needs and conventions of hospitality, culturally defined tastes, and community norms sometimes leads to odd paradoxes of hunger and waste, especially when food providers are insensitive to food culture. Having said that, it must again be emphasized that economic deprivation is clearly the single most important root of chronic or acute hunger.

Beyond Correlations

The race-hunger intersection can be viewed from other angles, as well. A web of subtle racist attitudes and racial/ethnic stereotypes among policy makers in the United States has affected the response to hunger, both domestically and internationally. As was noted some time ago by Linda Nilson, "political leaders tend to cast the poverty issue as primarily a problem of disadvantaged minority groups."[23] Certainly one reason why it is difficult to pass legislation that would increase funding for the food stamp program is its stigma as a "black" program.

There is also considerable evidence that racist assumptions about Third World peoples have influenced the evolution of foreign aid and development assistance programs (see chapter 5). Often these programs are premised on unspoken or unexamined assumptions about the lesser value, ignorance, distorted priorities, or corruption of recipient populations. These assumptions, in turn, promote a view that Third World countries should follow "our" example, often in contradiction to indigenous wisdom about such things as local agricultural conditions, social ecologies, and culturally appropriate organizational structures.

Race and hunger have occasionally come together in the arena of military adventurism. This was probably most clear during the recent famine in Somalia. The famine was due in large measure to a raging civil war that disrupted food production and distribution. As so often happens (despite international agreements to the contrary), food was used as a weapon of war. When the U.S. Marines invaded in late 1992, the ostensible reason was to secure famine-relief food distribution. But what were the unspoken reasons for the invasion? Barbara Ehrenreich, among others, observed that white racial chauvinism was no small contributor.[24] Nazir Ahmad (chapter 6) points out that, whatever the intent, the effect of the assault in Somalia buttressed a cultural belief in Western generosity and African need.

Hunger in Protest of Hunger

Since people of color have been disproportionately represented among the hungry, it is no surprise that they have sometimes drawn from their tragedies to design effective means of protest. Not only have people of color suffered hunger unjustly, they have used hunger to protest for justice. When the Clinton administration refused to let Haitian refugees enter the United States, for example, Randall Robinson, executive director of TransAfrica, launched a high profile twenty-seven day hunger strike that ended when the administration announced that it would stop the automatic forced repatriation of Haitian refugees.

One of the best examples of hunger fighting hunger was the protest fast of U.S. Representative Tony Hall, a member of the Congressional Black Caucus. He stopped eating on 3 April 1993 to protest the elimination of the House Select Committee on Hunger, which he chaired, and to raise consciousness in Congress of the plight of the 35,000 people who die of hunger-related causes daily.[25] His twenty-two day hunger strike gained widespread support, and thousands of letters from across the country poured into Congress. The result? Two new entities were created to continue and further the work of the Select Committee on Hunger—the Congressional Hunger Caucus and the independent Congressional Hunger Center. Both organizations have been instrumental in keeping the problem of hunger before the U.S. Congress and the media.

Race and Hunger: The Global Connections

The international link between hunger and racism is evident in the extent to which the international hunger line that divides the world into the well-fed and the hungry roughly corresponds to the international color line dividing Caucasian populations and peoples of color. Though it is, of course, a vast oversimplification, the countries of the Northern Hemisphere that are populated by Europeans or those of European descent tend also to be well-fed. In contrast, large numbers of people in the darker parts of the world suffer from undernutrition. This overlapping of the color and hunger lines is also evident in multiracial societies, such as the United States, South Africa, Brazil, and Guatemala, where hunger and racial disempowerment go hand-in-glove.

One of the primary historical roots of this pattern, of course, is colonialism and its legacies. This was recognized at the 1974 United Nations World Food Conference, which adopted the following language:

> The situation of the peoples affected by hunger and malnutrition arises from their historical circumstances, including social inequalities—including in many cases alien and colonial domination—foreign occupation, racial discrimination, apartheid and neocolonialism in all its forms, which continue to be among the greatest obstacles to the full emancipation and progress of the developing countries and all the peoples involved.[26]

Once again, what is evident to the casual observer is difficult to substantiate with reliable statistics. Most countries simply choose not to collect information about hunger among different racial or ethnic groups, and, if they do, they often do not wish to have such data distributed. When I first started working on this book, I consulted the *1991 CIA World Factbook* to obtain a list of countries where no single racial/ethnic group comprised more than 90 percent of the population. Having identified eighty-seven multiracial or multiethnic nations, I wrote to the Department of Health (by whatever name) within each requesting statistics about malnutrition and infant mortality (high infant mortality typically coincides with high rates of hunger) as distributed among the racial/ethnic groups. After one year, no statistics had been received.

Just as there are a few scattered reports about hunger among different racial/ethnic groups in the United States, so too there are a small number of studies reporting maldistributions of hunger among different racial/ethnic groups in selected countries. For example, in a study reported in the *Journal of the American Medical Association*, it was found that race was a significant predictor of malnutrition among rural children in Bolivia.[27] Hunger has been documented to be a significant problem for the Miskito Indians of Nicaragua,[28] the Mayan Indians of Mexico[29] and Guatemala,[30] and the aboriginal people of Australia.[31] In a study comparing four ethnic groups in Belize—the Maya, Mestizo, Creole, and black Caribbean—a clear rank-ordering of the racial/ethnic groups was observed, with, predictably, the Creole population being the best fed.[32]

Economics are again the primary determinants of who goes hungry. But again it is important to exercise some caution. Food is integral to culture, and the problems associated with malnutrition and hunger can be exacerbated by factors other than economics. For example, in a study of the Cree Indian and Inuit communities of northern Quebec, it was found that nutritional problems had more to do with disruptions in the traditional practices of hunting and fishing than with pure economics.[33] But as the Cree and Inuit food consumption patterns changed to accent more store purchased food, economics played an ever larger role in deciding who would go hungry.

Hunger, War, and Ethnicity

One of the most important forces creating a link between hunger and racial/ethnic status is war. The following excerpts from recent news stories indicate something of the scope of the problem:

> About 700,000 Burundians have fled the ethnic warfare in their central African country in recent months and are now suffering malnutrition and disease in refugee camps.
>
> *-The Financial Post, 22 December 1993*

> In Rwanda, Sierra Leone and Somalia, the DEC [the London-based Disasters Emergency Committee] says agricultural production has been affected by ethnic clashes. In Liberia, more than 150 children die daily due to malnutrition and a civil war that has compounded food deficit problems.
>
> *-InterPress Service, 13 December 1993*

> Thousands of ethnic Vietnamese who fled Khmer Rouge massacres in Cambodia have been stranded for months, suffering from disease and malnutrition, on a river border because the new government is blocking their return. ...Leiper [Director of the U.N. World Food Programme in Cambodia] said a U.N. survey had shown that about a quarter of the children living on the boats were suffering from malnutrition.
>
> *-Reuters Library Report, 19 August 1993*

> Donald Acheson, special WHO [World Health Organization] representative to the region, said Bosnian adults had lost an average of 30.86 pounds since ethnic fighting erupted in the former Yugoslav republic last March. ...WHO nutritionist Peter Hailey said many women were unable to breastfeed their infants because of poor nutrition and psychological trauma caused by the war.
>
> *-Reuters, 19 January 1993*

> Many child victims of Bhutan's "ethnic cleansing" policy have died

of malnutrition and disease in refugee camps.

-InterPress Service, 29 December 1992

A Sri Lankan church delegation called on Monday for a speedy end to ethnic violence in the north, saying shortages of food and medicine were causing an alarming increase in malnutrition.

-Reuters Library Report, 30 March 1992

One third of Tuareg children under five who have fled ethnic repression in Mali are facing serious malnutrition.

-Reuters Library Report, 6 March 1992

Food is often used as a weapon of war. And since racial/ethnic divisions are a major source of armed conflict, hunger often becomes divided along racial/ethnic lines. Hunger, of course, is not the only health problem associated with war. The juxtaposition in several of the above quotes of malnutrition and disease is no coincidence. Those who suffer from hunger are considerably more vulnerable to disease. Furthermore, in conflict situations, both food distribution and health care are readily disrupted. Racial and ethnic tensions are one of the primary roots of armed confict, and hunger is often both a deliberate instrument of war and an unintended consequence.[34] Though war is dwarfed by the legacies of colonialism as a distributor of hunger, it is certainly a significant contributor.

Summary

In this chapter, I have sketched some of the evidence that hunger and race are linked, both domestically and internationally. They are linked in the sense that disempowered people of color are disproportionately represented among the world's hungry, and they are linked in terms of people's attitudes, national policies, world history, and social programs. Other chapters in this volume will amplify some of the themes introduced here. To unlink race and hunger, we will need, among other things, to conceptualize malnutrition as a civil rights issue and racism as an issue of public health. We need to unite the constituencies of these concerns to mount a challenge to the status quo that works simultaneously on the attitudinal, legal, and political frontiers.

Notes

1. A good summary report on the extent of hunger is *Hunger 1990: A Report on the State of World Hunger.* Bread for the World: Institute on Hunger and Development, 1990.

2. Linda A. Wray, "Health Policy and Ethnic Diversity in Older Americans: Dissonance or Harmony," *Western Journal of Medicine* 157, no. 3 (September 1992): 357-361.

3. Charles Trueheart, "The Bias Most Deadly," the *Washington Post,* Tuesday, 30 October 1990, Sec. C, p. 7.

4. *Overcoming World Hunger: The Challenge Ahead: Report of the Presidential Commission on World Hunger,* Presidential Commission on World Hunger, March 1980.

5. William E. Coffer, "Genocide of the California Indians, With a Comparative Study of Other Minorities," *Indian History* 10, No. 2 (1987): 8-15. See, also, Julian Burger, *Report From the Frontier: The State of the World's Indigenous Peoples* (Atlantic Highlands, N.J.: Zed Books, 1987).

6. Jeffrey Shotland, *Full Fields, Empty Cupboards: The Nutritional Status of Migrant Farmworkers in America,* Public Voice for Food and Health, Washington, D.C., April 1989.

7. Eunsook T. Koh, "Clinical Signs Found in Association with Nutritional Deficiencies as Related to Race, Sex, and Age for Adults," *American Journal of Clinical Nutrition* 34, no. 8 (August 1981): 1562-1568.

8. "Less Equal than Others." The *Economist,* 14 February 1981, 23.

9. Andrew Hacker, *Two Nations: Black and White, Separate, Hostile, Unequal* (New York: Ballantine, 1992): 231.

10. Nutritional Status of Minority Children--United States, 1986. Centers for Disease Control, *Morbidity and Mortality Weekly Reports (MMWR)* 36, No. 23 (19 June, 1987): 366-369.

11. Steven Wineman, *The Politics of Human Services: A Radical Alternative to the Welfare State* (Boston: South End Press, 1984): 124-125.

12. Quoted in *Ebony,* (December 1992), 54.

13. "Public Aid," *Ebony,* (December 1992), 54.

14. George Anders, "Disparities in Medicare Access Found Among Poor, Black or Disabled Patients," *Wall Street Journal,* Wednesday, 2 November 1994.

15. This data is taken from *Current Population Reports, Consumer Income, Series P-60, No. 174: Money Income of Households, Families, and Persons in the United States, 1990,* table 34, p. 186.

16. Associated Press news release, Monday, 8 February 1993.

17. *Current Population Reports, Series P-60, No. 174,* table 34, p. 186.

18. Ibid. See also Vic Perlo, "Racism=Superprofits: Issues and Basic Facts," *Political Affairs* 71, No. 2 (February-March 1992): 1-6.

19. Gerald C. Wheelock & Gete Bekele, "Food Stamp and Health Program Participation Among Eligibles" (Paper presented at the Rural Sociological Society Meetings, 1985). See, also, Gerald C. Wheelock, & Gete Bekele, "Local Minority Status, Race and Age (Main Effects and Interactions) as Predictors of Food Stamp and Health Program Participation Among Eligibles" (Paper presented at the Southern Association of Agricultural Scientists, Rural Sociology Section, 1985).

20. Lina R. Godfrey, "Institutional Discrmination and Satisfaction with Specific Government Services by Heads of Households in Ten Southern States" (Paper presented at the Rural Sociological Society annual meeting, 1984).

21. Mary Douglas, ed., *Food in the Social Order: Studies of Food and Festivities in Three American Communities* (New York: Russell Sage Foundation, Basic Books, 1984).

22. It is also the case that racial/ethnic groups may not all respond the same when consuming similar foods. Kenneth and Virginia Kiple, for example, argue that the high death rates due to malnutrition among slave children were out of proportion to their caloric intake. The explanation may lie in different biological adaptations geared to survival in West Africa and North America. See "Slave Child Mortality: Some Nutritional Answers to a Perennial Puzzle," *Journal of Social History* 10, No. 3 (1977): 284-309.

23. L. Nilson, "Reconsidering Ideological Lines: Beliefs about Poverty in America," the *Sociological Quarterly* 22 (Autumn 1981): 547.

24. Barbara Ehrenreich, "Tis the Season for War," *Z Magazine*, February 1993, 6-7.

25. See, for example, Colman McCarthy, "Instead of Feeling Guilty about the Hungry, Hall Feels Responsible," *National Catholic Reporter* 29 (23 April 1993): 17.

26. World Food Conference, "The Declaration of the Eradication of Hunger and Malnutrition" (1974).

27. B. Wayne Blount, "Nutritional Status of Rural Bolivian Children," *Journal of the American Medical Association* 270, no. 5 (4 August 1993): 550-553.

28. M. R. Horner, "Malnutrition and Associated Factors in Preschool Miskito Indians in Nicaragua," *Ecology of food and nutrition* 10, no. 4 (August 1981): 213-220.

29. Curiel A. Avila, A. Chavez-Villasana, T. Shamah-Levy, H. Madrigal--Fritsch, et al., "Child Malnutrition in the Mexican Rural Environment: An Analysis of National Nutrition Surveys," *Salud Publica Mexicana* 35, no. 6 (November 1993): 658-666.

30. N. Hearst, "Infant Mortality in Guatemala: An Epidemiological Perspective," *International Journal of Epidemiology* 14, no. 4 (December 1985): 575-581.

31. F. J. Cameron, & G. D. Debelle, "Nutrition of Aboriginal Infants and Children in Murray Valley," *Medical Journal of Australia* 144, no. Supplement (23 June 1986): 5-8. See, also, M. Gracey, C. M. Anderson, & B. Brooks, "Low Birthweight and Impaired Growth to 5 Years in Australian Aborigines," *Australian Pediatric Journal* 25, no. 5 (October 1989): 279-283.

32. Carol L. Jenkins, "Demography and Malnutrition in Belize" (Paper presented at the annual meeting of the Illinois Sociological Association, 1981).

33. J. P. Thouez, A. Rannou, P. Foggin, et al., "The Other Face of Development: Native Population, Health Status and Indicators of Malnutrition--The Case of the Cree and Inuit of Northern Quebec," *Soc Sci Med* 29, no. 8 (1989): 965-974.

34. See Joanna Macrae and Anthony B. Zwi, "Food as an Instrument of War in Contemporary African Famines: A Review of the Evidence," *Disasters* 16, No. 4 (December 1992): 299-321.

CHAPTER 2

The Face of Hunger in America

Michele Tingling-Clemmons

Hunger is not racist and knows no color.[1]

Millions of children are hungry in the United States. According to the Community Childhood Hunger Identification Project (CCHIP),[2] a ground-breaking study by the Food Research and Action Center, 5.5 million children under the age of twelve—one in eight—are hungry in this country. More than 11 million—one in four—are either hungry or at risk of hunger.

These staggering numbers give only a small piece of the picture since the study, released 6 March 1991, surveyed only low-income families living in homes and apartments—not those doubled up, in shelters, or on the streets—and it was conducted prior to the big recession of the early 1990s. The numbers only reflect hunger among children under the age of twelve and in families with at least one school-aged child. What of the seniors, singles, and families with no children in residence? How well-off can a society be when one of every eight (a conservative figure at best—the real number is no doubt far higher) of its future leaders and workers is inadequately nourished during his or her developmental stages? What kind of a society will it be? More important for us to consider, what kind of a society is it now?

Hunger: A Function of Poverty

Can America survive without poverty? If the answer is no,

then in order for America to survive it must have some type of public benefits in order to regulate the victims of poverty, the permanent army of the unemployed. If the answer is yes, then everybody will have to be brought UP AND OUT OF POVERTY NOW! If we are to accomplish our overall goal of UP AND OUT OF POVERTY NOW, then we as victims of poverty need to know our history, know the objective processes, strategies and tactics to move forward. We are not fighting for a trickle down economy, but for society to work in our interests: to end homelessness, to provide health care and free and quality education for all, and to end hunger.[3]

-Annie Smart, National Anti-Hunger Coalition

Every thirty-five seconds a child is born into poverty in the United States. Children represent the poorest age group in the United States, a tragic distinction they have had for two decades.[4] According to U.S. Census Bureau data, 36.9 million Americans (14.5 percent) lived in poverty in 1992, up 3.3 million from 1990; this represents the highest number of people in poverty since the mid-1960s.[5] Furthermore, these figures do not reflect the full weight of our most recent recession, with its slowed economy, increased unemployment rate, rapidly expanded demand for food stamps and other public assistance programs, and budget crises at all levels of government. One in ten U.S. citizens is currently receiving food stamps,[6] and that number is, at present, continuing to escalate.

It is also important to remember that official poverty figures say little about poverty. They are based on the government's poverty line of $14,350 (Fiscal Year 1994) for a family of four. This definition of poverty, perhaps a statistical convenience, does not reflect "a realistic minimum level of living," according to Urban Institute economist Patricia Ruggles,[7] among others.

The poverty line was derived originally from information contained in a 1955 food-consumption survey that concluded that an average family spends about a third of its income on food. The Department of Agriculture then multiplied the price of a stringent, minimum-cost diet by three to establish the poverty line. Since its inception, the poverty line has been adjusted annually for inflation, but never for fallacies in the assumptions on which it is based. There have been "no adjustments...made for changes in consumption patterns, standards of living or even in the mix and relative prices of the goods and services that are available," notes Ruggles. Such an adjustment would have a major impact on the poverty line when one considers that today, two of every three low-income families spend almost half of their income on housing, while nearly half pay more than 70 percent, according to (prerecession) studies conducted by the Center on Budget and Policy Priorities in Washington, DC. Persons interviewed in a Gallup survey conducted in 1991 believed that a family of four needs $15,107 to have a minimum standard of living, an estimate similar to the recommendation of $15,000 made by Ruggles in congressional testimony.[8] At that time, the official poverty level for a family of four was only $12,700 per year.

Hunger is a condition of poverty. Living below the poverty line puts tremendous strains on a household budget, adversely affecting the ability to purchase a nutritionally adequate diet. Government surveys show that as income goes down, the nutritional adequacy of the diet goes down as well.[9]

The CCHIP study defined hunger as "the mental and physical condition that comes from not eating enough food due to insufficient economic, family or community resources."[10] While this is not a clinical definition, hunger is not a product of neatly controlled laboratory conditions, but of the real, oppressive, debilitating, dehumanizing, and thoroughly unnecessary poverty experienced by millions of families in our country.

Eight million Americans working full time receive food stamps...[11]

The Reagan-Bush policies were extremely successful during the 1980s in openly moving vast amounts of the country's resources away from the poor, near poor, and middle class to the rich. Between 1977 and 1988, according to *U.S. News and World Report,* the family income of the richest 10 percent of the population grew by 27 percent while that of the poorest 10 percent declined by over 10 percent.

At the same time that incomes of the poor were falling, government was cutting back on relevant assistance. Spending on programs that directly aided the poor dropped precipitously. Similarly, direct aid for cities fell by more than 60 percent, after inflation, during the decade; the federal share of city budgets plummeted from 18 percent in 1980 to 6.4 percent in 1990.[12] This has been accomplished through tax code changes and massive deregulation, best epitomized by the savings and loan fiasco, a multibillion dollar exercise in unrestrained greed that is being paid for by everyone except those who profited from it.

Racism: An Ideological Cover

The travesty of deepening poverty and shrinking assistance has been compounded and legitimized by an effective public "education" campaign that has kept the general public "ignorant, confused, and frightened"[13] about who is poor, where our resources have gone, and the source of the problems we face. One of the most effective tools in this campaign of misinformation has been racial innuendo.

The Reagan-Bush administrations countenanced and endorsed racism in various forums. They attacked affirmative action and the civil rights gains of the past thirty years; they promoted the idea that the majority of the poor and recipients of public benefits are people of color (a blatant lie, but one that makes the food stamp program unpopular by casting it as a black peoples' program); they played on the fears of whites by pushing the idea that blacks are dangerous through such highly publicized means as the Willie Horton campaign ads; and they failed to aggressively enforce the laws developed out of Southern blacks' struggle for voting rights.

Fraud, waste and abuse became watchwords of the Reagan-Bush years, used in almost every sentence mentioning food stamps. But the true fraud was in the actions of those administrations, which, with the consent and complicity of Congress, massively cut federal support of social service programs, such as welfare, health care, housing, employment, food stamps, and other nutrition support programs—all the while blaming so-called fraudulent recipients, whose greatest crime was simply being in need. The results of this image campaign can be seen a decade later in two highly symbolic events:

- A Los Angeles shopkeeper (Korean) shoots and kills an African American teenager in the back; she is fined $500 and assigned some hours of community service.

- An African American man in South Central Los Angeles is brutally beaten one night by police; the beating is captured on videotape and broadcast around the world. A mostly white suburban jury with no blacks finds the victim responsible for his broken skull/ribs/leg/ankle/arm and his own victimization; the batterers, therefore, are found not guilty.

America is the great melting pot...
Everybody on the bottom gets burned,
and the scum rises to the top...
-Charlie King, labor artist

To successfully pursue the divide and conquer plan,[14] the administration had to promote the idea that poverty and its associated ills—hunger, homelessness, unemployment, underemployment—were primarily or solely problems experienced by people of color. Contained in this deception is the implication that these conditions are somehow the result of character flaws among the victims and not a result of policies designed to benefit the rich at the expense of the rest—particularly the poor.

It is true that people of color, specifically African Americans, Native Americans, and Latinos, are disproportionately represented among the poor. But truth is gravely distorted when images of people of color are offered as standard fare in news broadcasts whenever stories pertain to poverty or hunger, homelessness or unemployment, welfare or food stamps, and teenage parents or fathers ignoring child support orders. Through such image management, whether deliberate or unintentional, whites have been steered away from thinking of poverty as their problem or, if they are in poverty, of uniting with others in the same situation. The impact of such image use becomes clearer still when one recognizes that illiterate and semi-literate adults in this country, who exist in unconscionable numbers, get a large share of their information from the broadcast media, particularly from television.

> The number of illiterate adults exceeds by 16 million the entire vote cast for the winner in the 1980 presidential contest. If even one third of all illiterates could vote, and read enough and do sufficient math to vote in their self-interest, Ronald Reagan would not likely have been chosen president.[15]

At the 1992 National Women's Survival Summit: Poor Women's Conference, "Under Attack But Fighting Back," a young white divorced mother on welfare from Marin County, California (a very wealthy area), testified that she had believed she was to blame for her situation until the day she arrived at the Summit and found that she was but one of millions of poor women in this country struggling to survive. This deception not only deters persons in poverty from organizing in their own behalf, but also effectively builds on the racism institutionalized in our economy and uses the perceptions perpetrated to justify government policies at all levels that criminally gut human services programs.

Civil Rights: The Unfinished Agenda

> The refusal to acknowledge those who are our sons or daughters, brothers, sisters, neighbors, fellow citizens, or former students, but whom we have relegated to statistical oblivion, holds some dangers that a sane society would not ignore. Societal denial of the crime by which it lives demonstrates political ineptitude and ethical betrayal; but it also tells us of that civic price that goes before a fall.[16]

Civil rights struggles of the 1960s are often trivialized as African Americans fighting for the right to sit next to whites in schools, department stores, lunch counters, bathroom stalls, buses, and trains. It truth, that was a largely irrelevant side effect. The true goal of the struggle was for decent living conditions and quality education for African American children; the right to eat, sleep, or sit wherever there were facilities (whether white people were there or not), whenever one chose, without being forced to search for one marked "Coloreds Only." The goal was to share in the benefits of this society—jobs, food, clothing, shelter—without having to document and reaffirm one's worth at every turn. The goal was to affirm that one was deserving of the decent quality of life that people of color have been systematically denied in this country ever since Europeans docked here, cheated and stole the land from the natives, and kidnapped architects, healers, teachers, leaders, scientists, artisans and other humans from Africa to build and develop it for them. This was at the core of the civil rights struggle. As Savina Martin stated at the first National Survival Summit, "Up and Out of Poverty Now," "We are the sons and the sisters and the brothers, grandchildren, nieces and nephews of the people who built this country and this is ours! We have a right to enjoy its fruits." Not only are African Americans the real source of wealth in this land, we are descended from the first humans, those who created civilization, writing, art, literature, science, medicine, culture, and cities.

Naming the Culprit

> An analysis of the first 5,000 arrests from all over the city revealed that 52 percent were poor Latinos, 10 percent whites and only 38 percent blacks.[17]
>
> "I'm from South Central L.A. and when the rebellion hit, not only were we angry, but it was the end of the month and didn't nobody have no money. So I went grocery 'shopping' and I'm glad, because my kids were hungry..."[18]
>
> -Reports on the 1992 Los Angeles uprising

The struggle to end hunger cannot be won if the conditions and basis for it—mo' profit, mo' profit, mo' profit—remain the guiding ethos of our economy, i.e., capitalism. But the struggle can and certainly must be engaged. Malcolm X stated the view of the victims of this economy—the hungry, the homeless, the oppressed, those who realize that they have nothing to lose by fighting back—when he said, *"By any means necessary."*

A look at the statistics of who actually participated in the April 1992 uprising in Los Angeles (as opposed to those who were the alleged "rioters" in news sound bites) should sound a warning bell for all thinking persons in this country. The oppression that people of color have faced in this country, the oppression that some workers and leftist organizations have tried to point out affect everyone, threatens the entire social spectrum and fabric. As long as anyone is hungry, homeless, or without other resources that are necessary to ensure more than bare survival (particularly in a country that flaunts its wealth as this one does), no one is safe from their just rage—or from finding themselves in the same dire circumstances.

Pastor Martin Niemoller died recently, but his words ring particularly true, and those who think themselves comfortable and safe would do well to pay heed to them and to remember that none are immune:

> In Germany, first they came for the Communists and I didn't speak up because I wasn't a Communist. Next they came for the Jews and I didn't speak up because I wasn't a Jew. Then they came for the

> trade unionists and I didn't speak up because I wasn't a trade unionist. Next they came for the Catholics and I didn't speak up because I was a Protestant. Then they came for me—and by that time there was no one left to speak up.

There are many who are made uncomfortable when the source of hunger is named directly—our economic system of capitalism, which puts profits before people. But avoiding the truth does not make it any less true. Unrestrained capitalism kills; it starves; and, yes, it undernourishes people of color disproportionately. Making this identification engenders fear, and struggling to change the status quo can amplify subtle fear into outright fright, because the brutality that is routinely reserved for those at the bottom of our economy can be turned against any who fight back; recall Denmark Vesey, John Brown, Geronimo, Sandino, Albert Parsons, Fannie Lou Hamer, Malcolm X, Martin Luther King, Jr., Medgar Evers, Leonard Peltier—and the list goes on. But anything worthwhile involves a risk. And the struggle is truly over our minds, hearts, bodies, and futures.

To move forward, we must remember our past. Just as knowledge about the African origins of humankind, culture, and civilization is liberating for persons of African descent (in reality all of us—but some are closer to the original than others), understanding about how real social change in our country has occurred is liberating for working people. It has occurred through struggles led by the disempowered themselves. This country was organized in the interests of white males of property. What was not in their interest had to be secured through struggle. The right to vote for everyone else (non-property-owning white males, women, slaves, and natives), social security, unemployment compensation, the eight-hour day, public education, the right to organize into unions, the minimum wage, and so on, were won by ordinary people organizing to change the status quo into something far more acceptable and just.

> Those who profess to love freedom and yet deprecate agitation are those who want crops without plowing up the ground. They want rain without the thunder and lightning. They want the ocean without the roar of its mighty waters. This struggle may be a moral one, or it may be physical, but it must be a struggle. Power concedes nothing without a demand. It never did, and never will.
>
> -Frederick Douglass, 1857

While the number of all children under six in the U.S. population remained relatively stable between 1968 and 1987, the number of poor children under six increased by 35 percent, according to the National Center for Children in Poverty.[19] One of every four children is born into poverty; one of every two black children and two of every five Hispanic children under six live in poverty, according to the most recent U.S. census data. Yet our leaders still try to maintain that we are the greatest country in the world. According to what or whom? Ask the woman on welfare who is penalized dollar for dollar if she tries to work her way off. Ask the union member who strikes to retain his health benefits but finds that exercising this right makes him ineligible for food stamps to feed his family. Ask the child who cries at the end of the school year because she will miss the school meals and for whom (because the summer food program only serves 16.2 percent of the low-income children who get school lunches during the year) summer vacation means hunger. Ask the family that cleans offices and earns so little that, despite being able to get food stamps, they must go back to a shelter after work. Ask the veteran who lost a limb "being all that he could be" for his country and now finds himself destitute and living on the streets after the parades are over. Ask the divorced mother whose food stamps run out after two and a half weeks, whose school board has refused to approve a school breakfast program, and who gets notes from the principal the week before standardized test day (on the results of which *his* performance is based) reminding her to make sure her child has a "hearty nutritious breakfast." Ask the mother who is denied prenatal care because she has no health insurance and no money, who watches her baby die before reaching the age of one. It is people such as these who, to my mind, define this country's greatness (or lack thereof) and on whom this country's future rests.

Racism *is* a public health problem that must be addressed. It *is* a key factor in determining the limits of one's circumstances and in determining who is poor, who is hungry, who is forced to do without a decent quality of life. As a victim, I do not diminish its importance in the least. But it is primarily a tool used to cloud the real struggle that goes on in this country—between the haves and the have-nots, the rich and the poor, those who produce the wealth and those who expropriate it. The struggle has many fronts, but they are all part of the same struggle. To effectively engage in the struggle for justice and win it, we must always keep our "eyes on the prize:"

I am the poor white, fooled and pushed apart,
I am the Negro bearing slavery's scars.
I am the red man driven from the land,
I am the immigrant clutching the hope I seek-
And finding only the same old stupid plan
Of dog eat dog, of mighty crush the weak.

O, let America be America again-
The land that never has been yet-
And yet must be-
The land where *every* man [sic] is free.

The land that's **mine**-
The poor man's, Indian's, Negro's, **ME**-
Who made America,
Whose sweat and blood, whose faith and pain,
Whose hand at the foundry, whose plow in the rain,
Must bring back our mighty dream again.

O, yes,
I say it plain,
America never was America to me,
And yet I swear this oath-
America **will** be!

-Langston Hughes, "This Mighty Dream"

Notes

1. Jose Mendevil, "What Columbus Day Means to Me," *Red Nations Movement*, January/February, 1992.

2. *Community Childhood Hunger Identification Project, A Survey of Childhood Hunger in the United States* (Washington, D.C.: Food Research and Action Center, March 1991), i.

3. "Which Way Welfare Rights?" *Voices from the Front* (Philadelphia, PA, April 1992), 2.

4. *Hunger in the United States* (Washington, D.C.: Food Research and Action Center, December 1993), 2.

5. Ibid., 3.

6. Ibid., 1-2.

7. "Studies Expose Destructive Myths About U.S. Poverty," *Community Change*, Issue 11, Fall/Winter 1992 (Washington, D.C.: Center for Community Change) 1.

8. Ibid., 1-2.

9. Ibid.

10. Op.cit., *Community Childhood Hunger Identification Project*, 2.

11. Becky Gallatin, Office for Church in Society, United Church of Christ, remarks at Interfaith/Impact Briefing, during introduction of workshop on childhood hunger, Washington, D.C., 7 April 1992.

12. "The War Against the Poor," *The New York Times*, p. A28, 8 May 1992.

13. Rick Tingling-Clemmons, personal communication with author, March 1991.

14. Utilizing the principle of divide and conquer along racial lines has its origins in the early days of this country's formation, when the powers that be were careful to highlight distinctions between white indentured servants and enslaved blacks to keep them from joining forces. This practice continues today as a standard employer strategy to combat union organizing efforts in the South, and has been institutionalized in many other areas as well.

15. Jonathan Kozol, *Illiterate America* (New York: Doubleday, 1985), p. 23.

16. Ibid., xvii.

17. Mike Davis, "In L.A., Burning All Illusions," *The Nation*, 1 June 1992, 243.

18. Anonymous mother testifying at People's Tribunal, National Women's Survival Summit, Poor Women's Conference, Oakland, California, 30 May 1992.

19. School of Public Health, Columbia University, New York, 1990, 15.

CHAPTER 3

Stereotypes of Africa in U.S. Hunger Appeals

Mutombo Mpanya

One night in 1981, while stopped in Denver, Colorado, on my way across country, I happened to see on television some very dramatic images of hunger in the Sudan. The short piece, sponsored by a hunger organization headquartered in the United States, ended with a captivating image: a glamorous movie star holding an emaciated child; standing beside them was a missionary who urged viewers to send in money to save the fragile lives of tortured children.

As an African, I had mixed feelings about what I had just seen. On the one hand, I was heartened that this organization cared enough about starving people in the distant land of Sudan to try to help. On the other hand, the way in which contributions to support that help were solicited seemed to diminish the dignity and individuality of the hunger victims.

By 1984, images of starvation had become common in the media, and the role of international hunger organizations in African famine relief had intensified. I began to ask myself how U.S.-based hunger organizations, as a community, represented Africa to their constituencies. I worried that, in the case of Africa, images of starvation and decay would reinforce old geographic and racial stereotypes, rather than help open Western minds to the realities and complexities of the African continent.

The Hunger Appeal Survey

To determine whether my concerns were based in reality, I conducted a survey. I gathered data from U.S.-based hunger organizations, including appeal letters, advertisements, magazines, news articles, annual reports, special field reports, and videotapes. The materials were collected from more than twenty-five agencies between 1984 and 1989. Most of the materials were designed for fund-raising; they asked implicitly or explicitly for monetary support for their African work. The data base contained videos, pictures, and texts that described African hunger victims, the context in which they lived, and the work the agency did with respect to the hunger situation.

The method I used to analyze the survey was content analysis. I counted and classified the descriptive words used to refer to Africa and the African people. To check my interpretations, I also designed a brief questionnaire that was given to a self-selected group of people throughout the United States who identified themselves as having a particular interest in Africa. After filling out the questionnaire, respondents were asked to participate in an in-depth group discussion about their perceptions of Africa.

In the materials I collected from hunger organizations, the issues most frequently discussed were emergency related: famine, drought, and civil war. Many of these problems were presented as simple and solvable, rather than complex and intractable. The major causes of the calamities were not explained in depth. The practical solutions offered were monetary support, the provision of technology, and education of the local people.

The results of the content analysis formed a clear pattern. In short, there were very few positive characterizations of Africa and the African people. There were exceptions, however. Two flyers described Africans as people who worked together and had a sense of human solidarity. In three cases, Africans were referred to as hard workers. One agency told the story of a crippled Ethiopian woman who saved her family through hard work and her skill as a weaver. Two agencies suggested in their flyers that some African governments made efforts to meet the health and nutritional needs of their people. In a few videos, attempts were made to show the diversity and complexity of Africa, and in some cases countries were described as potentially rich. Though the relationship between war and hunger was rarely directly exposed, some connections, such as the effects of war on the situation in Mozambique, were pointed out. In several cases, Africans were shown speaking for themselves and teaching each other. But these positive characterizations made up only a small fragment of the materials examined. The bulk of the images were negative.

Both the African continent itself and its people were described negatively as Table 1 illustrates. Africa was presented as the most endangered continent on earth, with unlivable conditions and the lowest quality of life in the world.

Table 1:
Descriptors of Africa from the Private Voluntary Organization Flyers: Groupings

Descriptors					
Countries				People	
Physical	Social	Economic	Political	Psychological	Biological
• drought	• minimal health service	• poor agricultural policies	• politically complex	• ignorance	• killed
• sand	• small health stations	• unrealized potential	• constant war	• irresponsibility	• tortured
• wind	• medical disasters		• continual terror	• vulnerability	• maimed
• uncertain rainfall	• populous		• turmoil	• incapability	• victimized
• cyclones	• great cultural heritage		• chaos	• ability to adapt	• starving
• floods	• unlivable conditions		• civil strife	• anguished	• perpetual death
• vagaries of climate				• suffering disintegration	• shortest life expectancy
• large, diverse terrain				• desperate	• highest infant mortality
• decay				• hopelessness	• widespread hunger
• cursed				• unsuccessfully eking a living	
• stricken					
• adverse conditions					

The Africa depicted had unavoidable potential for disaster. Countries seemed to be constantly at war, in the midst of turmoil and chaos. At times, the descriptions of the African people took on a primitive, savage quality, as when it was told that some people in Mozambique subsisted on leaves and wore clothes made of grain sacks and tree bark.

Reading the hunger organizations' flyers, one is left with the overall impression that Africans lead miserable lives; that they are needy, displaced, nomadic, or homeless people; that they are starving, weak, and frail; and that they lack technical knowledge and do not take the initiative to solve their own problems. These images of Africans are images of a people who are not the artisans of their own destinies and who are ultimately irresponsible and inept.

Photographs in hunger organization flyers suggested passivity on the part of Africans. About 20 percent of the subjects pictured were sitting down; close to 25 percent were pictures in which Africans were receiving something from an aid worker; another 10 percent were smiling children. Most of the photographs suggested distance from the subject; only 8 percent were close-ups. In videotapes and films, Africans generally were not shown speaking for themselves. With incredibly few exceptions, the narrators and hunger experts were Western white males. African women were shown as beasts of burden, always bending with a hoe or carrying a heavy load. Most of the material suffered from over-generalizations, whereby the black starving child of Ethiopia became the symbol of an entire continent.

The questionnaire and group discussion data reinforced the findings of the content analysis conducted on the hunger organizations' materials. More than 60 percent of the respondents agreed that, in their minds, Africa was associated with coups, corruption, starvation, and warfare. Close to 52 percent of respondents thought that, due to poor nutrition, most African children were less intelligent than American children.

In short, both the content analysis and survey results suggest that hunger organizations promote a generally negative, stereotypic image of Africa. This does not mean, however, that the publicity materials lacked a positive side. While the image of Africa was, for the most part, belittling, the hunger agencies portrayed themselves with descriptions and images that were quite positive. Agencies presented themselves as playing an important role in providing solutions to hunger and other community development issues. They, readers or viewers were encouraged to believe, provided African countries with needed resources and expertise; they worked hard and were committed to action; they were successful in their efforts; they were helpers who had witnessed the suffering of the African people and had become a voice for the voiceless.

Hunger Organizations in Africa: A Brief History

Before commenting further on the survey results, it is helpful to place the issue of negative African stereotyping in historic context. The problematic representation of Africa is not new in the Western world. In fact, it is as old as Western culture itself. In Greece, Rome, and among the Christians of the Middle Ages, black Africans, represented as savages with low social status, were depicted as slaves, domestics, comic dwarfs, singers, dancers, acrobats, soldiers, and mercenaries. In many Christian depictions of the Passion of Christ, the executioner is a black African. A black slave, Simone of Cyrene, carries Jesus's cross.

A countertrend of images, however, was also present in the classical age as an undercurrent. Greeks, Romans, and Hellenistic Alexandrians used the image of the black African to represent prestige, beauty, and human fulfillment. Africans were associated with fertility, as in the black goddesses "Isis the Black" and the "Black Madonna." The black Magi held prestige and knowledge, and Homer chose Ethiopia as the ideal place for the Banquets of the Gods.[1]

More recently, in the eighteenth and nineteenth centuries, British intellectuals, scientists, and colonial officers described Africans to the British public as inferior beings. The black African was portrayed as mentally limited and culturally deprived (see chapters 5 and 7). While Africa was associated with the wealth of gold, spices, and ivory, it was commonly held that these riches caused laziness. The continent was often talked about in terms of intolerable heat, monstrous animals, and strange diseases.

The literary writers who created the image of the noble savage—cheerful, peace-loving, and hospitable—understood that, though noble, the savage remained inferior. Even Christian humanitarians who opposed slavery and sought to help Africans as fellow human beings often saw Africans as the cursed sons of Ham, the fallen people. These perceptions were shared by most Europeans well into the beginning of the twentieth century.[2]

Politically and economically, the historical image of Africa may be related to Western exploitative interests. Belief in the inferiority of the African played an indispensable ideological role. If the black continent is savage, imperialism can call itself civilizing. Overall, the reasons behind the negative portrayals of Africa always have had more to do with the stereotyper's interest in Africa than with the reality of Africa itself.

Hunger Organizations and Negative Stereotyping

What we call hunger organizations belong to a group of organizations called PVOs, or private voluntary organizations. They are nongovernmental in nature and rely heavily on grants and voluntary private contributions for funding. Many PVOs do development work; others provide famine relief; some do both.

Hunger relief organizations have been in Africa for hundreds of years. At the time of the Portuguese explorations of Africa in the sixteenth century, church agencies already existed to help local populations. In the Kingdom of Congo, for example, the agencies concerned themselves with issues of health and education, as well as food production and evangelization. In Ghana, they worked in agriculture, producing cotton and coffee. These organizations also engaged in business and sometimes worked directly under a European government. In the nations of Liberia and Sierra Leone, private organizations took former slaves as refugees. In the nineteenth century, a community called Freetown, populated mostly by freed slaves, was formed in Kenya. Church organizations, which helped the community with food production, maintained a political administration over it.

Today, there are about 600 private voluntary organizations in the United States, close to 300 of them have hunger and aid programs in Africa. This represents about 3,000 projects in diverse areas, including food production and disaster relief. These organizations have inherited a legacy of negative stereotyping and have, in turn, often added to it. In the wake of the African food crisis of 1984, the image of Africa in the popular mind was still one of backwardness. Politically, Africa was associated with corrupt leaders—Bokasa, Idi Amin, Dada, and Mobutu. Africans were now starving people, international beggars, waiting—bowl in hand on a parched earth—for salvation to come from the outside.

The Hunger Survey: Discussion

Given that only about thirty hunger organizations were selected for study, and due to the self-selected nature of the individuals surveyed, it is fair to ask whether my results reflect an accurate picture of images portrayed through hunger appeals and whether those images reflect broader views among the U.S. public. The hunger survey was a preliminary investigation and, admittedly, not a scientifically rigorous study. Still, there are reasons to believe in its essential veracity.

Hunger organizations are not homogeneous. They vary in size, financial resources, strategies and philosophy, and specific interests. The organizations featured in the survey were not chosen randomly, but according to the likely influence they had on the American public's perceptions of Africa and its people. I deliberately focused on the largest and most visible of the hunger organizations. Similarly, the self-selected individuals surveyed were considered acceptable on the assumption that if those with an interest in Africa harbored negative images, those with little or no knowledge of the continent would do worse. If the results are not a precise reflection of the images portrayed or perceived, they nevertheless provide us with strong indications of the general motifs in common use.

Though any representation of a diverse continent will be limited, one should ask to what extent the images of Africa projected by hunger organizations reflect those images by which African societies wish to be known. In

Kenya, for example, people have worked around the idea of *Harambee*—or "pulling together." In Tanzania, *Ujamaa*—or "familihood" has been a unifying concept. In other countries, similar mottos or slogans represent the guiding idea around which the society works. With the exception of one or two flyers that mentioned African solidarity, most of the materials made no attempt to represent Africans to the U.S. public in a way that included African self-images.

The problems emanating from negative media images of Africa and the African people are not limited to their impact on the Western audience. As U.S. and European footage of African hunger is broadcast in African countries—as it often is—Africans come to see themselves through the eyes of Westerners. When U.S.-based hunger organizations try to sell images of African need to their domestic market, those same images invariably work their way into African media, shaping African self-understanding. The more-or-less positive and nationalistic self-images of local solidarity and a lively people are being slowly eroded by the Western image of starvation and decay. A new struggle has arisen in the African mind, the struggle for a positive and self-created self-image. Because of the dominance of the Western world and its global media technology, Africans are increasingly likely to internalize the negative stereotypes.

One of the most critical questions that must be asked is why hunger organizations—organizations ostensibly concerned with the promotion of human dignity and self-determination—use negative, often racist, stereotyping in their appeals. Why are race and hunger linked in this way?

For some agencies, the negative depiction of Africa may be related to an attempt to be objective. They provide the U.S. public with negative descriptions on the grounds that this is what they themselves witnessed in a specific region. However, this benign explanation calls for closer scrutiny. The issue is not simply one of objectivity, but also of fairness, and the two are not unrelated. When providing an image of Africa that applies to less than 10 percent of the African reality, one should—in the interest of both objectivity and fairness—give the audience a sense of the context in which these images are applicable. With so many existing stereotypes of Africa, objectivity should mean tackling those biased images rather than reinforcing and adding to them. Hunger organizations could work toward exposing these stereotypes and toward a sense of balance and real objectivity.

It is often argued that people give with their hearts and not with their heads. Some hunger organizations may employ negative images of Africa in the belief that such images evoke human sympathy and paternalism more readily than do positive images and, thus, generate more income for the agency. There is probably some truth to this claim. But it is questionable whether money and emergency resources are what is most needed. In the last three decades, billions of dollars have been spent, but the situation is deteriorating. It could even be argued that the more aid money that is transferred to

Africa, the worse the situation becomes, especially if the money creates large debts or exaggerated impressions of a charitable white, Western world.

During the 1984 Ethiopian food crisis, most of the affected population died before emergency food arrived. Of the survivors, many succumbed during the 1987 famine, to which Western response was much weaker. It is not clear that emergency resources and money are viable long-term solutions to the problems in Africa.

Perhaps the most fundamental reason why hunger organizations use the negative African image is to place it in opposition to their own image. Unlike the Africans they seek to save, the agencies portray themselves as highly responsible and diligent. The agencies' personnel, mostly of European descent, are portrayed as dedicated and hard-working; they have the technical competence to improve the livelihood of the African people; they work efficiently and effectively under very difficult African conditions. This polarity of negative African and positive organizational images—images often intentionally or unintentionally pitting black African hunger against white Western affluence—while unfounded in reality, does serve a practical purpose. Many managers of U.S. hunger organizations apparently feel they must create positive institutional images to elicit support from the Western public and that this is best done by way of contrast. The images of Africans and those of the hunger organization are symmetrical: if the African is weak, the agency is strong, and so forth. The question then arises, to what extent have these agencies created Africa in their own counterimage?

If it is true that the image of self and other are socially constructed, an organization could reasonably put forth an image of Africa and an image of self that would promote understanding and cooperation. These images would not only be more fair, but also likely more accurate, bringing the Western world closer to an understanding of African hunger problems. While emphasizing similarities and projecting images of Africans as fellow human beings, differences need not be ignored or glossed over, but recognized for what they are.

Let me conclude on a personal note. I grew up in a village of 1,000 people in Tshikapa, Zaire. There were no soldiers, policemen, prisons, or criminals. Everyone had enough food to eat; there were no beggars. Children, elders, and sick people were all taken care of by their families. People grew their own food, built their own homes, and created their own arts and entertainment. Of course, my village was not Korem in Ethiopia, or any other village, but this image of peace and self-sufficiency is as valid and real an image of Africa as any other.

Notes

1. Jean Vercouter, et al., *The Image of the Black in Western Art, 2 vols.* (Cambridge, Mass.: Harvard University Press, 1976).

2. Philip D. Curtin, *The Image of Africa, British Ideas and Action 1780-1850* (Madison, Wis.: University of Wisconsin Press, 1961).

CHAPTER 4

Race and Poverty in the Psychology of Prejudice

David L. L. Shields

> There was here a Nazi extermination camp between July 1942 and August 1943. More than 800,000 Jews from Poland, USSR, Yugoslavia, Czechoslovakia, Bulgaria, Austria, France, Belgium and Greece were murdered. On 2 August 1943, the prisoners organized an armed revolt which was crushed in blood by the Nazi hangmen.

These stark and startling words are inscribed in stone near the small village of Treblinka in Poland. They stand testimony to the brutality that emanates from the topic of this chapter—prejudice. It is a gruesome reality, but more tragic yet is the fact that the same inscription, with only minor modification, could be placed most anywhere on earth. The current rate of extermination by hunger exceeds that which occurred in the Nazi camp referred to in the quote above. And most of those who die are people of color.

My discussion of the interplay between race and class in the psychology of prejudice is not meant to imply that such monumental social problems as racism, hunger, homelessness, and poverty can be reduced to issues resolvable at the level of individual psychology. Hunger is not a charity issue to be solved by diminishing people's prejudices and increasing their compassion. Racism is not just about attitudes. Hunger and racism are justice issues, and adequate responses will involve major social, economic, political, and legal changes far more than changes at the level of the individual psyche.

Why, then, a chapter on prejudice in a book on race and hunger? The reason is simple. Despite the systemic nature of these problems, it is people who design, support, and maintain social systems, and individual prejudices and structural inequalities reinforce one another. While social transformation will come primarily from the power of victims' revolts, cooperation from at least a minority of those in privileged groups is also essential. If allies are to be recruited for the effort to stamp out hunger and racism, and if opponents are to be understood, then an analysis of individual psychology needs to complement an analysis of social structures. If we are to move beyond preaching to the choir, we need to understand how widely shared racial prejudices sustain the prevailing ideologies that justify hunger.

Just as racism and hunger intersect historically and geopolitically, so do they intersect within the psyche of most who reside in the dominant class of the so-called First World. To amplify this point, the chapter is divided into two main sections. The first provides a summary of the psychology of prejudice. The second section explicitly links racial prejudice to problems of poverty and hunger, both domestic and international.

The Psychology of Prejudice

In this first section, five basic questions are used as scaffolding to construct a model of the psychology of prejudice: What is the psychological structure of prejudice? What are the main cognitive, affective, and behavioral characteristics of prejudice? Why are prejudices resistant to change? How are they learned? And, finally, who are the prejudiced?

What is the Psychological Structure of Prejudice?

All prejudices share a common underlying psychological structure that has been designated *hierarchical dualism* (Shields, 1986). In brief, prejudice builds on the nearly universal human tendency to *dualize* experience, that is, to perceive reality as consisting of opposite or opposing forces, categories, or principles. For example, to understand hot, we pair it with cold. Some dualisms, such as hot and cold, are simply descriptive. But many dualisms are value-laden: one side of the dualism is valued, the other disvalued. When prejudice is manifest, the disvalued sides of value-laden dualisms are used to generate negative stereotypes of targeted out-groups, and the positive sides of the dualisms are used to generate images of one's own group.

To better understand these propositions, it is helpful to reflect on the cognitive maps we employ to understand reality. It often has been observed that the human mind perceives the world through a set of culturally defined dualisms. Among the most common dualisms in Western culture are the following pairs:

mind	/	body
spirit	/	matter
masculine	/	feminine
active	/	passive
rational	/	emotional
autonomous	/	dependent
strong	/	weak
clean	/	dirty
competitive	/	cooperative
white	/	black
success	/	failure
win	/	lose

In the popular mind, the poles of each dualism are perceived as opposites. In reality, however, this is something of a simplification, as the poles of the dualisms define ends of spectrums of overlapping possibility rather than bipolar, mutually exclusive alternatives. Dualisms such as these, all of which are of the value-laden variety, are influential in how we perceive and understand people. To understand the characteristics of people, we employ the socially available categories of thought, such as the above dualisms. Since opposites do not easily exist together, it is commonly believed that a person will naturally exhibit characteristics of one pole, but not the other. For example, a person can be a "mind" person (e.g., a scientist or a professor) or a "body" person (e.g., an athlete or a construction worker), but rarely both. A person can be either level-headed (i.e., rational) or emotional (i.e., irrational), but the two are thought to be in opposition. If one is masculine, then one cannot be feminine. A person can be independent or dependent, but not both simultaneously. And so on.

As noted before, these dualisms are not simply descriptive. Through the influence of culture and socialization, we come to embrace one pole of each dualistic pair as more valuable than the other pole. In our culture, masculinity is valued over femininity, activity over passivity, and so on. Stated in yet another way, the dualisms elaborated above have come to be associated with the three basic value dualisms:

the moral dualism:	good (or right)	/	evil (or wrong)
the knowledge dualism:	true	/	false
the aesthetic dualism:	beautiful	/	ugly

We are now in position to describe the psychological structuring of all forms of prejudice. All prejudices feed off prevalent cultural dualisms to generate stereotypes of an out-group. The negative pole of prevalent dualistic pairs is used to generate negative generalizations (stereotypes) that are applied to all members of a targeted group. For example, the mind/body dualism underlies the belief that blacks are naturally better athletes, but worse students, that they are hypersexual, but cognitive underachievers.

While the negative pole of dualisms is projected onto the outgroup, the positive side is used to stereotype the characteristics of one's own group. European Americans, for example, tend to claim rationality, morality, autonomy, and the like for themselves.

Because diverse forms of prejudice share a similar psychological structure, it is not surprising to find that a person who has a strong prejudice against one group is more likely to have prejudices against other groups (Bierly, 1985; Ray & Lovejoy, 1986).

What Are the Cognitive, Affective, and Behavioral Characteristics of Prejudice?

The word prejudice is derived from the term prejudge. Prejudice involves a judgment formed before and with indifference to the attainment of adequate information. As one aphorism states, "Prejudice is a vagrant opinion without visible means of support." The noted prejudice researcher Thomas Pettigrew (1982:3) defines it as "an antipathy accompanied by a faulty generalization. It may be felt or expressed. It may be directed toward a group as a whole, or toward an individual because he or she is a member of that group." Prejudice is a complex phenomenon with cognitive, affective, and behavioral dimensions. An elaboration on the following four points will help us better understand the dynamics of prejudice:

1. *Affectively, prejudice incorporates an unfounded dislike for groups and their members.*

Prejudice has a strong affective component. A prejudiced person has a negative affective response to the targeted out-group. The source of the negative affect is a topic of considerable controversy, the details of which need not concern us here. Suffice it to say that prejudice often works as a salve for unresolved emotional turmoils. Within the psychology of prejudice, inner difficulties are confused with outer realities. By externalizing the internal source of affective discomfort, the individual gains an illusory feeling of control over the problem. For example, if a person is apprehensive about his own professional competence, he may repress his true feelings and transform them into an attack on affirmative action programs.

One major affective source of prejudice is the pervasive human need for positive self-regard. People want to feel good about themselves. By providing denigrated "straw" comparison groups, prejudice provides a vehicle for enhancing self-esteem.

The affective dimension of prejudice is, without doubt, one of its most important components. Unfortunately, affects are notoriously difficult to quantify and study. It is difficult to reliably determine, for example, if one person feels more or less strongly about an issue than another or in a qualitatively different manner. Thus, many prejudice researchers, while acknowledging the importance of affect, focus their attention elsewhere (cf. Apostle, Glock, Piazza, & Suelzle, 1983).

2. *Cognitively, prejudice is exemplified in stereotypic thinking.*

Prejudicial thinking involves perceiving social groups through stereotypes. To an extent, however, the formation of stereotypes is inevitable. Stereotypes are one product of a normal and necessary cognitive process. With prejudice-based stereotypes, however, the underlying cognitive process is amplified and systematically distorted as a consequence of the affective dimension of prejudice. To elaborate on these points, let us look at the cognitive processes we use to make sense of the world.

Every moment our brains are bombarded with hundreds of sensations. To reduce the stimuli to manageable proportion, we organize sensory input into meaningful categories, or what Piaget called schemes (Piaget, 1936/1963). While mental categories enable us to decipher meaning from experience, they carry two disadvantages. Categorization requires that a considerable portion of the available stimuli be tossed into our mental junk drawer. A great deal of potential information is necessarily and unconsciously ignored. Second, there is a natural and universal tendency to conclude that objects included within a category are more alike than objects perceived as belonging to different categories. For example, if I categorize people into racial/ethnic groups, I will tend to maximize what the people *within* one racial/ethnic group have in common and minimize what people *across* racial/ethnic groups have in common. Stated in psychological jargon, the cognitive act of categorization invariably produces an *accentuation effect* such that similarities within categories and dissimilarities across categories are overemphasized (Tajfel, 1984).

In prejudicial thinking, experience is categorized to accord with the antipathy felt toward an out-group. The prejudiced person's attention is highly focused on people's race, gender, class, or other parameter of group difference, and the perceiver is likely to overestimate the similarities of people belonging to the same categorized groups and underestimate the ways in which people in different groups are alike. Furthermore, the group to which one believes oneself to belong is invariably used as a focal category around which other person categories are designed. The combination of a salient self-categorization system with the inevitability of the accentuation effect creates a clear gulf between the "we" and the "they."

When the prejudiced person uses salient, undifferentiated categories to think of out-groups, we speak of stereotypes. Stereotypes, which can be defined as preconceived and oversimplified notions about some aspect of reality, are cognitive tools for restricting our awareness about members of out-groups to grossly oversimplified categories that may or may not reflect a small element of truth.

The accentuation effect invariably creates overgeneralizations about members of identified groups. But not every overgeneralization is appropriately considered a stereotype. A stereotype is an overgeneralization that simultaneously serves the cognitive need for simplification and the affective need for alleviation of frustration and/or enhancement of self-esteem. Thus, affective needs augment the accentuation effect and channel it systematically in the direction of prejudice against out-groups. It is an unfortunate reality of human psychology that the human need for positive self-regard is often met through a process of social comparison, whereby one's own group is elevated and comparison groups denigrated.

In their influential book, *The Anatomy of Racial Attitudes*, Charles Glock and his colleagues (Apostle, et al., 1983) distinguish between three important components of the cognitive dimension of racial prejudice, or what they prefer to call racial attitudes. "In effect, white racial attitudes are made up of how black-white differences are perceived (perceptions) and accounted for (explanations) and how the deprived status of blacks in society is responded to (prescriptions)" (p. 18). Glock was concerned with racial attitudes or prejudices, but his analysis is likely applicable to most other forms of prejudice as well.

Thus far, we have been emphasizing the perceptual dimension of prejudice. Perceptually, prejudices are rooted in the process of categorization, which leads to an accentuation effect, which, in turn, leads to the formation of stereotypes. Stereotypes are the lenses through which group differences are perceived. Stereotypes may relate either to characterological traits (e.g., intelligence, ambition, and moral strength) or social structural position (e.g., social status, opportunities, and class).

Perhaps more important than the filters through which one perceives group differences, however, are the explanatory categories that people employ to account for those perceived differences. Glock found that there are consistent patterns in the way various individuals explain perceived racial differences.

The modes of explanation for perceived racial differences depend on the forces that people believe are most influential in shaping human behavior. Glock identified six explanatory modes. The first two attribute racial differences to forces beyond human control—either God or nature, modes respectively designated *supernatural* and *genetic*. People who use one or the other of these modes believe racial differences are innate and irreversible. In contrast, those who adhere to the *individualistic* mode of explaining racial differences conceive of racial differences as a product of individual decision.

The relative disadvantaged position of African Americans, for example, is explained as a result of blacks failing to use their free will to better themselves.

Finally, there are two modes of explanation that account for perceived differences sociologically. Adherents of the *radical* mode of explanation attribute observed differences to the effects of white racism, both historically (slavery) and contemporaraneously (discrimination). Those who employ the *environmental* mode similarly trace black disadvantages to slavery, but attribute ongoing disadvantages, not to white racism, but to a legacy of systemic social disadvantages. From this perspective, the problems of poor African Americans stem primarily from their class, not their race. Poor whites and poor blacks both have to struggle to get ahead, and social conditions make it difficult for them to do so.

In his classic book, *Blaming the Victim*, William Ryan (1971) maintained that the privileged in society are able to live comfortably with poverty and discrimination because they consider these phenomena to be caused by their victims. Several of the explanatory categories identified by Glock would seem to fit this "blame the victim" mentality, though Ryan did not explicitly consider the full range of alternative explanations identified by the Glock research group. In any event, though Glock's research group resists the term prejudice (Apostle, et al., 1983, pp. 7-19), it seems feasible to designate as prejudiced those individuals who (a) *perceive* characterological and/or social system differences between groups in stereotypic ways, attributing negative stereotypes to out-groups (that is, the out-group is believed to possess either negative character traits or a disadvantaged social position), and (b) *explain* these differences by appeal to supernatural, genetic, and/or individualistic causes. Significantly, Glock found that the "radicals" and "environmentalists" were most inclined to be intolerant of discrimination and supportive of institutional efforts to eliminate it.

To summarize, the cognitive dimension of prejudice is rooted in processes of perception and explanation. These processes build on an inescapable and normal process of categorization and the equally inescapable and normal accentuation effect that accompanies it. Prejudice is an amplification and systematic distortion of normal, but nonetheless misleading cognitive processes.

3. *Behaviorally, prejudice is expressed in willingness to engage in discriminatory practices.*

Discrimination does not always follow prejudice. Nonetheless, prejudiced people are more likely than others to act in a hostile, demeaning, or discriminatory way toward out-groups. Because of this association, social scientists have often measured the severity of prejudice by noting the extent to which a person condones negative acts against out-groups (e.g., Adorno, et al., 1950; Bogardus, 1925).

Thomas Pettigrew (1982) identifies four overlapping levels of increasingly discriminatory behavior. The first is *verbal hostility*, such as making the targeted group the brunt of humor. At the next level, *avoidance behavior* is condoned and interaction with out-group members is eschewed. *Differential treatment* of groups is openly accepted at the third level. Finally, the most severe form of behavioral prejudice is *assaultive behavior*, where members of out-groups are physically attacked.

An analysis of discrimination in terms of individual prejudice is clearly inadequate. Though all aspects of prejudice reflect group phenomena as well as individual dynamics, this is particularly true of discriminatory behavior. When one moves in focus from the individual to the social group or society, discrimination needs to be analyzed not only in terms of individual psychology, but also in terms of group dynamics, social practices, and distributions of social power.

Since our focus in this chapter is on the psychology of prejudice, the social question becomes: How is it that an individual comes to act as a group member, as an extension of a particular group? Social identity theory is particularly useful in addressing this question (e.g., Hogg & Abrams, 1988; Tajfel, 1984; Turner, et al., 1987). According to social identity theory, individuality is comprised largely of a patchwork of group identifications, though an element of personal identity derived from specific relationships is also recognized. Individuals engage in group behavior when the situation makes salient aspects of important group identifications that the individual has incorporated in his or her identity. For example, if a European American finds herself in a group of Asian Americans, she is likely to become highly conscious of her racial/ethnic identity. Discriminatory behavior, even when carried out by an individual, is really a form of group behavior, because it intrinsically reflects perceived group beliefs, attitudes, or norms that the individual has embraced through an identification with a reference group or groups. White racism, for example, is a consequence of white individuals adopting the prejudices and behavioral norms that they associate with others who share a perceived racial/ethnic identity. Thus, when an individual acts in a discriminatory way, that person acts simultaneously as an individual and as an extension of a group to which the individual belongs.

4. *The affective, cognitive, and behavioral dimensions are mutually reinforcing.*

Prejudice and discrimination work in a vicious circle to reinforce one another, and they do so on both a personal and institutional level (Allport, 1954; Pettigrew, 1982). The negative affect associated with prejudice accentuates stereotypic thinking, "blaming the victim" explanations of disadvantages, and demeaning action. Members of groups who have been stereotyped may also partially internalize the stereotype (Hamilton & Trolier, 1986; Word,

Zanna & Cooper, 1974), or, put on the defensive, they may respond in a hostile or self-effacing manner that may also have the effect of reinforcing stereotypes (Allport, 1954).

Why Are Prejudices Resistant to Change?

Not too many years ago, it seemed prejudice was on the wane. The civil rights movement of the 1950s sounded the trumpets against racism; in the 1960s, students poured into the streets and campus squares protesting against (among other things) the ethnocentrism of the Vietnam War; women, in the 1970s, challenged one of the most deeply rooted prejudices of all—that lodged within the intimacies of male/female relations. A spirit of hope moved within the chaos of these decades, and many looked for a more just and humane world. But during the 1980s, the tide seemed to turn, and dreams of harmonious human relations washed away like so many sand castles beneath growing waves of intolerance and bigotry. Today, hardly a week passes without the newspaper delivering another tragic story of bigotry, racial strife, or ethnic conflict to our doorstep.

In his monumental work, *The Nature of Prejudice*, Gordon Allport (1954) wrote: "Perhaps the most perplexing problem in the entire field of human relations is this: why do so relatively few of our contacts with other people fit in with, and satisfy, our predominant affiliative needs, and why do so many find their way into sentiments of hatred and hostility?" (p. 365). Allport was convinced that our desire to love is more fundamental than our desire to hate, and yet the latter often gains the upper hand. To understand the persistence of prejudice, we need to look at its functional utility. Though others could no doubt be identified, five functional utilities of prejudice stand out and account for much of the stubborn persistence of prejudices.

1. *Displacement of negative affect*

Life is abundant with challenges, ambiguities, and stresses. Prejudices help people deal with these frustrations (Chabassol, 1970; Duckitt, 1985; Grossarth-Maticek, Eysenck & Vetter, 1989). When we are unable to directly confront the cause of our upset—either because to do so would threaten something we value or because we cannot even name the source—then tension grows and we seek some form of outlet. Enter the scapegoat. Hovland and Sears (1940) were the first to propose a comprehensive theory of scapegoating. They suggested that frustrated majority-group members who cannot safely aggress against those responsible for their frustrations, or who cannot identify the source of the frustration, tend to displace their aggression onto out-groups, particularly when out-groups are relatively defenseless. Prejudices turn out-groups into dumping grounds for negative emotions that we have not been able to resolve or release elsewhere. The group that becomes the target for scapegoating is typically one that is paradoxically both relatively powerless and threatening. Below, we shall discuss how the poor and hungry fit this paradoxical set.

2. *Simplified attributions*

Attribution theory contributes to our understanding of prejudice by highlighting that people want not only to understand or categorize the world, but also to render it predictable (Harvey & Smith, 1977; Hewstone, 1983; Kelley, 1967). To make sense of our world and life circumstances, to render them predictable, we make causal attributions. Such intuitive or naive causal models enable us to behave adaptively. In reality, of course, a complex web of causal factors are operative, but prejudice reduces this complexity through two types of simplifications. In the case of out-groups, simplification occurs by overestimating the role of those qualities within the person's control when the factor to be explained is negative: "Juan (an Hispanic American) is unemployed because he hasn't tried hard enough to hustle a job." In the case of one's own group, simplification occurs by stressing external circumstances as the cause of negative occurrences: "John is unemployed because of the recession." Prejudices can be difficult to relinquish because of their functional utility in attribution processes.

3. *Self-concept enhancement*

One of the most important psychological functions of prejudice is the enhancement of one's sense of self-worth. Social comparison is the basic process through which self-worth is established. To determine the extent to which one is good at something or has a quality or trait that is desirable, the person engages in a process of comparing the self to others. By comparing oneself to others, or—as social identity theorists emphasize—by comparing the groups that one identifies with to groups one does not identify with, one gauges one's own behavior, abilities, status, traits, and the like. To elevate one's sense of self-esteem, the process of social comparison must conclude with a favorable verdict rendered on the self. Prejudices guarantee this outcome in advance.

4. *Moral justification*

Prejudices reflect a moral reasoning that divides people into categories of good and bad, right and wrong. This dualistic thinking allows moral corruption, through processes of externalization and objectification, to be comfortably located outside one's own skin and inside the skins (preferably of a different color) of others (see Staub, 1989). This simplistic morality is remarkably successful at maintaining prejudiced people's sense of moral integrity, even while they engage in the most inhumane behaviors.

5. *Socioeconomic advantages*

Another important reason why prejudices continue to flourish is because prejudice pays—literally! Of course it doesn't pay equally, as sociologists Jack and William Levin (1982, p. 130-131) note:

> There is a strong tendency for those in the lower segment of the majority group to benefit from discrimination and prejudice at the level of the personality. Prejudice makes them "feel better" about their difficulties. It allows them to displace aggression, protect self-esteem, and reduce uncertainty. In contrast, the upper segment of the majority group is much more likely to benefit at the level of the social structure. They reap economic benefits in the form of paying lower wages, controlling production costs, protecting their advantaged power position, acquiring land, and so on.

Prejudice and discrimination function to funnel economic resources disproportionately to the upper class. But the upper class would not be able to appropriate the resources of the majority if they did not obtain the cooperation of the majority in their own oppression. For this reason, an ideology promoting the notion that society functions as a meritocracy is peddled in the media, in cultural practices such as sports, and in educational and civic organizations. In a meritocracy, reward corresponds to the combination of talent and effort. Those who are well positioned in society promote the idea that they achieved their position as a consequence of hard work and personal characteristics, though the reality is far removed from any such explanation. However, many in the majority accept the status quo, not because their material interests coincide with the wealthy, but because they derive psychological benefits from the prevailing systems of prejudice and discrimination. In short, whether the payoff is primarily psychological or material, those of us who are not lower-class lesbians of color have some powerful motives to maintain the status quo.

How Are Prejudices Learned?

Learning dynamics are quite complex, and I will not attempt a comprehensive analysis here. Nonetheless, a few key points related to the process of acquiring prejudices can be highlighted:

1. *The early environment is central.*

The child's early intimate environment is one of the most influential contexts for lifelong learning. In many cases, the home is the most influential single source for the early formation of prejudices, though schools, religious organizations, and other institutions play a role. Early caretakers encourage the development of prejudice in two ways. In the first instance, these socializers communicate their own values. Thus, children are taught the ethnocentrisms of the influential adults in their lives. Equally important, prejudices are indirectly fostered through child-rearing practices that lead to chronic fear, suspicion, and hostility—affects that often form the irrational core of prejudice. And when parents treat their children in a rigid, authoritarian manner, children learn to view human relationships in terms of hierarchy and power, rather than in terms of reciprocity and sharing. Though there has been considerable critique of this "authoritarian personality" approach to prejudice (e.g. Billig, 1976; Brown, 1965), the basic contention that rigid child-rearing practices augment children's prejudices is sound.

2. *Sexism is paradigmatic.*

Sexism may play a particularly important role in the early formation of prejudices (Shields, 1986). One of the major developmental tasks for maturing children is to learn their group identifications. Children must master the complex of relationships that defines the social nexus in which they live. In this process, the child learns his or her gender, race, nationality, social class, religious affiliation, etc. Of all the group identifications eventually learned, gender identity is the first to consolidate. As children develop gender awareness, they also learn a rudimentary way of relating themselves to someone who is "different," i.e., someone of the other gender. If children learn to relate to "the other" as an equal, they may be more inclined in the future to assume a basic equality between people of various group identifications. Unfortunately, children more often learn to relate hierarchically. Boys learn that maleness is more valued and associated with greater social power than femaleness, while girls learn that their identify is tied to identifying themselves with relevant males. This pattern of hierarchical relationship is easily duplicated when the child learns of others who are different from himself or herself. In this way, the early experience of sexism paves the way for other forms of prejudice.

3. *Prejudice is learned in phases.*

Prejudice does not enter the child's heart and head in full blossom. It develops through a fairly regular sequence (Allport 1954/1979). The first phase consists of what Allport calls *pregeneralized* learning. The child does not yet have stable ideas about group identifications and, consequently, negative attitudes are attached to labels, the referents to which are ambiguous in the child's mind. Let me illustrate. I remember when I was a young child asking my parents, "What am I, a Democrat or a Republican?" After my parents provided the identifying labels, I knew names for the favored and disfavored though I had no idea whatever who the labels identified. Similarly, a young child may hear disparaging remarks about "those blacks," "welfare queens," and "immigrants," and long before the child knows who these people supposedly are, negative attitudes are formed.

In a second phase of prejudice development, the child learns to identify the members of the stigmatized group. By this time, the person usually enters a period of *total rejection,* during which out-groups are thought about almost exclusively in negative terms. Members of out-groups have few if any positive attributes, and all members of out-groups are similar. Some people never grow beyond this phase of prejudice, but, for most, prejudice moves to a phase that is more subtle and nuanced.

Total rejection gives way to the period of *differentiation.* Out-groups are imaged in terms of selected negative stereotypes, but the person does not necessarily assume that members have no good qualities. Thinking of themselves as fair-minded, these prejudiced people nonetheless persist in harboring negative stereotypes, though they are often hidden beneath a veil of affirmations about selected positive characteristics. Similarly, the person exhibiting this form of prejudice may readily acknowledge that many people in the stigmatized group do not exhibit the characteristics that the person associates with that group. Such people, however, are exceptions and an endless number of exceptions can be tolerated without modifying the underlying assumptions.

Who Are the Prejudiced?

Though researchers have designed numerous ingenious experiments to discover the characteristics of prejudiced people, surprisingly few generalizations can be made. Three generalizations, however, have received overwhelming support.

1. *Prejudiced people generally have a low tolerance for ambiguity.*

This point is well illustrated by a classic study in the investigation of prejudice (Frenkel-Brunswik, 1949). In this experiment, people were shown a series of similar drawings. The first was of a cat. In each of the succeeding drawings, however, the figure looked progressively less like a cat and more like a dog. After presenting each picture, the experimenter asked, "And what is this a picture of?" The results of the experiment showed that those people who scored high on a measure of prejudice kept insisting the picture was a cat long after less prejudiced people said they didn't know or said that it was a dog. This was but one of numerous experiments demonstrating that prejudice is associated with a low tolerance for ambiguity. Prejudiced people take the fuzziness out of life.

2. *Prejudiced people have low self-esteem.*

The finding that prejudiced people have low self-esteem is one of the most consistent reports from the literature (Bagley, et al., 1979; Bagley, Verma & Mallick, 1981). Prejudiced people generally do not feel good about themselves. This negative self-evaluation creates a yearning for personal validation. Unfortunately, one way that people enhance their feelings of self-worth is to compare themselves with others considered inferior. Prejudice guarantees that comparisons with out-groups will always come out in one's favor.

3. *Prejudiced people have a familiar face.*

Nathan's famous parable to King David of ancient Israel (II Samuel 12) is a good illustration of this point. After King David "knew" Bathsheba and then had her husband killed, the court prophet, Nathan, narrated a story to David about two men, one rich and the other poor. The poor man had one treasured possession, a young lamb, that he treated like family. One day the rich man received a guest. Not wanting to take a lamb from his own abundant flock, he stole the poor man's lone lamb, had it slaughtered, and prepared it for a feast. King David was irate. He demanded the rich man's name. Nathan replied, "You are the man!"

We are the prejudiced! True, most of us are not guilty of gross discrimination, but we are not thereby innocent. Prejudice works on what might be called the *pyramid principle*—the blatant prejudices of the few are magnifications of the latent prejudices of the many (Shields, 1986). The fact that most of us abhor the actions of the Ku Klux Klan does not mean that latent racist attitudes within us do not contribute to a social climate that facilitates more radical expressions of racism. If we are honest, we will see that extremist groups are like amusement park mirrors that take our reflection and exaggerate it to ugly proportions. The pathology of the Klan member is not random; it feeds from the everyday racism that few in the majority culture even recognize.

We need to look at our own values and lifestyles and see how they may contribute inadvertently to the depersonalization of others. Do we use white and black, for example, as symbols of good and evil? Do we laugh at humor based on stereotypes? Is "cleanliness next to Godliness"? Do we think it is appropriate for women, but not men, to lose their family name when married? Is God Father and not Mother? Essed (1991) writes poignantly about "everyday racism," the subtle (at least to dominant-culture whites) means by which racism is enacted and learned in interpersonal dynamics. Only by becoming sensitive to the subtle ways in which our own actions and behaviors reinforce prejudices can such major social problems as racism, classism, sexism, homophobia, ageism, militarism, and nationalism be addressed.

Prejudice, Race, and the Domestication of Hunger

Now that we have summarized the psychology of prejudice, it is time to turn our attention more directly to the topic of this chapter: the connection between racial prejudice and hunger. I will do so by addressing three topics: hunger and epistemology, the domestication of hunger, and racial prejudice as a source of hunger.

Hunger and the Epistemic Break

One of the great myths about hunger is that it can be adequately studied objectively. In the academic halls of the great universities, hunger, when it is not ignored, is turned into a *topic*, a problem to be investigated. It is subjected to theoretical analysis, statistical manipulation, and policy review. Scientific papers are delivered at professional meetings, dissertations are written, and careers are made in the study of hunger. In the corridors of government, hunger, when it is not ignored, is turned into a topic for partisan debate. Politicians issue position statements, bureaucrats shuffle papers and people, and technocrats design assistance programs like an architect designs a building. I am not suggesting that these are entirely barren efforts, but by themselves they fail to come to grips with the most basic challenge posed by the existence of hunger. To genuinely *know* hunger, one must break with the objectivist mode of knowing, returning to it only after experiencing the subjective immediacy of hunger's threat.

Hunger is ugly and tragic. The hungry person, simply by virtue of his or her existence, is a fundamental protest against the moral integrity of our society and culture. More basic yet, the ravaged bodies of the hungry call into question our own humanity. How can we claim full personhood when we have allowed such a situation of massive suffering to go uncorrected? Hunger cannot be studied objectively because our very soul is called into question by the approaching victim of hunger. Until we are grasped in our innermost core by the wrenching protest of the walking death called hunger, until we are pulled into a struggle of solidarity and militant resistance, until we are ready to burst with an anguished outcry of "Stop, this can't go on!" then we cannot *understand* hunger. We misunderstand hunger when we turn the hungry person into one more object of study.

When we understand hunger in its full immediacy, we are grasped by a inescapable truth: hunger is a threat. Hunger is a political threat because the existence of the hungry is a stinging indictment against the political status quo. Hunger is a social threat because the hungry, having little to lose, are likely to fight by whatever means necessary to disrupt the social order. Hunger is a personal threat because to unflinchingly perceive the realities of hunger is to confront one's own inhumanity. Despite the overt powerlessness of the hungry, hunger itself is a profound and omnipresent threat. And so hunger must be domesticated. For the status quo—political, social, and personal—to remain, hunger must be tamed. Prejudice becomes a vehicle to domesticate hunger.

Prejudice and the Domestication of Hunger

For prejudice to reduce the threat of hunger effectively, the hungry must be assimilated into a category laden with negative stereotypes. Consequently, the images of the hungry are colored. Dominant-culture whites perceive the hungry as people of color, mostly black. This is true on both a global and domestic level. Despite the fact that the majority of the world's hungry live in Asia, it is African hunger—black hunger—that is the prevailing stereotype. When the hungry are colored black, the principles of attribution that characterize prejudicial perception come into play. The reader will recall that when negative events occur, blame is placed on the victim if that person is a member of an out-group. Correspondingly, the hungry themselves (or, by extension, their parents or their governments) often are blamed for their plight. African people, and hungry Africans in particular, are thought to lack sufficient industriousness or knowledge or integrity. Of course, massive hunger does not readily fit this paradigm. Consequently, when the severity of hunger is extreme and the numbers of hungry immense, such as in a large-scale famine, then the stereotype shifts to that of helpless children bantered about by the cruel but impersonal forces of nature (cf. Mpanya, chapter 3). In either case, hungry people are not viewed as equals; they are not encountered as full human persons with dignity, individuality, and competence.

The coloring of hunger is evident in the domestic context as well. When the U.S. Postal Service released a "Help End Hunger" stamp in 1987, the stamp featured three faces—one white, two of color. The reverse would have more closely approximated reality. Despite the fact that the majority of the poor in the United States are of European descent, poverty is equated with race in the public imagination. Most public depictions of welfare mothers, ghetto dwellers, and soup kitchen clients reflect racial imagery. So pervasive is this that even poor whites are often seen through "colored" lenses. It is a fighting insult in the African American community for one black person to call another an Oreo, someone black on the outside, but white on the inside. When poor whites are thought about, however, they are often perceived as *yogurt-covered raisins:* white on the outside and black on the inside.

Racial Prejudice as a Source of Hunger

It is an indisputable reality that people of color are disproportionately represented among the hungry, both on a global scale and in the United States. So are women. It is certainly no coincidence that both groups are frequent targets of prejudice and discrimination.

The problem of racism is not just individual and attitudinal. It is important to emphasize that once prejudices have had an impact on the structuring of social, political, and economic systems, continuing discrimination need not depend on the continuation of explicit or overt prejudice. Continued social stratification depends only on a lack of explicit and effective resistance to prejudice and discrimination.

When prejudices are widespread among a socially dominant group, social structures and practices evolve that consolidate power differentials into institutionalized, invisible discrimination. For example, college entrance exams may appear innocent of prejudice, yet cultural differences and poor schools leave many racial/ethnic minorities ill-prepared to take them. The results: a segregated society in which whites are educated for high-status jobs and people of color are told where to find the unemployment line.

The combination of capitalism, patriarchy, and racism in contemporary North American society guarantees that social power is wielded to the disadvantage of all those who are not part of the privileged power elite. Capitalism depends on social stratification. Both racism and patriarchy function on the economic level to provide a class of people with lowered economic expectations. In the context of a world and domestic economy characterized by an increasing gap between rich and poor, preparation for low positions in the economic hierarchy translates to preparation for poverty and the potential for hunger.

Prejudice is a cause of hunger. It is a cause of hunger because it generates discriminatory practices that channel economic resources away from people of color. It is a cause of hunger because it marginalizes the poor, removing them from view and thought. It is a cause of hunger because it perpetuates an ideology that blames victims for their plight, thereby dismissing the indictment that hunger presents to the dominant culture. And it is a cause of hunger because it interferes with the formation of alliances among poor people themselves and between the poor and people of greater economic resources.

References

Adorno, T. W., Frenkel-Brunswik, E., Levinson, D., & Sanford, R. N. (1950). *The authoritarian personality.* New York: John Wiley.

Allport, G. (1954). *The nature of prejudice.* Reading, MA: Addison-Wesley.

Apostle, R., Glock, C., Piazza, T., & Suelzle, M. (1983). *The Anatomy of Racial Attitudes.* Berkeley: University of California Press.

Bagley, C., Verma, G., Mallick, K., & Young, L. (1979). *Personality, self-esteem and prejudice.* Westmead, England: Saxon House.

Bagley, C., Verma, G., & Mallick, K. (1981). Personality, self-esteem and prejudice. *Journal of Personality Assessment, 45,* 320-321.

Bierly, M. M. (1985). Prejudice toward contemporary out-groups as a generalized attitude. *Journal of Applied Social Psychology, 15,* 189-199.

Billig, M. (1976). *Social psychology and intergroup relations.* New York: Academic Press.

Bogardus, E. S. (1925). Measuring social distances. *Journal of Applied Sociology,* 299-308.

Brown, R.J. (1965). *Social psychology.* New York: Free Press.

Chabassol, D. (1970). Prejudice and personality in adolescence. *Alberta Journal of Education Research, 16,* 3-12.

Duckitt, J.H. (1985). Prejudice and neurotic symptomatology among White South Africans. *Journal of Psychology, 119,* 15-20.

Essed, P. (1991). *Understanding everyday racism.* Newbury Park, CA: Sage.

Frenkel-Brunswik, E. (1949). Intolerance of ambiguity as an emotional and perceptual personality variable. *Journal of Personality, 18,* 108-143.

Grossarth-Maticek, R., Eysenck, H.J., & Vetter, H. (1989). The causes and cures of prejudice: An empirical study of the frustration-aggression hypothesis. *Personality and Individual Differences, 10,* 547-558.

Hamilton, D. L., & Trolier, T. K. (1986). Stereotypes and stereotyping: An overview of the cognitive approach. In J.F. Dovidio, & S.L. Gaertner (Eds.), *Prejudice, discrimination, and racism* (pp. 127-163). San Diego: Academic Press.

Harvey, J.H., & Smith, W.P. (1977). *Social psychology: An attribution approach.* St. Louis: Louisianna: Mosby.

Hewstone, M. (Ed.) (1983). *Attribution theory: Social and functional extensions.* Oxford: Blackwell.

Hogg, M.A., & Abrams, D. (1988). *Social identifications: A social psychology of intergroup relations and group processes.* New York: Routledge.

Hovland, C., & Sears, R. (1940). Minor studies in aggression VI: correlation of lynchings and economic indices. *Journal of Psychology, 9,* 301-310.

Kelley, H.H. (1967). Attribution theory in social psychology. In D. Levine (Ed.), *Nebraska symposium on motivation.* Lincoln: University of Nebraska Press.

Levin, J., & Levin, W. (1982). *The functions of discrimination and prejudice* (2nd ed.). New York: Harper & Row.

Pettigrew, T. (1982). Prejudice. In T. Pettigrew, G. Fredrickson, D. Knobel, N. Glazer, & R. Ueda, *Prejudice.* Cambridge, MA: Harvard University Press.

Piaget, J. (1936/1963). *Origins of intelligence in children.* New York: Norton.

Ray, J.J., & Lovejoy, F.H. (1986). The generality of racial prejudice. *Journal of Social Psychology, 126,* 563-564.

Ryan, W. (1971). *Blaming the victim.* New York: Random House.

Shields, D. (1986). *Growing beyond prejudices: Overcoming hierarchical dualism.* Mystic, CT: Twenty-Third Publications.

Staub. E. (1989). *The roots of evil: The origins of genocide and other group violence.* New York: Cambridge University Press.

Tajfel, H. (ed) (1984). *The social dimension: European developments in social psychology.* Cambridge: Cambridge University Press.

Turner, J.C., Hogg, M.A., Oakes, P.J., Reicher, S.D., and Wetherell, M. (1987). *Rediscovering the social group: A self-categorization theory.* New York: Blackwell.

Word, C.O., Zanna, M.P., & Cooper, J. (1974). The nonverbal mediation of self-fulfilling prophecies in interracial interaction. *Journal of Experimental Social Psychology, 10,* 109-120.

CHAPTER 5

Racism in Foreign Policy and Development Programs

Percy Hintzen

The United States is the breadbasket of the world. Whenever and wherever mass starvation strikes, there U.S. foreign assistance arrives to deliver aid and relief. Moreover, the United States, through its development assistance programs, works to eliminate the underlying causes of hunger—illiteracy, technological backwardness, institutional ineptitude, and so on.

These are popular ideas promulgated by the U.S. government and the mass media. In this chapter, I will offer an alternative view of U.S. foreign policy as it relates to development and hunger. I will suggest that foreign aid and development assistance are not charitable vehicles of diplomacy undergirded by benevolent and humanitarian notions. Rather, they are weapons. They are weapons used in the pursuit of narrow national interests, and they are undergirded, not by altruism, but by notions of white supremacy.

Unilateral Developmentalism

To speak of development policy and foreign aid in terms that are conventionally understood may constitute a dangerous, if tacit, endorsement of a number of myths upon which rests a system of racial domination that has lasted almost five hundred years. It is crucial to keep in mind that the idea of development policy, in its application, pertains exclusively, and not surprisingly, to those countries that lie outside of the North Atlantic. At its root is the notion of *unilinear developmentalism* whereby Western Europe and North America[1] are considered to be at the apex of human intellectual, cultural, political, social, economic, and technological achievement. The descendants of Western Europe, who constitute the dominant majority in these regions, are located at the top of a development pyramid. Located in subordinate positions are the various non-European populations, communities, and groups. The position of each on the pyramid relates to its degrees of closeness to the Western European ideal, defined in terms of all or a combination of moral, ethical, charactological, and genetic traits.

The myth of racial superiority is at the root of unilinear developmentalism. Both have combined to fashion the ideological basis of the foreign policies and structures of diplomacy of North Atlantic nations as these apply to countries where the dominant majority is neither European nor European-descended. The roots of the present concept of unilinear developmentalism extend deep into our colonial heritage. Speaking of the period of colonial expansion that was accompanied by the "Europeanization of the world," historian Paul Gorden Lauren argues that, during this time, "international relations increasingly became interracial relations as well, particularly when so much power was held in the hands of those [meaning Europeans] with such intense and explicit racial ideologies."[2] Referring to Europeans and North Americans, Lauren further observes that:

> The majority supported, participated in, or benefitted from colonization, slavery, immigration restrictions, imperialism, and the propagation of racial ideologies. These people enslaved the black, excluded the yellow, dispossessed the red and brown, and subjugated them all. These developments occurred not on the fringe but rather at the center of Western civilization, as demonstrated by the active participation of many of its greatest philosophers and thinkers, explorers and soldiers, scientists and scholars, clerics and even missionaries.[3]

To this day, even domestic race relations are perceived in terms of foreign relations. Persons of color living in the North Atlantic are never fully accepted as citizens of their own countries. This is just as true for original inhabitants of the land, such as Native Americans, for groups that have made, singularly, the most important contribution to their countries' development, such as African Americans, and for migrants and their descendants. De facto exclusion from citizenship is supported by the same myths that undergird the ideology of white supremacy in the international system and the benefits derived therefrom.

The Twin Foundations of Foreign Policy

In what is conventionally considered to be foreign policy, the notion of unilinear developmentalism and its undergirding myth of racial superiority has led to two complementary, even though seemingly contradictory, sets of concepts and practices. One is a racist version of *noblesse oblige,* admirably represented by Rudyard Kipling's "The White Man's Burden." Accordingly, the obligation falls upon Europeans to civilize the "new caught, sullen peoples, half-devil and half-child" whose origins lie outside Europe.[4] The contemporary variant of the white man's burden is found in efforts by the West aimed at ensuring the political and economic development of the Third World through programs of multilateral and bilateral foreign aid and developmental assistance. The stated aim of these programs is modernization through the establishment of "democracy" and through the "rationalization" of the economic behavior.

The second set of concepts and practices defining Western foreign policy is constructed around the theme of national interest. The core idea is that European civilization needs to be protected to prevent its descent into the Hobbesian "state of nature." There is much more to this than mere justification for racial domination. The life of the "primitive" or the "savage" is characterized, among other things, by that of absolute equality. The danger to civilization rests in the consequences of such equality. Hobbes represented such consequences in terms of a state of existence where life becomes "poor, solitary, nasty, brutish and short."

If the very institutions and culture of the world outside the West, i.e., of "primitive" people, become threatening, Europeans need to develop collective institutions to prevent incursion of these non-European peoples, their ways of life, their ideas and values, their institutions, and even the contaminating effects of their genes. This is the fundamental idea embodied in the principle of protection of national interests, a cornerstone of the foreign policies of Western nations as they relate to the world outside of the North Atlantic.

Since the end of the nineteenth century, the ideology of racial superiority has supported notions, preeminent in the secular ideas of Europeans, of a global struggle for existence. This struggle became firmly identified as a racial one in the philosophical discourses of nineteenth-century European scholars. Among the latter were Social Darwinists such as Herbert Spencer and Thomas Huxley of Great Britain, Austria's Ludwig Gumplowicz, Russia's Nicolas Danielevsky, and American William Graham Sumner. All interpreted human history as a brutish struggle for survival and racial relations as a biological and cultural contest defining the potential for human progress. The widespread perception of the innate inferiority of non-Europeans that these and other "scholars" helped to fashion has been internalized, reinforced, and sustained in the central core of values, beliefs, and ideas of modern European society. It serves, continuously, to justify and legitimize different codes of conduct and standards of behavior when such codes and standards apply to persons whose origins are located outside of Europe.

At the heart of the foreign policy complex, therefore, is the idea of the innate inferiority of people of color, their culture, and their institutions. This idea undergirds the twin notions of developmentalism and protection of national interests. It is from this perspective that the contradiction contained in the idea of the modernizing (read civilizing) mission of development becomes evident. How can those who are innately inferior realistically become the objects of a civilizing mission?

Praxeologically, this contradiction turns out to be the most important feature in the myth of development. The possibility of Third World development is negated at the outset by the idea of innate inferiority. It is this negation that legitimizes white supremacy, racial domination, and racial privilege. Contemporary manifestations of "The White Man's Burden" provide moral legitimacy for intervention into and control over the affairs of people of color throughout the world. Ironically, intervention becomes "necessary" for development and modernization. Any resistance is interpreted as indisputable evidence of the irredeemable inferiority of people of color. Such inferiority, linked to the "organic, inherited, biological differences of race,"[5] becomes the central justifying principle in their subjugation and exploitation.

If development equates with civilization, which it does, and if Europeans and Europeans alone are capable of civilization, then it is sheer delusion to speak of development policy in terms conventionally understood, i.e., as policies designed to better the conditions of those to whom they are addressed. Rather, the idea of development has, from its inception, provided a thin veil with which to hide European expansionary and exploitative designs upon the populations and resources of the world outside of Europe. The consequences of exploitation and expansion are uncontestable: extermination and enslavement, dispossession, despoliation, and destruction, poverty and hunger, and all the other maladies of Europe's civilizing mission. Translated, development becomes underdevelopment, and aid becomes destruction.

How, then, have foreign aid and intervention, the two central pillars in the foreign policies of the West toward the Third World, retained their legitimacy in the face of their incontestable history of despoliation and destruction, exploitation and extermination? The legitimizing force of the twin but contradictory concepts of unilinear developmentalism and national security derives its power from the rooting of these concepts in the idea of the biological superiority of Europeans. By rooting themselves in racist ideology, often only subtly expressed, development "assistance" and foreign "aid" can continue to be seen as viable, despite their actual historical consequences of misery, hunger, and exploitation. The innate inferiority of people of color, not contradictions in the programs, accounts for the lack of any civilizing and modernizing outcome of European efforts. Thus, conditions of hunger, poverty, disease, desperation, and powerlessness persist despite the moral and ethical conduct of Europeans in their civilizing mission.

The Doctrine of White Supremacy

The doctrine of white supremacy[6] supports and sustains the position of a small group of dominant Europeans that has managed to appropriate for itself a combination of power, privilege, wealth, and prestige that enables it to maintain hegemonic control over the rest of the world's population. Those whom they dominate, exploit, and control comprise a resounding majority of the world's population. They are primarily poor and powerless, and many are hungry, as well. While most are people of color, the dominated include within their ranks groups of Europeans themselves who are defined out of the system of privilege because of attributes such as class, religion, gender, and patterns of association and ideology. While these attributes relegate them to the station of undesirable, the myth of race acts as a basis of *political* unity that, in many instances, preempts any strategic alliances between disadvantaged Europeans with non-European populations.

Development Policy, Foreign Aid, and the United States

The United States happens to be the most recent international flag-bearer of the doctrine of white supremacy. It is, thus, the latter that frames the context for its foreign policy. As such, there is nothing uniquely "American" about the formulation and implementation of its development and aid policies. Institutionally, the United States remains an integral part of a North Atlantic alliance of European (in the racial sense) interests. This is quite evident in the position of the United States at the head of the Organization for Economic Cooperation and Development (OECD), comprising the 22 richest Western countries, along with Greece, Turkey, and Japan. The OECD is responsible for coordinating the economic policies of the capitalist industrialized countries, as well as the terms of their relationship with countries outside of Europe.

Militarily, the international domination of the North Atlantic is maintained and sustained through the North Atlantic Treaty Organization (NATO). Formed ostensibly to protect the "free world" against the now defunct Warsaw Pact communist states, NATO has been the hub of the post-World War II imperialist and neocolonialist military campaigns from Vietnam to Iraq. These campaigns are now threatening Libya, Cuba, and possibly Syria and North Korea, under the aegis of the United Nations Security Council, which has become a surrogate for European interests.

One needs only to look to the composition of the Security Council to find evidence of its solidarity with European perspectives. Of the five permanent members of the Council, the United States, Great Britain, and France are

North Atlantic countries. Russia has replaced the defunct Soviet Union as a permanent member. The efficacy of China, the only non-European country (despite the Asian landmass of Russia) on the Council, has been severely undermined after its decision to use the military to suppress popular dissent in Beijing in 1989. China has become strategically dependent upon the United States administration in its efforts to prevent economic and diplomatic retaliation for what is generally perceived as its suppression of the civil and political rights of its population. This strategic dependence has eliminated any chance that it can use its position on the council to challenge European dominance.

The principles of conduct that apply to relations within the North Atlantic bloc of nations, where Europeans and their descendants comprise the dominant majority, are fundamentally different from those that inform relations with countries outside of the bloc. President Theodore Roosevelt, the primary architect of twentieth century U.S. policy toward the latter, was quite clear in his rejection of the application of "rules of international morality" to non-European populations whom he considered to be "savages" and "beasts." He thought it of "incalculable importance" that lands "should pass out of the hands of their red, black, and yellow aboriginal owners, and become the heritage of the dominant (white) world races."[7] His position is at the very heart of the principle of national interests that has been the centerpiece of U.S. twentieth century foreign policy. Thus, national interests come to mean the right to control and dominate non-European populations and appropriate non-European resources. This "right" undergirds policies for development and foreign aid, even though camouflaged by the modern day notions of *noblesse oblige.*

U.S. Food Aid

The principles of white supremacy thus remain central in all issues of foreign relations across the "north-south" divide. This is particularly evident in development and foreign aid programs. An archetypical example is the U.S. food aid program, considered to be the most humanitarian component of the foreign aid package. Passed into law in 1954 under Public Law (P.L.) 480, the language that provides the rationale for the program, which has now become the largest food aid program in the world, constitutes an exemplary statement of the objectives of the aid policies of the U.S. government. The primary goal of the program was to get rid of a glut of grain stocks. The glut itself had been produced by a government program that purchased all the excess production by U.S. grain farmers as a means of maintaining prices. By 1959, government stocks had grown to a point where they were valued at U.S. $7.7 billion. The costs of storage were so exorbitant that a way had to be found to dispose of the surplus that did not have a depressive effect on prices. It was this crisis of overproduction that forced the development of a consolidated food aid program.

It was evident from the start that American grain farmers were to be the primary beneficiaries of this program of foreign food aid. It was equally evident that the intention of the United States was to employ the food distributed under the program as an instrument of control over recipient governments and their populations. These intentions were clearly spelled out in P.L. 480's statement of objectives. Accordingly, the aims of the program, in order of priority, were: 1) to get rid of surplus stocks, 2) to maintain U.S. farm incomes, 3) to develop markets abroad for U.S. farm products, 4) to gain political influence abroad, and 5) to serve humanitarian purposes.

With the implementation of P.L. 480, food became a political weapon employed by the U.S. government in pursuit of its national interests. Under the program, surplus food is provided to friendly governments and denied to those seen to be acting against U.S. interests.

The objective of securing markets, to the extent that it has been successful, comes at the cost of the destruction of domestic food production in recipient countries.[8] Over time, this has become one of the primary causes of hunger, as domestic production of food declines in the face of competition from North American grain provided as a grant to compliant governments. Once hooked on U.S. food aid, recipient countries and populations become extremely vulnerable. As the food aid program shrinks with increased international demand for U.S. farm products, as new priorities emerge in U.S. foreign policy that cause redirection of food aid to other countries, or as governments fall into disfavor for one reason or another, populations find themselves at increasing risk of major food shortages. Given its potential to inflict widespread hunger, the threat to suspend food aid has become a strategic weapon in the arsenal of control. It is employed to force governments to accede to the demands of U.S. and North Atlantic national interests.

Foreign Aid is Foreign Policy

The U.S. government is quite unapologetic in its position that the purpose of foreign aid is the promotion of its own national interest. In justifying the Foreign Affairs Budget request in 1990, for example, then-Secretary of State James Baker was quite definitive in explaining the purpose of U.S. foreign assistance programs. Baker argued that:

> Daily, all over the world our foreign affairs programs promote America's fundamental values. From the refugee officer in Thailand to the aid worker in Pakistan to the trade negotiator in Geneva, our business is representing America's interests to the world.
>
> The investments we now make... —all these are essential investments in our future. These investments will secure for us a leadership

> role in the next century. They will ensure that the world of the future is one in which our fundamental values continue to flourish.

In other words, the objective of funding allocations in the foreign affairs budget of the United States is to ensure the continued dominance of the United States and its values. This intention is clear in its budgetary allocations. In fiscal year (FY) 1991, the State Department requested a total of $20.8 billion in discretionary budget authority. Of this, $9.7 billion was for economic aid and $5.1 billion for military aid. A considerable portion of this aid request ($8.5 billion) was for "security assistance" described by then-Secretary of State Howard Baker as the best "vehicle at our disposal...to provide timely, flexible support to our allies and friends around the world."[9] Such assistance, much of which goes to Israel and Egypt, is perceived in strategic terms and contains the entire $5.1 billion military aid package.

What is the effect of this pattern of allocations for countries outside of Europe? Penny Lernoux, a prize-winning journalist, reported on the consensus of opinion in Latin America, as expressed by one of Brazil's former Planning Ministers, Joao Goulart, as to the real intent of the foreign aid package of the United States. In Goulart's words, "'development' was a myth invented by the industrialized nations to con the Third World into footing the bill for the American (and European) way of life."[10] Goulart was speaking in light of the experiences of the 1960s, when a major program of aid and development assistance was launched by the United States. The specific intent of this Alliance for Progress was to prevent a reoccurrence of a Cuban-type revolution in another Latin American country. In this regard, the idea of self-determination and the right of the populations of Latin America to choose their own systems of government and international allies was never a consideration. As with P.L. 480, the consequences of this developmental package was the intensification of economic exploitation. In its implementation, it:

> meant essentially a series of foreign, mostly U.S., loans for industrial infrastructure and large inputs of foreign investment. The loans have so burdened the Latin-American countries that many are now spending an average 25 percent of their foreign earnings just to service the debt. As for foreign investment, far from creating the millions of new jobs promised by the advance publicity, nearly half this money went to take over existing Latin-American industries. By the end of the "decade of development," 99 percent of the loans made by AID to Latin-American countries were being spent in the United States for products costing 30 to 40 percent more than the going world price.[11]

There are a number of observations to be made from the foregoing discussion. The United States saw the objectives of development assistance in terms of its own self-defined national interests. These, in turn, contained no notion of self-determination for the people of Latin America. Finally, the strategy fashioned for protecting these national interests was implemented in such a way as to intensify the exploitation of the political economies of Latin America for the benefit of U.S. business.

No New Marshall Plan

U.S. aid and development assistance to Latin America differed at its very core from the United States' Foreign Aid program to Europe after World War II. Under the Marshall Plan, the United States transferred U.S. $17 billion over four years, equivalent to around 1.5 percent of U.S. Gross National Product, for the rebuilding of Europe. Here, the primary and paramount concern was the restoration of Europe's devastated physical capital stock. The ideological basis for such assistance was rooted in the notions of mutual respect and a perceived uniformity of interests. Its roots went back to the Atlantic Charter, signed in 1941 by President Theodore Roosevelt and Prime Minister Winston Churchill. The charter had, as its centerpiece, the idea of self-determination and human rights.[12] It was explicitly understood, nonetheless, that these principles applied to Europeans (in a racial sense) and not people of color. After signing the charter, Prime Minister Churchill made it absolutely clear that "these principles do not apply to British colonial territories."[13] Needless to say, these territories were located in Africa, Asia, the Caribbean, and the Pacific. Churchill's frequent assertions as to the inferiority of persons of color were legendary: "Why be apologetic about Anglo-Saxon superiority?" he once asked rhetorically, "We are superior."[14]

Thus, a double standard prevailed when principles of human rights, equality, self-determination, and justice were raised and acted upon. This was particularly evident in the organization of international affairs. It was out of the question that these principles applied to persons of color. Senator James Reed of Missouri expressed such a sentiment quite succinctly: "Think of submitting questions involving the very life of the United States to a tribunal on which a nigger from Liberia, a nigger from Honduras, a nigger from India ...each have (sic) votes equal to that of the great United States."[15]

Hence, the ideological basis informing the Marshall Plan was fundamentally different from that which informs U.S. policies of aid and development to countries outside of Europe and North America. It is evident that principles of equality and self-determination that apply to Europe do not apply to countries outside of the North Atlantic.

Ideological Resistance

There always have been challenges to the ideology of white supremacy. Most recently, such challenges have come in the wake of the acquisition of strategic resources by countries and groups outside of Europe. These resources have been employed to challenge North Atlantic dominance. Perhaps Japan has been most successful in employing its enormous financial resources and technological expertise in efforts to break through the North Atlantic megalith. Nonetheless, the country remains wealthy without power and privilege. More recently, it has become quite vulnerable to a political and economic backlash. A virulent racist campaign of scapegoating, conducted primarily by North American political and economic elites and in the North American media, places blame for existing economic problems unequivocally on the unprincipled practices of the Japanese government and its export sector. This campaign is quite reminiscent of similar attacks against the "Yellow Peril" of "subhumans from the Far East" conducted at the beginning of the century. The latter resulted in the exclusion of Japan from effective input in international affairs solely on the basis of race. It was such exclusion that set the stage for Japan's entry into World War II in 1941.[16]

China's policy of enforced isolation from Western influences after the Communists took power in 1949 paid tremendous dividends in its ability to support powerful challenges to white supremacy. Lacking in wealth and with limited technological expertise to complement its power and prestige within the non-Western world, its effectiveness was severely compromised. China's decision to make strategic alliances with the West and to couch its foreign policy in terms designed to enhance its access to Western technology have eroded its ability to act autonomously in international affairs. This has virtually destroyed its effectiveness as a challenge to white supremacy. The country now seems to be losing its prestige and its struggle to preserve its economic, political, social, and cultural autonomy against the Western juggernaut.

During the 1960s and 1970s, challenges to white supremacy came in the form of the development of "Third Worldism." They were initiated at the Asia-Africa Conference held in Bandung, Indonesia, in April 1955. At the time, countries outside of the North Atlantic alliance were able to exploit the bipolar cold war confrontations in attempts to chart independent courses in their affairs. They used the conference to organize a collective face in their relations with the Western industrialized nations. By the 1980s, however, this collective multinational challenge to white supremacy collapsed as country after country found itself under tremendous economic pressures. Many of their economies had collapsed because of the growing debt burdens that stemmed directly from the program of development and aid pursued by the West. Economic crises were exacerbated by the international recession brought on by the Arab oil embargo of 1973, which began to produce huge balance-of-payments deficits for oil-importing nations. The weakening position of the Soviet Union and Eastern Europe added to the crisis. The potential for support in efforts to challenge the power of the Western industrialized nations all but disappeared with the collapse of European communism and the subsequent dissolution of the Soviet Union in the late 1980s.

Debt and the Destruction of Resistance

During the 1980s, U.S. development policy came to be tied, integrally, to international public policy. The latter took the form of multilateral debt management programs of *structural adjustment* administered cooperatively by the World Bank and the International Monetary Fund (IMF). In short, countries that agree (invariably under pressure) to structural adjustment regimes hand over considerable economic decision-making power to Western-trained IMF economists, who prescribe increased focus on export earnings and curtailed government spending on such programs as food and transportation subsidies. In the words of Walden Bello, executive director of San Francisco's Institute for Food and Development Policy, such programs have become "terribly efficient debt collection mechanisms."[17]

The administration of President Ronald Reagan effectively used its control of the World Bank and the IMF to break international challenges to white supremacy. One of its targets was the quasi-official coalition of countries in the Third World called the Group of Seventy-Seven which had emerged out of the Bandung Conference. The goal of the coalition was to change the terms of the relationship between the "North and South." To do so, the group petitioned for a "New International Economic Order" whose objectives, as outlined by economist Paul Streeten, were aimed:

> partly at removing biases in the present rules, partly at the exercise of countervailing power where at present the distribution of power is felt to be unequal, and partly at counteracting biases that arise not from rules but from the nature of economic processes, such as the cumulative nature of gains accruing to those who already have more resources and the cumulative damage inflicted on those who have initially relatively little.[18]

Efforts to establish a New International Economic Order were the particular targets of the Reagan administration. The World Bank and the IMF were the instruments of its demise. According to Bello, in the 1970s and 1980s, "the (World) Bank virtually functioned as an extension of the State Department and the Treasury Department" of the United States.[19] He continues:

> There were three principal ways in which Washington blatantly employed the Bank to promote its interests. First, it deployed its power and influence at the Bank to punish countries with which it had political disputes and reward those that followed its political

> leadership. Second, the U.S. used the Bank to discourage Third World countries from pursuing development paths that would lead to more economic independence, and to more tightly integrate them instead into a world capitalist order dominated by the United States. Third, with the onset of the international debt crisis, The World Bank became a central element of the debt collection strategy that the Treasury Department put together to salvage the interests of the New York banks at the expense of Third World living standards.[20]

The attacks on efforts aimed at self-determination succeeded with enormous consequences. They resulted in a deepening of the exploitation of Asia, Africa, Latin America, the Caribbean, and the Pacific. The net transfer of financial resources from these countries to the industrialized West amounted to U.S. $155 billion during the 1984-90 period, according to figures provided by the United Nations.[21] The consequences of intensified exploitation have been evident particularly in Africa and Latin America. Per capita income in the former has declined to the level of the 1960s. Both continents are caught in the throes of severe crises of health, education, welfare, and malnutrition. They have seen the return of diseases such as malaria, cholera, and tuberculoses, long thought eradicated. To this has been added new and even more deadly diseases, such as AIDs. Millions of Africans are dying annually from the effects of malnutrition and chronic hunger, which are on the increase.

The fact of pervasive European (in the racial sense) control over Third World countries through the medium of international public policy is undisputed. As an example, of the forty-four countries of sub-Saharan Africa, thirty-two were under the control of World Bank and/or IMF through structural adjustment regimes imposed upon them as a condition of the management of their international debt at some time between 1980 and 1990.[22]

Thus, the modern version of the white man's burden is alive and well in all these programs. The Development Group for Alternative Policies, Inc., makes this observation about the bilateral and multilateral agencies that administer and implement U.S. policies of aid and development:

> There exists an arrogant belief in these institutions that Northerners know what is best for Africans, typified by the claim of an US AID economist that "a revolution" is being "imposed from without" in Africa by a group of donors and international institutions...Only in Washington and in a few other Northern capitals is the myth alive that adjustment is working in Africa, or, for that matter, elsewhere in the Third World. Any other set of development policies, after so prolonged a period of failure would have been ridiculed and jettisoned by the assistance agencies.[23]

The arrogance is born out of the ideology of unilinear developmentalism undergirded by the myth of racial superiority. The application of the Marshall Plan to post-war Europe worked for a very fundamental reason: its intention was the rebuilding of Europe without impinging on the rights of self-determination and on the human rights of Europeans. Thus, when European governments came under the control of socialist and communist regimes after World War II, the type of overt and covert intervention into their affairs that has become standard fare for countries outside of the North Atlantic was considered unthinkable. The United States' strategy for national security was one of cooperation with those countries that had not become members of the Warsaw Pact, whatever the ideological orientation of their governments. This was despite an almost universal move to democratic socialism in Western Europe and the participation of Communist parties in government. To combat the threat posed by the Warsaw Pact, the United States chose to increase its military defense, particularly its strategic forces, and to intensify its intelligence-gathering capabilities in an escalating cold war. In other words, the twin principles of sovereignty and self-determination were meticulously honored in relations with Eastern Europe. Meanwhile, the United States and its allies went on a rampaging campaign in Asia, Africa, Latin America, and the Pacific to "protect" these regions from communism. In the process, almost every country has been touched by outright warfare, low-intensity conflict, interventions, invasions, economic embargoes, assassinations, etc., the likes of which were never seen on European soil in the North Atlantic's strategy of defense against the communist threat.

With the collapse of communism, the United States and its European allies have not missed a step in finding new justifications for policies of domination and control. Terrorism, the drug war, human rights violations, and the absence of democracy have become the new bogeymen of foreign policy. Singly and collectively, they justify continued policies of intervention and practices of withholding development assistance and foreign aid. Meanwhile, the North Atlantic Alliance is engaged in a mad rush to provide a Marshall Plan type bailout program for Eastern Europe. On 26 April 1992, finance officials from the United States, Japan, Germany, Britain, France, Italy, and Canada unveiled a $24 billion assistance package for Russia alone. Moreover, they indicated strong support for using the World Bank and the IMF to coordinate a package of Western assistance that could exceed $150 billion for the former Soviet Union. This figure "would rival in today's dollars the amount of aid the United States provided under the Marshall Plan after World War II to rebuild Europe."[24]

Brian Willson, codirector of the Institute for the Practice of Nonviolence in San Francisco, explains the continued need for white supremacy:

> the West's insatiable consumption appetites, protected by military and covert forces, require exploitative policies threatening the well-

> being of the majority of humankind and other species. Americans alone—representing only 5 percent of the world's population—consume nearly half of its resources. Yet three quarters of the world's "underdeveloped" population are limited to but 15 percent of its resources. Last year, some 40,000 children died every day in the world for lack of nourishment while Americans spent $5 billion on diets.[25]

Wilson went on to point out that "our collective appetites require the majority of the world's people to remain poor." This is at the heart of U.S. foreign policy. The principles of white supremacy continue to justify actions done in the pursuit of Western hegemony; such actions ensure the continued impoverishment of those who are not European, their exploitation, the appropriation of their resources, and an international racial division of labor.

Notes

1. For the purposes of this chapter, North America is considered to comprise the United States of America and Canada. While Mexico is conventionally included as part of North America, its history, culture, structures of social organization, and ethnic composition make its location meaningless except in a strict geographical sense. I would prefer to consider Mexico as part of Mestizo-America. As such, Mexico probably is better identified with Central rather than North America.

2. P. G. Lauren, *Power and Prejudice: The Politics of Diplomacy of Racial Discrimination* (Bolder: Westview, 1988), 42.

3. Ibid., 43.

4. R. Kipling, "The White Man's Burden," in *Rudyard Kipling's Verse* (New York: Doubleday, 1939).

5. Lauren, op. cit., 44.

6. Historian George Fredrickson, in his discussion of the emergence and development of the ideology of white supremacy, defines it as "the attitudes, ideologies, and policies associated with the rise of blatant forms of white or European dominance over 'nonwhite' populations...It involves making invidious distinctions of a socially crucial kind that are based primarily, if not exclusively, on physical characteristics and ancestry...It suggests systematic and self conscious efforts to make race or color a qualification for membership in the civil community" (George M. Fredrickson, *White Supremacy: A Comparative Study in American and South African History.* New York: Oxford University Press, 1981:xi).

7. T. Roosevelt, *The Winning of the West*, in *The Works of Theodore Roosevelt*, 20 vols., (New York: Scribners, 1926), 57-58.

8. Cf. W. W. Murdoch, *The Poverty of Nations* (Baltimore: Johns Hopkins University Press, 1980), 101-105.

9. J. Baker, "U.S. Foreign Policy Priorities and FY 1991 Budget Request," *Current Policy No. 1245* (Washington, D.C.: U.S. Department of State, Bureau of Public Affairs, 1990), 8.

10. P. Lernoux, *Cry of the People* (Harmondsworth: Penguin, 1980), 33.

11. Ibid., 33.

12. Cf. Lauren, op. cit., 136-150.

13. Lauren, op. cit., 139.

14. Lord Charles Moran, *Winston Churchill* (London: Constable, 1966), 131, 559.

15. R. Stone, *The Irreconcilable* (Lexington: University of Kentucky Press, 1970), 88.

16. Cf. Lauren, op. cit., 44-75.

17. W. Bello, "Disciplining the Third World: The Role of the World Bank in U.S. Foreign Policy," *memeo* (San Francisco: Institute for Food and Development Policy, 1992), 15.

18. P. Streeten, "Approaches to a New International Economic Order," in Charles K. Wilber (ed.), *The Political Economy of Development and Underdevelopment*, 3rd ed. (New York: Random House, 1984), 478.

19. Bello, op. cit., 2.

20. Bello, op. cit., 2.

21. United Nations, *World Economic Survey, 1991* (New York: United Nations, 1991), 68.

22. A. E. Elmendorf and W. Roseberry, "Structural Adjustment: What Effect on Health? On Vulnerability to HIV?" (Paper presented at the Ninth International Conference on AIDS, Berlin, June 10, 1993).

23. "Arrogance and Ignorance: Development GAP," Interpress Service, 3 (May 1991), 1.

24. Martin Crutsinger, "Rich Nations Agree on Help for Russia," *San Francisco Chronicle*, 27 April 1992, 9.

25. Brian Willson, "American Way of Life is a Big Threat to the Planet," *San Francisco Chronicle*, 29 October 1990, 12.

CHAPTER 6

Multilateralism, Racism, and the Culture of Altruism

Nazir Ahmad

In this chapter, I am interested in probing the connection between hunger and poverty, on the one hand, and implicit racism in international agencies, on the other. Since this is a quite broad topic, I have chosen to make it more manageable by focusing specifically on two types of multilateral institutions—large development or aid agencies and the media. Some readers may be surprised that I would choose to include the media as one of my selections, but the media is a powerful molder of international norms and values. The growing concentration of media ownership by a small number of transnational conglomerates makes it an important institution to examine in connection with our topic. My approach in this chapter is deliberately conversational; I combine autobiographical reflection and cultural critique. My main point can be summarized succinctly: these international institutions are often unconscious of their racism and, despite an appearance of multiculturalism, often promote policies and practices that work to the detriment of poor people of color.

International Aid Agencies

The issue of multilateral development agencies and racism is a complicated one for at least two reasons. First, it gets complicated due to our own illusions about what these organizations really are. Without knowing much about them, we have vested these international agencies with our intentions, hopes, and ideals. We expect these agencies, with their great charters and compelling rhetoric, to actually implement policies reflecting a common vision of a better life for humanity. And sometimes when we hear the speeches given at the United Nations and other such fora, we are tempted to think that maybe that is indeed the case. If this chapter accomplishes nothing else, I hope it will dispel this illusion.

Second, the theme of multilateral aid agencies and racism is complicated because the flaws of international institutions cannot simply or strictly be analyzed in terms of racism, as we typically understand that word. In fact, if participation meant representation, then, at least superficially, multilateral agencies are nondiscriminatory, because they incorporate considerable racial/ethnic diversity. Nonetheless, racism does exist in these agencies, and this has an impact on the realities of world hunger.

Let me begin to approach our theme by offering a trivial, but symbolically powerful, anecdote. At least twice in the past decade, there have been demonstrations outside the United Nations by its employees. I remember walking by one of them in 1987, and I distinctly remember one big poster. It read: "Let's march today, and let us show our anger and outrage. It simply cannot continue this way." For a brief moment, I felt quite inspired. If the United Nations' employees themselves were standing outside protesting what was going on in the world, I thought, then maybe their idealism was going to take some concrete shape and have some effect. Then I discovered that the demonstration--quite a lively one, quite a multiracial one, as well--was about lowering U.N. employee parking-garage fees, and not about improving the welfare of the poor! The parking fees had been hiked from $20 to $80 a month. Outrageous? Perhaps, though neighborhood parking normally went for about $300.

Similarly, in 1991, there were demonstrations by employees of the United Nations. This time, these idealistic people working to create a more just and united world took to the streets to vocalize their demand for higher wages. Maybe higher wages were in order; that is not my point. The issue has to do with values and priorities and mindsets. It has to do more with what was not being protested than with what was.

Perhaps we are not ready to endorse the specific hierarchy of priorities and values that predominate in international agencies, but that does not make them guilty of racism. What about racism? If you simply look at the crowd in and around the United Nations, or walk into any office associated with it, you may well be pleasantly surprised by the rainbow of people, both in the general work force and among those in charge. The same is true of most international development agencies. Walk into any room--the chances of finding a non-white are quite high. You'll find senior officials who are

African, Asian, or Latin American--holding high posts with considerable perks and privileges. Therefore, can we conclude that there is no racism in these institutions?

Implicit Racism

I believe there is considerable racism in most international institutions, but it is a racism of neglect rather than of intent. It is subtle, it is underlying, and it is difficult to detect with conventional lenses. If we define racism as deliberate exclusion from a position, privilege, or organization based on skin color, then we would have to conclude that most international public organizations are remarkably nonracist. But if we judge these organizations in terms of the impact of their work, we would have to conclude that, too often, people of color have borne the harshest part of economic and political changes, including those orchestrated by international aid agencies. In other words, despite a presumed lack of such intent, an uncanny racial bias exists in the consequences of many actions and policy decisions of multilateral agencies. This, of course, is a generalization, and, thankfully, one also finds exceptions to this.

As an illustration, let us consider the World Bank, by any standard a powerful designer of economic change in many poor countries. I've had two different occasions to work at the World Bank, and each time I was impressed by its intellectual firepower and financial resources. I was also impressed by how little overt racism existed there. The first time, I worked for a Kenyan, who reported to an American, who reported to a Pakistani. Another time, I reported to an Israeli, who reported to an Australian, who reported to a gentleman from Ghana. The Bank has developed the remarkable ability to overcome at least the more obvious forms of racism.

In light of the apparent multiculturalism in the Bank's chain of command, some observations seemed incongruent. One stood out with particular poignancy. Given the preponderance of staff from the Third World, I expected the entire organization to be infused with a sense of urgency and personal commitment to end poverty and injustice. Afterall, hunger is torturously killing people of color at such a rate that an outside observer (perhaps a newcomer from Mars) could plausibly conclude that the dominant North was engaged in a worldwide policy of "ethnic cleansing" by its inattention. But, somehow, it seemed that despite the representation of races, nations, and peoples, there was something even more powerful that made most employees conform to a rather uninspired state of being.

During the mid-1980s when I worked at the Bank, I found little sense of the urgency or impatience that our situation warranted. Most of us intellectually realized that we were losing the battle against poverty, but this realization alone made little difference to our everyday choices and routines. I remember on numerous occasions feeling that we were suspended in an ethical vacuum, unsure of our personal commitments and psychologically distanced from the realities of poverty in our home countries. I remember feeling that many of us had lost our idealism and had become just cogs in an international bureaucracy that viewed development as its job but not its passion and dream. To understand the genesis of this reality, I think we need to examine the socialization process that occurs within most such agencies.

Most international agencies maintain that their best employees give up their national loyalties to become professional international civil servants. There is much to be said for eschewing national chauvinism and becoming global in one's orientation. But this particular process of socialization has a shadow side, as well. In the process of assimilating into this faceless international bureaucracy (with its own notions of careers, promotions, professionalism, and perks), many of us lose a sense of why we got into this line of work in the first place. This confusion is further exacerbated by the jargon and convoluted rhetoric that are the daily currency of many agencies. The process of conforming can become a process of deforming. I suspect that this rootless existence of some people (such as many of those inhabiting transnational agencies) is in part responsible for the insensitivity and maladroitness of many policies.

A number of months before the United Nations took action in Somalia, a most-senior African official of the United Nations appeared on "Nightline" and defended his organization's lethargic response to the crisis of Somalia. The kinds of procedural, bureaucratic, and jurisdictional excuses that he presented could have come out of a Franz Kafka novel. While people were being slaughtered and starved on an unfathomable scale, he was passing the buck from one agency to another. His attitude would have made even Max Weber, the master of modern bureaucracy, cringe in disbelief. Just imagine what a difference a timely intervention by the United Nations might have made. As countries such as Somalia and Rwanda (among many others) lurch into ever-deepening crises, the leaders and officialdom of the United Nations seem ever so paralyzed, unclear about their own objectives and caught in the cross fire and politicking of member-states. Because the values and principles of the United Nations are rhetorically recited but inadequately internalized, the organization repeatedly finds itself following the path of least resistance.

Socialization and Implicit Racism

How is it that we, people of goodwill and of color, who have been entrusted with the representation os the world's conscience, have become so immune to the realities of hunger, poverty, and injustice? A partial explanation of this paradox might lie in psychological reflections offered by people such as Albert Memmi and Frantz Fanon. Memmi, in his landmark book, *The Colonizer and the Colonized*, and Fanon, in *Black Skin, White Mask* and *The Wretched of the Earth*, grasped a fundamental truth: one's skin color is a weak indicator of one's ethnic identity and pride. Those who watched the confirmation hearings for Supreme Court Justice Clarence Thomas may also have been reminded of this.

Memmi, in his analysis, probes the impact of the encounter between the West and the colonized nations. He compellingly depicts the powerlessness and dehumanization of the indigenous populations that resulted from this unequal interaction. Memmi maintains that in a context of such powerlessness, it is not surprising that there emerged a group of people who decided to mimic the oppressors—and to serve them. There is an irony to this: those among the oppressed who do the oppressor's dirty work frequently find themselves at war with their own consciences. They may be at war with their own consciences, but the lure and security associated with the status quo usually prevail.

Many of us who were born privileged in the colonial or postcolonial Third World have our own split identities. Frantz Fanon tells a story that echoes through the halls of many of our personal memories. He talks about growing up in Martinique in a very elite family, being told that he was French, and finally showing up in Paris to study psychiatry, quite enamored of the French. He thought of himself as a part of that culture, only to discover that as far as *they* were concerned, he was only an imposter.

A number of years ago, a *New Yorker* magazine cartoon depicted a cocktail party with some humans and a dog milling about. The dog had joined the conversation, was bow-tied and suited, and was standing on its hind legs, while holding a wine glass with its forelegs. The caption was: "He thinks he is one of us." I suspect that many of us—people from developing countries working in international aid organizations—may really be the dogs of the development cocktail party if we uncritically accept and join the status quo.

In the bureaucratic trenches of the United Nations and other multilateral agencies, staff from Third World countries become alienated from their own roots. They become disconnected emotionally, if not always cognitively, from the social conditions prevalent in the cultures and societies from which they have come. These people, in a sense, are in an in-between land. They are people who exploit the fact that they're interested in poverty; they claim certain expertise, credibility, and even a certain exemption from accountability because they come from poor countries. Yet their social consciousness is not reflective of their roots. They studied development mostly in Western institutions; they work in elite circles where Western modes of thought are normative; many do not even have social contacts apart from the affluent. It is not surprising that they are hesitant to disrupt the status quo. They are beneficiaries after all of the very system of affluence and poverty that they purport to change. It is an unholy arrangement, where righteousness and peddling poverty become a source of financial and positional reward.

When I was originally approached to contribute a chapter to this volume, the topic was to be my country of origin, Bangladesh. I was very tempted, but

I had to decline that particular topic. It would have bordered on the disingenuous for someone who has lived in the United States for nearly twenty years to claim expertise or any deep knowledge of Bangladesh. I am familiar with some of those realities, but my own views are in many ways influenced by my own privileged upbringing and subsequent migration to the West. I can sympathize, but I cannot totally empathize, with the plight of the poor in Bangladesh. I told the editor that if he wanted an analysis of race and hunger there, he should not expect intermediaries like me to speak with a great deal of authenticity. But you see, I was invited to write the chapter not only because I am originally from Bangladesh, but also because in many ways I am more like the audience of this book than like those I was asked to write about. The sad truth is that I know your game and language well enough that if I claimed profound expertise on Bangladesh, you could not tell otherwise. Paulo Freire aptly observed that the poor are spoken of, spoken for, and spoken to, but seldom do they get a chance to speak for themselves.

The International Development Elite

The development elite are a powerful group, and I say this without being pejorative. Owing to their power, it is imperative that we understand how their ideas for global solutions to global problems are being developed. Who is developing these ideas? Which institutions influence the direction of these ideas? Whose ideas are likely to gain support and whose are likely to be neglected? And, finally, what characteristics define this multiracial, multicultural, and yet surprisingly uniform development elite?

There is much to commend about those who inhabit the inner sanctums of international development organizations. They all recognize that our planet and its people grow more fragile and precarious by the day. They are all convinced of the importance of such fundamentals as basic human rights, the need for peace, the concept (in principle) of sustainable development. No one argues that hunger is a justifiable condition. Few actively promote racism. Still, there are aspects of their ideology, their culture, and their view of development that I find troubling and that, in turn, lead to a toleration of hunger and poverty among people of color in this world.

Not long ago I was on a plane to Washington D.C., sitting next to a West African development expert returning from a mission to another West African country.[1] While describing his activities, he started referring condescendingly to his host countrymen as "those people." Somewhat perplexed, I asked him, "Sir, where are you from?" He replied firmly, "I'm from Washington D.C." But I queried further, "Is that where you were born?" "No," he replied. As the conversation progressed, we talked about his roots, upbringing, and professional experience. As we talked on, he concluded, "You know, I guess you are right. I'm really one of them, but I am not sure anymore because *I can no longer relate to them.*" Therein lies the rub.

Nowhere is the implicit racism of international aid bureaucracies more evident than in the ways in which we support a veritable army of foreign experts in developing countries. Where technical skills combined with common sense, compassion, and a spirit of appreciative inquiry is necessary, we bring in high-paid, self-promoting "experts" who tell "them" at best what they already know, but in a language that is no longer accessible. By creating this new caste of development experts, we have confused rather than eased the path to social progress.

As a consultant myself, I have a healthy regard for the value of independent perspectives and expertise. But I also know that too often the advice provided by outside experts on development is not worth the paper it is presented on—and certainly not worth the bill that comes with it. Furthermore, I submit to you that too large a portion of the international technical assistance is driven by a sense of white superiority (however subtle) and donor nationalism, rather than the actual needs of development. Those of you who have worked in the development field know only too well the phenomenon of itinerant, Western consultants who spend the first half of their extended visits learning from those on the ground and the second half of their tenure pontificating to those from whom they have just learned.

Right now, there are about 80,000 foreign (read Western) experts in Africa, and it costs a minimum of $150,000 a year per person to keep them there. I ask you, how many of these so-called experts know more about Africa than their African counterparts? The European Development Fund, which was set up as Europe's conscientious response to the crises in their old colonies, has foreign expatriates running about 90 percent of its projects in Africa, the Caribbean, and the Pacific. Throughout the Third World, we spend a staggering $15 to $22 billion a year—a third to a half of all bilateral and multilateral foreign aid money—to support Western experts, who live like nobility and speak nobly of the poor. By overpaying expatriates and a select group of privileged nationals, we are practicing a kind of foreign aid apartheid, all the while preaching the good words of self-determination, self-reliance, and progress at the grassroots. Is this really the best way to engender indigenous capabilities? Foreign expertise can be helpful and well worth its price tag, but only if such expertise is focused on critical needs and rapidly builds self-sustainability.

The Ideology of Development

Just as in Manifest Destiny, or Christopher Columbus's "discovery" of the Americas, or the British "civilizing" India, all modern development paradigms, capitalist as well as socialist, start with a model of an ideal world that is defined in European materialist terms. It assumes that all people of the world are on the same path, with the white West leading the way and the nonwhite Third World following.

The dominant paradigm is captured by W.W. Rostow's book, *The Stages of Economic Growth.* Although Rostow himself was far more cautious and understood subtleties, those who took his mantle basically reduced the countries of the world and their economic history into stages of economic "growing up." First you have infancy, the stage that a number of countries are said still to be in. Then you develop certain infrastructure to facilitate private capitalism and a certain necessary concentration of productive capital. As you continue to develop, you move in a straight line until, finally, you're ready to "take off" economically. I don't quite know where, but at some point, a country reaches the nirvana of development. This is the basic formula, admittedly simplified and caricatured, that all so-called Third World countries are asked to follow.

Have you ever wondered what this "development nirvana" would look like? How many McDonald's should it have? How many Nintendo games per household? How many cable channels and tanning salons? I know I am being facetious, but less so than you think. The fact remains that the current development paradigm simply tries to mimic (but not challenge) the economic, cultural, and social transformations that the Euro-based industrial societies went through, presumably toward similar ends. Development assistance, as currently formulated, is designed to help people do the best they can within rigid constraints. It is designed to help people play the modern economic game, and to play it more efficiently; it is not designed to reinvent the game or alter the balance of power.

I want to emphasize that the problem is not one of a lack of good intention or good will. The same kind of arrogance and the same kind of unconsciously racist assumptions come from people whose individual moral character is beyond reproach. Let me illustrate. Consider Larry Summer, the former chief economist of the World Bank and now the Under Secretary of the U.S. Treasury. A distinguished academician, Summer recognized that the West had a severe pollution problem and a high cost for health care. Following a certain logic inherent in a certain economic worldview, Summer came up with a quite rational yet ethically unacceptable alternative: the West could export its toxic wastes to poor countries, where both life and land were cheap.

In summary, multinational development organizations exhibit a cultural affinity toward a Western, primarily European, view of development. The people of color in these organizations are largely from affluent classes who have been educated in Western or Western-influenced institutions. Many of them have become psychologically distanced from the histories and conditions of the popular struggles in their countries of origin. They have gone through a process of socialization that has dulled their idealism and tempered their sense of urgency.

Racism and the Media

I refer to the mass media as multilateral organizations because, as Noam Chomsky and even those in the mainstream point out, we are in the midst of the globalization and concentration of media control around the world. And I think it is important that we do not focus on multilateral aid agencies in isolation, but rather look at the broad cultural context that shapes their (and our) views.

According to contemporary development ideology, despite whispers to the contrary, development is something that we do to the poor. Progress is something that is done to them. Those who it is done to really have no say. It puts human beings in the position of having to receive, react, and conform. And we support this imposition through a culture of arrogant altruism.

The Media and the Culture of Altruism

According to the popular image, development assistance is an altruistic burden shouldered by the generous West to help the helpless and often ungrateful Third World. This viewpoint persists despite the demonstrable fact that most foreign aid creates a net economic benefit for the donors. Therefore, it is not surprising that at times of economic difficulties in affluent nations, foreign aid becomes a favorite scapegoat. This misinformed view of foreign aid endures because it ultimately reinforces Western claims of moral superiority. The truth is, this "altruism" is without sacrifice. It is ultimately self-serving. This culture of altruism finds no small measure of its legitimacy through the mass media.

One of the best illustrations of how the media builds and reinforces this culture is the portrayal it offered of the U.S. intervention in Somalia in the fall of 1992. If one were to believe the popular media, both print and electronic, the U.S. Marines invaded the African country of Somalia to relieve the severe famine taking place and to restore civil order. Both of these, of course, would be purely altruistic motives. But a number of facts do not fit well with the descriptions and images offered the American public.

First of all, we were rarely told that the crisis in Somalia was largely one of our own making. After all, those weapons shouldered by Somali pre-adolescents were supplied from our arsenals. In the 1980s, we supplied more than $100 in military aid for every man, woman, and child in Somalia, at a time when the country was terrorized by a cruel dictatorship.[2] Yet more important, the invasion itself had numerous counterproductive effects. For example, instead of dealing with traditional leaders, such as community elders, the U.S. invasion force dealt exclusively with the Somali warring military leaders, thereby strengthening the position of the very people we claimed to be putting under wraps. We stated that our aim was to restore peace, but the internal peace negotiations, which had advanced to a critical stage, including plans for pivotal meetings between elders and intellectuals, collapsed in the wake of the Marines' invasion.[3] Finally, the famine itself, well into its second year, was already beginning to ebb about the time the Marines were storming the beaches of Mogadishu under the glare of camera lights. In fact, the death toll had fallen by 90 percent between July and November.[4]

So why did the Marines invade? It is undeniable that some of the motivation and support came from our genuine concern. A number of influential strategists seemed to believe that in the post-cold war era, the military's immense logistical capabilities could be mobilized for humanitarian assistance. We also thought that it would be a relatively easy and painless venture to undertake. In addition, some have cynically observed that the Somalia intervention, conducted as it was in front of the world media, provided a perfect public relations showcase for the modern U.S. military. Whatever the complex mix of motivations, it is certainly the case that the media circus that surrounded the troops further reinforced traditional, negative stereotypes of Africans. Why, for instance, did the media refer to "tribal wars" and "warlords" in Somalia but not in Ireland or Bosnia?

Media Racism and the Victims of Famine

To illustrate further how the mainstream media reinforce a racially premised culture of altruism in the West, let us reflect on the coverage of the Ethiopian famine of the early 1980s. The Ethiopian famine was, you may recall, one of the hottest topics during 1984 and 1985 in both the electronic and print media. Largely as a result of massive coverage, hundreds of thousands of people from Europe and the United States were moved by compassion to contribute generously to the relief effort. Thousands of children saved money from school lunches to donate to starving children in Ethiopia. Rock musicians galvanized a generation of young people through a trans-Atlantic "Live Aid" concert designed to benefit African hunger relief. All in all, it was a remarkable and inspiring demonstration of compassion and generosity.

But, it is essential to add, the outflow of altruism was tinted by no small dose of racism. When all was said and done, one was left with a clear impression of white generosity and black need.[5] Hidden behind the veil of generosity were issues of structural injustice that went unaddressed. To illustrate the point further, it is helpful to probe how it is that the Ethiopian story ever achieved prominence in the first place.

Have you ever wondered how, of all places, Ethiopia visited you in your living room, appealing to your conscience? When we scrutinize the story behind the first telecast of the Ethiopian famine, we uncover a jolting truth: mortifying hunger among people of color is, with few exceptions, not considered newsworthy. So let's look at how Ethiopia came into our consciousness. The story begins, not with journalistic success, but with an aborted effort to bring Ethiopian hunger to world attention.[6]

Early in 1984, Bill Blakemore, an ABC journalist stationed in Rome, heard that there was a major crisis emerging in Ethiopia. He contacted ABC headquarters in New York and told them about the drought and looming famine and requested permission to travel with a film crew to the site. Permission was denied. Blakemore persisted and eventually was told to gather secondhand clips from other journalists and send them back for consideration. Discouraged, Blakemore (according to his own account) thought with justifiable cynicism: "There are people dying, but they're only black."[7] Nonetheless, he followed instructions. He gathered his footage, sent it to New York, but never received a reply.

Six months and thousands of deaths later, Michael Buerk, a BBC journalist normally stationed in Johannesburg, traveled to Ethiopia with a film crew and made a tape, which was quickly aired in Britain. The report so impacted the British viewers that they donated $10 million to relief agencies. None of the major media outlets in the United States, however, picked up the story.

Buerk returned to Ethiopia later that year. He found the famine had worsened monstrously. As his film crew shot footage of the famine, a child died on camera. In the village he visited, people were dying at the rate of one every twenty minutes. In his narrative, Buerk described it as "a famine of biblical proportion." On 22 October, he flew with his film crew back to London, and his story aired the next day on the BBC. The pictures were startling, the narrative jolting. It was one of the decade's most poignant and piercing pieces of broadcast journalism. In response, the phones of relief organizations rang off their hooks.

NBC had an exclusive arrangement with the BBC that gave it the right of first refusal for BBC international television reports. NBC's London bureau, knowing the value of the story, notified New York, but it found the New York management unresponsive. Apparently, the New York brass were operating according to a widely observed (but implicit) decision principle in television journalism that Peter Boyer, a *Los Angeles Times* bureau chief, summarizes as "the more distant the place and the darker its people, the slimmer a story's chances of making it on the air."[8]

It would certainly be a mistake to place the entire blame on network producers. Producers do not achieve their high-power positions by accident. One essential skill that they all possess is a keen ability to predict what is of interest to the viewing public. Though they clearly make mistakes, the Ethiopian story being one, they have a well-honed skill for reading the public mood. As a rule of thumb, the rules they use to decide what to place on the air are fruitful guides to understanding the culture of the intended audience. It is enlightening, then, to learn from a senior U.S. television executive that the operative geographic and racial math goes something like this: "One dead fireman in Brooklyn is worth five English bobbies, who are worth 50 Arabs, who are worth 500 Africans."[9]

As a result of the resistance of the NBC management to viewing the BBC footage, Joseph Angotti, NBC's general manger of news in Europe, personally called New York from London, insisting that they at least take a look at the tape. Paul Greenberg, executive producer of "Nightly News," consented and the tape arrived by satellite just as the news crew was busily completing work for the evening's broadcast. As the tape began to feed into the New York monitors, work in the newsroom came to a halt, as everyone watched in stunned silence. Though there was lingering debate about whether to show the BBC piece or a tape about Cadillacs belonging to the Rajneesh of Oregon, Tom Brokaw settled it by insisting on the Ethiopian story. That evening, 23 October, after the famine was already many months long, the starving Ethiopians visited the living rooms of America.

After the initial U.S. broadcast, the public response was tremendous. Belatedly, dozens of additional stories were done by all the major networks. NBC ran an unusual full-page advertisement in the *Washington Post*, congratulating itself on its famine coverage. Ethiopia, in a sense, became the latest television icon. Even Ronald Reagan, the coldest of the cold warriors, who previously refused all aid to Ethiopia, relented to the power of the medium that had created him. Under the weight of public opinion and congressional pressure spearheaded by the late Mickey Leland, he authorized humanitarian aid to Ethiopia.

Before we congratulate ourselves about how generous and concerned we once were about Ethiopia, let us remember that Ethiopia entered our consciousness and energized our commitments due to happenstance; and even with these factors going for it, the story was told only after untold human misery went unreported for lack of interest. The eventual airing of the Ethiopian tragedy was a result, in part, of someone preferring that story over one about some fringe leader in Oregon who loved Cadillacs. If we are serious about being global citizens, we cannot rely on such belated accidents. And I assure you that, while some network personnel admitted to being spooked by the blistering success of a story that they themselves had earlier rejected as unmarketable, few people in the media have changed the way stories are evaluated and selected.

If Peter Boyer is correct in his summation that "the more distant the place and the darker its people, the slimmer a story's chances of making it on the air," then we need to reflect on the media's image of the U.S. population's interest. Let us not forget that the media is an incredibly powerful institution that shapes our mind, shapes our soul, and shapes our interpretations of the world. I have a great deal of respect and awe for the potential of modern media, but so far it has failed to demonstrate enough courage or vision to be trusted. We cannot allow the pundits of the media to unilaterally shape our agenda any more than we can allow the experts of development.

Media and the Trivialization of the Third World

The media punditry prevail because we permit them to reduce complexity to sound-bite simplicity. And in the process, we neglect some fundamental truths. All you have to do is listen critically to the respectable popular media and you will notice it for yourselves. Let me give just a few brief examples, in case you thought that the delay in reporting on Ethiopia was an unfortunate exception. A number of years ago, my college-mates and I were watching the CBS "Evening News," and Dan Rather introduced his story something like this: "Vietnam, the war that took 55,000 precious human lives..." This sounded so poetic and poignant that it took me a few seconds to comprehend the implications of his words. You see, I thought of Vietnam first as a country with a rich and colorful civilization and as a site of war second. And 55,000 precious human lives? What about the hundreds of thousands of Vietnamese who were slaughtered during the same war? Could he mean that only the lives of the U.S. soldiers were precious? And did Dan Rather not know that the body count of the U.S. dead was almost double the 55,000 he cited, if all the U.S. veterans of the war who died from suicides, mysterious single-car accidents, and psychological trauma were included? I believe that Dan Rather had no intention to mislead us, but in the process of making the short sound bite, he left out some vital and pertinent facts.

Let me give you other brief examples. At the end of the Persian Gulf War, National Public Radio hosted a panel to discuss the media coverage of the war. A number of journalists criticized the manner in which the Pentagon spoon-fed news to the media, which, in turn, regurgitated it to the public. But toward the end of the program, the moderator (a distinguished journalist whom I admire) prefaced her last question by stating, "But given that only a few lives were lost in this war, do you think...?" Again, you see, she inadvertently but nonetheless inexcusably implied that the 140,000 Iraqis who died in the war (about 100,000 of whom were buried alive) did not fit into our census of human lives. Abraham Lincoln, during the bitter Civil War, constantly stressed the need for magnanimity upon military victory. But how can we be magnanimous if we don't even acknowledge our actions?

Finally, let me offer a more personal example. Some of you may recall that there was a massive tidal wave in my native Bangladesh in 1991 that took over 200,000 lives. All public telecommunications lines to the country were out, and the news media was my sole source of information on the calamity. I turned on the local television news that night, and near the end of the broadcast, the anchor spent perhaps twenty seconds mentioning that a huge tidal wave had swept through Bangladesh, killing many thousands. The item was immediately followed by the weatherman, who did his human interest introduction by quipping that the weather of San Francisco was so much more appealing to tourists than that of Bangladesh. I suspect that if London had been the site of the catastrophe, it would not have been so quickly glossed over and then used as a backdrop for humor.

The World Beyond Racism

The theme of this book is racism and hunger, so I wanted to first express my views on this intersection. As I have outlined, I believe that there is indeed a pattern of implicit racism that has shaped the dominant ideologies of development (of both left and right) and the practices of the media. It is a racism that leads to a dulling of our sense of moral outrage, to the point that we quietly tolerate hunger among massive numbers of people of color. Ultimately, however, I am not at all certain that solving the racism problem alone will get us far enough.

In the long run, it is quite conceivable that race will diminish as a prime human differentiator. Instead, class, education, wealth, access to information, and cultural orientation may play the lead roles in separating the haves from the have-nots, the helpers from those chosen to be helped. We must be skeptical of solving the race problems without addressing the fundamental question of how the poor and the weak of all races might gain equitable access to resources, power, and opportunities on a global scale.

Senegalese economist Samir Amin observed in 1975 that in a world of an emergent multinational elite, differences of ethnicities would be overcome by the convergence of economic interests, shared worldviews, and a "Western" consumption-driven lifestyle.[10] Jacques Attali, the controversial and extravagant former president of the European Bank of Reconstruction & Development, also observed the same phenomenon—of what he called the "affluent nomad."[11] This nomad has no national identity or responsibility, but is able to claim the whole world as his or her own, connected by the best communications technology, consumerist culture, and ease of travel for those who can afford it.

The growing unification of the affluent of the world across national, cultural and racial boundaries through the power of technology, investment, and market integration poses an interesting situation for those who are advocates for the poor. I believe that this process of realignment can also create opportunities to redefine perspectives and priorities. The challenge before us is to harness the power of these same technologies to work toward a new "people-centered multinationalism," bringing together people of concern and goodwill from across the world (including businesses and governments, when appropriate). We, too, can collaborate across national, linguistic, and ethnic boundaries. Organizations such as the Institute for Global Communications (providers of PeaceNet and other progressive computer networks) are hard at work creating a communications infrastructure that will allow nongovernmental organizations and private citizens to effectively reach and communicate with one another. Organizations such as Business for Social Responsibility are working to be similar catalysts in the for-profit sector.

I was asked recently whether I supported the idea of the United Nations, and I said that I did, unequivocally. But to me, the United Nations is not the existing edifices in New York and Geneva. Lofty as their goals were, the founders of the United Nations made one fundamental error. They assumed that we lived in a world where member governments would automatically represent the best interests of their peoples. We have learned that most governments care first about securing and staying in power, second, about enriching themselves, and only third about improving the well-being of their people. Given this hierarchy of priorities, it is not at all surprising that the United Nations, as an organization, despite spurts of efforts, has made only limited headway in solving the endemic problems of poverty, hunger, racism, civil war, and other human-rights violations.

So is there hope in all this? Is multilateralism bound to fail, and should all of us just look inward, circle our wagons, and forget about the rest of the world? The answer to this question depends on your point of view. As you may have heard, the optimist sees the glass as half full; the pessimist sees it as half empty. But the activist simply takes the glass, empties what isn't needed, and fills it with what is more useful. I would recommend, that instead of abandoning multilateralism, we redefine it with a new covenant between the leaders and the led. There will not be a better time than now for beginning this recasting. We have now a rare moment in human history, when the dominant paradigms of yesterday are clearly not working. In the despair and anxiety that one finds in so many places lie the potential seeds of hope and the germination of change. It is time for all of us, as people of concern and goodwill, to reach out to international institutions and internationalist individuals, to governments and popular movements, to leaders and the led, and articulate a new global ethic—one based on the principles of justice, accountability, humility, and the cultivation of curiosity and openness. Often imperfect organizations can be transformed, but only if there is a clarity of vision and a commitment to change.

Those of us who have had the privilege of education and access to opportunities have a special obligation to help transform the institutions in which we work. To be a change agent from inside is especially difficult, because it is much safer and comfortable to *go along to get along*. For us to be effective as change agents, according to the brilliant Edward Said, we must be thinking people motivated not by financial reward or approval of superiors, but rather by a deep sense of care and affection. Our problem, Said observed, is to "deal with the impingements of modern professionalization...but not by pretending that they are not there, or denying their influence, but by representing a different set of values and prerogatives."[12] As we edge toward a new future and a new millennium, we must remember that the struggle for global change requires each of us to participate, including those with whom we disagree the most. After all, few of us are true heroes or true villains. We are simply people with a whole lot of different concerns, who want to live and create some meaning in our lives—and in the process, hopefully, to leave the world a better place than we found when we arrived. That is the promise that we must fulfill, because otherwise we will perish. Are we ready to seize the new day?

Notes

1. The word "mission," so commonly used by development professionals, is revealing. It comes from the colonial days, when colonizers thought that the natives had to be convinced of their own ignorance and imbued with superior European Christian values and views.

2. See Stephen R. Shalom, "Gravy Train: Feeding the Pentagon by Feeding Somalia," *Z Magazine*, February 1993, 15-25.

3. R. Omaar, and A. de Woal, "Saving Somalia Without the Somalis," *Africa News*, 21 December 1992—5 January 1993, 4.

4. Ibid.

5. It is interesting to note that the pivotal role of African American churches and leaders in mobilizing support for Ethiopia was generally neglected in the media.

6. The following information is drawn from Peter J. Boyer, "Famine in Ethiopia: The TV Accident that Exploded," *Washington Journalism Review*, January 1985, 19-21. It is remarkable that even in this excellent piece, there is no mention of Mohammed Amin, Michael Buerk's African colleague, who was instrumental to this story being developed.

7. Ibid., 19.

8. Ibid., 19.

9. Ibid., 19.

10. Samir Amin, "Accumulation and Development: A Theoretical Model," in *Review of African Political Economy*, Vol. 1, No. 1 (1975): 9-26.

11. Jacques Attali, *Millennium: Winners and Losers in the Coming World Order* (New York: Times Books, 1991).

12. Edward W. Said, *Representations of the Intellectual* (New York: Pantheon Books, 1994).

CHAPTER 7

Getting at Hunger's Roots: The Legacy of Colonialism and Racism

Kevin Danaher

Anyone who has tended a garden knows that if you don't pull a weed out by its roots, it is certain to grow back. Hunger is a similar phenomenon. If we only address its surface manifestations—the bloated bellies and shriveled limbs of starving children—we will be fighting a war without end. This essay argues that to dig out the roots of hunger, we must first find them, and to find them, we need to examine the history of colonialism and how it built hunger into the world economy as a structural feature.

In 1984, my partner, Medea Benjamin, and I were traveling in the Guatemalan highlands interviewing peasant families about land issues and repression by the military. One of the Indian women we met told us that soldiers had come to her home one night and hacked her husband to death, right in front of her and her three children. The military said he was a subversive because he was helping other peasants learn how to raise rabbits as a source of food and money. I tried to understand this but I couldn't. I asked the woman to explain how teaching peasants to raise rabbits could be considered subversive.

This illiterate peasant woman proceeded to give us one of the best lectures I have ever heard on structural inequality and the need for structural change to eliminate hunger. "Look," she said, "the plantations down along the coast that grow export crops are owned by generals and rich men who control the government. A big part of their profit comes from the fact that we peasants are so poor we are forced to migrate to the plantations each year and work for miserable wages in order to survive. If we could feed ourselves, through raising rabbits or any other activity, we would never work on the plantations again. If that happened, the bosses would lose the source of their riches. So, given this system, helping peasants learn how to raise rabbits is subversive."

The struggle against hunger is crucial to us all because it holds the secret to all struggles for social justice. No greater gap can exist between human beings than that between people who are well fed and those who are physically and mentally weakened due to inadequate nutrition. Divisions of race, gender, religion, and nationality are real enough, but none is as stark as that between the satiated and the hungry. If we can overcome this human chasm, we can overcome all others.

The antihunger movement must expand to become a mass movement, or it will never achieve its goal of eliminating hunger. To reach beyond its current constituency, the movement must develop a broader appeal. Those who are morally concerned about hunger and feel compassion for the poor are easy converts. But they are a minority. To reach a wider audience, we must appeal to more than a sense of charity.

Charity is based on a sense of "other"—the giver of charity feels a separateness from the recipient. The words altruism and alienation come from the same linguistic roots. Solidarity, on the other hand, is based on a sense of shared interest. The dictionary definition of solidarity is "complete unity, as of opinion, purpose, interest, feeling." The person expressing solidarity understands that building friendships across social boundaries is in one's own self-interest.

The difference is illustrated by different orienting questions. Those operating from a simple charity perspective ask, "How can we feed all the hungry?" Those operating from a solidarity perspective ask, "What changes need to be made in the social order so that the hungry will be able to feed themselves?" The latter question, if handled correctly, can appeal to both sides of the political spectrum.

The importance of the distinction can be seen at the policy level. The charity perspective of doing for others what they are presumed incapable of doing for themselves is behind much of the degrading and dependency-creating programs of the modern welfare state. At their best, these programs offer opportunities to people who are temporarily down on their luck. But often they incarcerate people's spirits by locking them into dependency on the state for handouts.

In contrast, a solidarity perspective is behind efforts to create independent, self-sustaining organizations controlled by the poor themselves. Solidarity is a more fundamentally democratic impulse than charity. While charity can often perpetuate the relationship of wealthy giver and impoverished receiver, solidarity seeks to break down the very structures that maintain divisions between the powerful and the powerless.

Within the antihunger movement, we need to be vigilant about our own motivations. Feelings of guilt do not liberate—they paralyze. Feelings of solidarity lead us toward a goal that most great religions aspire to: achieving oneness with other living things.

This is not just a spiritual dilemma. There are many practical questions about how we can help people in affluent countries develop a sense of oneness with the poor of the world. In the conclusion of this essay, we provide some suggestions for ways to educate Americans about their shared interests with the hungry.

Reconceptualizing Race

Making sweeping generalizations about the effects of racism on hunger can be very misleading. Human beings do not exist as representatives of simplified racial categories. A person of any given race is simultaneously of a particular gender and class, and carries cultural baggage specific to his or her particular national or ethnic group. Isolating race as a factor is an intellectual process that cannot be duplicated in reality. The difficulty comes in trying to develop an analysis that can capture the reality of how people actually exist: as a complex matrix of race, class, and gender inequalities.

Race should not be thought of just in terms of skin color. Operationally, throughout history, race has been more than a difference in color. Definitions of race have been tied to power imbalances that have allowed one group to impose a definition of "inferior other" on a less powerful group. In this chapter, I use the term race in a broadened sense, as when historians refer to the "Irish race." History clarifies the point.

What outsiders usually call the Irish potato famine and the Irish call the Great Starvation (1846-1848) is just one case that debunks simplistic notions of race as it relates to hunger. It would be difficult for an outsider to tell who was whiter, the Irish peasant starving in the countryside or the British landlord sitting in his parlor counting rent money. Without going into great detail, the essential facts of the case are these.

The Irish potato crop suffered a combination of epidemic diseases, resulting in a reduced crop in 1845, a very small crop in 1846, and a total crop failure in 1847. This produced hundreds of thousands of deaths from hunger and related diseases; the exact casualty toll is still not known to this day. Due to starvation and emigration, the population of the country was cut by one-third in a decade. The rural population shrunk by more than half.

But most of these deaths were unnecessary. During the famine years, Ireland produced sizable crops of corn, cattle, and other foods not effected by the potato blight. The amount of food exported from Ireland for profit during the years of starvation would have been more than adequate to feed all the people. Landlords and tax collectors made no concessions for peasants hit hard by natural disaster. The collectors even took advantage of the occasion to demand payment of arrears from previous years. Hence, the Irish saying: "God sent the blight; but the English landlords sent the famine." What ultimately defined the situation was power: British elites were powerful enough to impose famine on the Irish countryside, and the Irish toiling classes were not powerful enough to prevent it.

Reducing the concept of race to skin color cannot tell us why thousands of black-skinned Ethiopians starved to death in the early 1970s and again in the mid-1980s, while other black-skinned Ethiopians survived those years quite comfortably. As in the Irish case, while millions of Ethiopians died for lack of food, large amounts of Ethiopian beef and other foods were exported for profit—under both Haile Selassie's "capitalist" regime in the 1970s and Mengistu Haile Mariam's "socialist" regime in the 1980s.

Other historical examples abound. When the German Nazis massacred millions of Russians in World War II, the carnage was facilitated by the German belief that the Russians—every bit as white as Germans—were *untermenschen* (subhuman). When the state of Biafra attempted to secede from Nigeria, the ensuing war touched off widespread starvation among the Biafrans. The black rulers of Nigeria and their white backers in Washington and London did not lose much sleep over the many black Biafrans who perished. During World War II, when the government of India took massive amounts of food from Bengal province to feed British and Indian troops fighting the Japanese in nearby Burma, it left the people of Bengal vulnerable to a famine that eventually killed millions.

Those in power may share the same physical characteristics as those who go hungry. Only by incorporating into the analysis other axes of power, such as class and gender, can we arrive at an accurate understanding.

In most cases of severe mass hunger, we can make the following generalizations about who suffers and who does not:

- The most vulnerable to hunger and starvation are those farthest removed from wealth, political power, and weapons. This usually means women and children. Access to any one of these three hunger-retarding characteristics can be used to overcome the lack of the others. For example, rural bandits in Mozambique during famines in the 1980s were not wealthy and did not have access to state power, but they had guns and were willing to employ force ruthlessly to take what they wanted from whoever had it. Few of these bandits starved to death, although thousands of Mozambicans were expiring from hunger.
- Skin color alone cannot always tell you who will go hungry and who will not. Black American journalists and doctors in Ethiopia and Sudan during the famine years of the 1980s did not starve, despite sharing the same skin color as those who were starving. The class status of these professionals

protected them from hunger. Another example is that despite the fact that the ruling elite of the United States is white, the majority of Americans going hungry are also white, not black. The white skin of U.S. policymakers does not seem to give them great concern for all of the white people going hungry.

o On the other hand, most of the people going hungry in the world are people of color. But this is not due to any innate inferiority of these people. It is a historical legacy explored in the next section: white people inhabited that small section of the planet (western Europe) that generated an acquisitive economic and military system that, for the past 500 years, has conquered the rest of the earth, plundered its resources, and forcibly integrated Third World economies into the capitalist world system in a dependent way.

The fact that there is widespread hunger in economically developed countries such as the United States, proves that the problem cannot be fully understood using the nation-state as the main unit of analysis. Due to the "trickle-down" of empire, people without money in the United States do not experience the same severity of hunger as those without money in Sudan, but the key defining relationship of exploiter and exploited is the same. The trick is to avoid being fooled by the physical form exploitation takes and see the underlying structure of injustice that lies hidden beneath the surface.

This is why it is so important to understand the historical roots of global hunger. Without this understanding, many people believed the mass media portrayal of drought as the key cause of famine in Ethiopia in 1984-85. While no one would deny the importance of severe weather in wrecking Ethiopian agriculture, we must ask what historical processes brought the Ethiopian peasantry to such a level of impoverishment that a natural disaster could push them over the edge. In recent years, there have been droughts in Australia, England, and the United States, but these countries did not experience famine because they had sufficient economic reserves to purchase and distribute food resources. The Ethiopians—and many others in the Third World—have been so drained of resources over the centuries that they have no reserves to fall back on.

What Drove the Process of Colonization?

Many of us know that the impact of colonialism was evil. But if we fail to understand what drove the Europeans to conquer the world, we are left with an impression that these crazy white people just got it in their heads one day to rape the planet and then did it. This view is just as racist as thinking that colonial Europeans were innately superior to people of color and therefore somehow deserved to take over the world.

For Europeans to dominate the globe, there were several requirements. There needed to be a revolutionary economic system that could provide the dynamism and force to conquer the rest of the earth. There also needed to be an instrument of conquest: mobile weaponry powerful enough to let this small minority strike out across the globe and seize control of other cultures. And finally, there needed to be an ideological system that would justify the smashing of other cultures and the pillage of their wealth. In the fifteenth and sixteenth centuries, the nations of western Europe were putting together this powerful combination.

The Economic Engine

Northwestern Europe in the fifteenth and sixteenth centuries was unique in that it developed a system of economic organization that provided (1) a driving force to motivate entrepreneurs to seek greater profits at all costs, (2) a way to generate large surpluses in order to fund expeditions and conquests, and (3) a class of people—capitalists—with a need and desire to break apart the old social order.

By the 1400s, Europe was making a transition from feudalism to capitalism. While there had been long-distance trade under feudalism, that trade involved relatively small amounts of mainly luxury goods consumed by a minority who could afford them. The dawning of capitalism saw the emergence of long-distance trade in mass-consumption items, such as textiles. It would be a defining characteristic of the capitalist epoch that globe-spanning trade would link far-flung corners of the world in a dependent way with the financial and manufacturing centers of Europe.

The expansive dynamic of this new system can be seen by comparing its anatomy to trade under previous systems. Under precapitalist trade, producers would trade commodities for money and use that money to buy other commodities they needed. The key determinant in this type of trade was the qualitative value of the commodities: the specific uses of the product vis-a-vis the needs of the purchaser (a farmer buys a shovel to dig with, a toolmaker buys corn to consume). But under the new system, capitalists used their money to buy commodities to sell for a greater amount of money. The specific uses of the commodity were irrelevant; what mattered was its quantitative value—being able to sell the commodity for an amount of money greater than the purchase price. This gave the new economic system an inherent dynamic of expansion for expansion's sake. Obstacles to expansion had to be smashed. Competitors had to be pushed aside or gobbled up.

By pillaging the Americas of gold and silver and harnessing the labor of millions of African slaves, the early European capitalists amassed huge fortunes that provided the initial capital for the industrialization of western Europe. Corporate empires that survive to this day, such as Barclays Bank and Lloyds of London, accumulated their initial capital in the slave trade.

This new economic system that was beginning to encircle the world with its trade and conquest produced a new class of people with the desire and ability to constantly increase their wealth. The original capitalists often behaved more like pirates and plunderers than what we think of today when we see a corporate capitalist in a three-piece suit. The system demanded that they "accumulate capital!," and there were very few international legal obstacles to hinder the early entrepreneurs from doing whatever they could to gain more money. Greed was elevated to a high social value.

The Military Tools

The economic driving force would not have been enough, by itself, for Europeans to conquer the planet. They also needed the military capability to overcome many different cultures, some of them quite skilled in the arts of war.

On the eve of the European explosion that would thrust it to all corners of the globe, the Europeans were themselves besieged by the Ottoman Turks. The invading Turks had penetrated southeastern Europe to within the outskirts of Vienna, thanks in large part to the superiority of Turkish cavalry vis-a-vis the cumbersome and less maneuverable cavalry of the Europeans.

Just in the nick of time, Europeans made several advances in military technology that allowed them to escape the grasp of the Ottoman Empire and embark on global conquest. The Atlantic powers, especially England, made great use of navigational innovations such as the magnetic compass. More important, they developed the war-making power of sailing vessels (as opposed to the traditional galleys powered by oarsmen).

"By turning wholeheartedly to the gun-carrying sailing ship the Atlantic peoples broke the bottleneck inherent in the use of human energy and harnessed, to their advantage, far larger quantities of power. It was then that European sails appeared aggressively on the most distant seas."[1]

Probably the most crucial European military development was the ability to mount cannons on sailing ships. The Turks were fond of huge siege cannons that packed a wallop when smashing the walls of a city, but these behemoths were unwieldy in the field, used large amounts of gun powder, took a long time to reload, and could not be mounted on ships. The Europeans developed lighter cannons that were more versatile in the field and could be mounted on ships.[2]

The combined innovations in gun technology and naval technology would be central to the next several hundred years of colonization. And, as we saw recently in the Gulf War, the ability to project destructive power far from one's own shores is still key to controlling the resources of others.

The Ideological Lubricant

Lubricating these economic and military impulses was a European ideology of racial and spiritual superiority. The profit motive was abetted by the prophet motive.

Christopher Columbus exhibited the kind of blind arrogance of power that led to the enslavement and impoverishment of millions. In his diaries, Columbus remarks on how kind and generous the natives were and how they seemed to be leading an idyllic existence. Yet his immediate thought was, not how to learn from them, but how to subjugate them.

> They do not bear arms, and do not know them, for I showed them a sword, they took it by the edge and cut themselves out of ignorance. They have no iron. Their spears are made of cane...They would make fine servants...With fifty men we could subjugate them all and make them do whatever we want.[3]

In his *Brief History of the Destruction of the Indies,* the Catholic priest Bartholomé de Las Casas records that the Spanish pounced on the Indians "like wolves after days of starvation."

> For 40 years they have done nothing but torture, murder, harass, afflict torment and destroy them with extraordinary, incredible, innovative and previously unheard of cruelty...Some natives they hung on a gibbet, and it was their reverential custom to gather at a time sufficient victims to hang 13 in a row, and thus piously to commemorate Christ and the 12 Apostles.

Some 50 million Indians of the Americas perished within fifty years of Columbus landing in the Caribbean. Ninety percent of the indigenous population was wiped out by murder, disease, and famine within the first century and a half. It is the greatest demographic collapse in human history.

The brutal treatment of Third World peoples is not so surprising when one considers that the dominant Christian ideology of the day viewed all of nature—including "savages"—as mysterious at best and hostile at worst. The church did not encourage scientific investigation of nature. It was sufficient for believers to know that God had given to human beings "dominion" over the natural world and all its creatures. For the average European of that era, nature—whether in the form of rivers, mountains, animals, or strange peoples—represented an antagonistic force to be controlled.

The ideology of racial superiority was already firmly in place and now served as rationale and spiritual fuel for the horrors of the "civilizing" process. As Pope Alexander VI decreed in a papal edict of 1492:

> The Catholic faith and Christian religion, especially in our times shall be exalted, broadened and spread in every part of the world, salvation shall be sought for all souls, barbarian nations shall be subdued and led back to the faith.

By definition, those who believed in Christ as the incarnation of God the

Father were superior to nonbelievers because Christians had knowledge of the ways of God, the most important knowledge of all. Thus, conquering non-Christian people and forcibly incorporating them into the Europe-centered world economy was a "civilizing" process that was deemed to be in the best interests of the victims.

The Impact of Colonization

Third World areas now suffering widespread hunger were feeding themselves quite well before they were forced into the capitalist world economy starting in the sixteenth century. Cases of starvation, such as famines in China, were episodic and largely due to natural causes, unlike the chronic hunger of today, which stems from structures of political and economic inequality.

In Asia, Africa, and the Americas, indigenous civilizations had developed cultures with a reverence for nature. Their agricultural systems were far more sustainable than the ones that would be introduced by the Europeans. Aside from some limited burning of forested areas, pre-Columbian civilizations did not wreak havoc on their environment.

This all changed with the arrival of the colonizers. Indigenous models of development were pushed aside or destroyed by the Europeans. The colonizers made few attempts to learn from the cultures they were displacing. Entire civilizations in the Americas were exterminated through forced labor, murder, and disease. Genocide against Native Americans dovetailed with the increasing importation of African slaves to do agricultural labor. Millions died in the process of being captured and transported to the "new world," and tens of millions more barely eked out an existence as chattel.

The social destruction was matched by ecological catastrophes. When English colonists accidentally brought some rats to the Caribbean, it unleashed "one of the most spectacular ecological disasters of the age."[4] The rats—previously nonexistent in the islands—multiplied and spread throughout the region. They nested everywhere and nearly ate the colonists into oblivion.

The Europeans used the broad expanses of Africa and the Americas to introduce cattle grazing on a scale unknown in Europe. The vast herds were soon eating up all the vegetation in sight, making it even more difficult for indigenous people to forage for survival.

Economic Restructuring

The ecological disasters brought by the Europeans were surpassed in their negative impact by the way Third World economies were twisted and distorted as they were incorporated into the capitalist world system. In a centuries-long process by which they subjugated the peoples of Africa, Asia and Latin America, European colonizers disrupted farming and herding patterns that had fed generations of indigenous people in sustainable ways. The best farmland was seized by the colonizers to produce export crops, such as sugar cane, tobacco, cotton, coffee, tea, cocoa, rubber, and cattle. The choice of crops and the way they were produced were in the interests of wealthy outsiders, with little thought to the needs of local people. This outward orientation stifles the development of Third World economies to this day.

The colonial model of export agriculture ravaged the soil, reducing large areas to semidesert. Millions of acres of brush and trees were cleared, robbing the soil of organic replenishment. Export crops such as peanuts, cotton, and tobacco, absorbed large amounts of nutrients from the soil. After each year's harvest, the soil was left bare and unprotected.

Contrary to the model of export agriculture they preach to the Third World, the colonizing countries of the North continue to produce a wide variety of food crops, even subsidizing their production with large infusions of government money. But the colonizers imposed on the Third World a form of agriculture focused on growing export crops for outsiders rather than food for local people. Two big problems with the export crops are (1) if they fail to be sold on the world market, they cannot simply be eaten by the local producers, and (2) consumers in the first world can forego the product if tastes change or the price rises too high.

Seizing the best land for export crops not only degraded the natural resource base, it also impoverished the rural majority. Most indigenous families could not sustain themselves on the inferior land left to them without resorting to questionable practices of overgrazing, deforestation, and failing to leave land fallow long enough to recuperate. The many farmers who could no longer compete either went to work on the large colonial plantations or migrated into the cities, where they swelled the ranks of the homeless and unemployed. Thus, the destruction of family farming created a large, low-priced labor pool for colonial employers, and it set in motion a cycle of grinding poverty for most Third World people.

The African slave trade—the largest forced migration in history—shattered the labor supply of West Africa by taking away millions of the youngest, most able-bodied workers. Although some African states had practiced slavery prior to the European invasion, it was a paternalistic form of slavery focused primarily on providing services for local rulers. This was drastically different from the slavery of global capitalism, driven by huge profits and greed.

The profits from the slave trade—over 300 percent at its height—were crucial in funding the industrialization of Europe. Cities, such as Liverpool, that were hubs for industrial development got their initial boost from the slave trade. The industrial revolution in England was based on textiles, and the raw material (cotton) came largely from the slave plantations of the Americas.

While the plundering of Third World areas enriched Europe, the Third World was being crippled economically and socially. The distribution of locally produced goods was interrupted by the colonizers. Local products were replaced by European goods, often by violent methods. In India, for example, the British colonizers went so far as to hack off the thumbs of Indian loom operators so they could no longer produce local cloth in competition with British textile exports.

The Belgian Congo—now Zaire—is an area eighty times the size of Belgium. During the late eighteenth and early nineteenth centuries, Belgium amassed a fortune from wild rubber production in the Congo using African labor. King Leopold II's henchmen regularly maimed and disfigured Africans who did not meet the quota of rubber production imposed by colonial edict. Africans who tried to organize resistance were disciplined by being forced to watch their children having hands or feet hacked off. To prove to their managers that they were enforcing the rules, field bosses would collect and smoke-cure amputated limbs of the Africans for later display to colonial officers, such as Sir Henry Morton Stanley, who was King Leopold's main agent in the Congo. Some historians estimate that through a combination of the slave trade, overwork, and disease, the Congo's population was reduced by 8 million people during King Leopold's reign (1865-1909).

Market forces dictated that private and government money from Europe be invested in export crops that could earn big profits, rather than in food crops for local populations. Infrastructure, such as ports, railways, and communication links, was constructed with the central goal of taking resources out to the major markets of Europe and (later) North America. One distinguishing characteristic of a developed economy is multiple linkages among different sectors. In an underdeveloped economy, the major linkages are from key extractive sectors (mining the soil through export crops or mining the earth through mineral extraction) out to the major industrial markets of the North.

Today, we can still see the debilitating effects of the Third World's status as raw material producer for the industrialized North. For example, most African countries are dependent on exporting a narrow range of unprocessed minerals and agricultural products. Thirty-seven African countries (with more than 60 percent of Africa's population) get over half their total export earnings from primary commodity exports. Twenty of these countries get between 90 and 100 percent of export earnings from primary commodities.

World market prices for these raw materials fluctuate more than prices for industrial goods, making economic planning impossible. Relative to those of manufactured goods, raw material prices also tend to stagnate or decline over time. For example, from 1950 to 1984, agricultural commodities lost, on average, more than 1 percent of their value per year, while manufactured exports from industrial countries benefitted from increases of between 5 and 11 percent.

Another obstacle to Third World development is the concentration of market control in the hands of relatively few transnational corporations.

Table 1 shows that world markets for major Third World exports are dominated by a small group of large corporations.

Table 1

Corporate Control of Global Commodity Trade, 1980

Commodity	Percentage marketed by 3-6 largest corporations
corn	85-90
coffee	85-90
cocoa	85
tea	80
pineapples	90
bananas	70-75
sugar	60
cotton	85-90
forest products	90
copper	80-85
iron ore	90-95

Source: *UNCTAD Statistical Pocket Book,* p. 48.

The combination of price inequalities and corporate monopolization guarantees that Third World countries will suffer widespread hunger until there are major changes in the structure of the world economy and major changes in the power structures of Third World countries.

Cooptation of Local Elites

Perhaps the greatest tragedy of all was the cooptation of Third World elites. During the transition to the postcolonial state following World War II, very few Third World leaders sought to radically change the extractive structures of the colonial economy, despite much populist rhetoric to the contrary.

In the transition to postcolonial rule, the local petite bourgeoisie (professionals, small businessmen) was in most cases the only class capable of leading the struggle for independence. Lacking any revolutionary consciousness, this class sought primarily to replace the retreating colonizers in the leadership positions at the top of society.

The colonial model of capital accumulation created closer links and greater shared interest between Third World ruling classes and their northern counterparts than between those same Third World rulers and their subordinate classes. While it is true that government agencies, corporations, and banks of the major industrial countries have continued to extract wealth from the Third World, they are abetted by local elites and postcolonial state institutions.

It should not surprise us that people living in big houses, riding in limousines, and working in air-conditioned offices produced policies that have impoverished the mass of Third World peasants and workers. And now that the economic failure has reached the horrific proportions of mass hunger, we are being asked to believe that the same transnational alliance of elites that created the crisis in the first place will implement some policy reforms that will somehow resolve it.

We are not saying that Third World ruling classes have no disagreements with their northern counterparts or that they have the exact same material interests. Many governments in the Third World have struggled to increase local ownership of economic resources, but in general, the evidence shows that most Third World elites have struck deals with their counterparts in the North. A recent observation about Mobutu Sese Seko of Zaire could apply to many Third World leaders.

> Mobutu had paid his dues: he mortgaged his great slab of Africa to the Western strategic interest and, in return, the West gave him free rein to pursue his visions, to act without mercy in the name of power.[5]

To give credit where credit is due, leaders in some underdeveloped countries have put great emphasis on education and health care. But a disproportionate amount of Third World health-care expenditures are for high-technology services that mainly benefit urban elites. And formal education is of little use if it doesn't help graduates find decent jobs.

When local elites come into conflict with the elite of the wealthy nations, sheer power is another factor that must be considered. When a postcolonial Third World government is attempting to mediate a conflict between international capital and local workers, the power of international capital will generally force the Third World state to be a conveyor belt for the interests of foreign elites. Powerful outsiders, such as the International Monetary Fund and the World Bank, can get Third World rulers to make changes of a magnitude that could not be achieved by most Third World toiling classes.

This understanding of structural bias is essential if we are to move beyond a simple instrumental critique of Third World policy errors. The elites in charge of Third World states cannot be expected to implement an effective development strategy based on institutional structures that were created to transfer wealth upward in the class structure and out of the Third World.

Yet the crucial and complex relationship between Third World elites and the ruling strata of the major industrial countries has not received the research attention it deserves. An entire research agenda needs to be constructed specifying precisely how the ruling strata of Third World nations are linked to the generals, politicians, and elite business leaders of the industrialized countries. The key units of analysis in this research should not be things (states or classes), but rather the processes through which the ruling strata of first world and Third World interrelate and develop dependence on each other. Only by moving beyond the simplistic North versus South conceptualization and understanding whose class interests are served by the current system and its component processes can we grasp the real roots of the problem.

Cultures of Resistance

Although history provides many examples of human brutality and suffering, there are also many inspiring cases of people fighting back against difficult odds. It is hard to find a place and time where there was oppression without resistance.

The very first incidents of barbarism by Columbus and his cohorts against Native Americans were staunchly opposed by some people, including the Catholic priest Bartolomé de las Casas. His book, *History of the Indies*, published in 1542, documents the struggle against Spanish brutality in the Americas. The Dominican priest Antonio de Montesinos shocked his Spanish congregation by warning them:

> you are living in deadly sin for the atrocities you tyrannically impose on these innocent people [the Indians]. Tell me, what right have you to enslave them? What authority did you use to make war against them who lived at peace on their territories, killing them cruelly with methods never before heard of? How can you oppress them, and not care to feed or cure them, and work them to death to satisfy your greed?[6]

Slaves suffering the worst oppression imaginable mounted resistance in a wide variety of ways. They ran away to form maroon societies, living in the wild in groups ranging into the thousands. They sabotaged the work process on plantations and refused to work at a fast pace. When their owners split up families, slaves developed alternative kinship systems to care for their young. And, eventually, slavery was hastened to its grave by the constant rebellions by the slaves, which raised the cost of the system to the slaveholders.

Although the British have tried for 900 years to subdue the Irish, the victims refuse to give up. Priests and nuns in Latin America often pay with their lives for preaching a democratic gospel that seeks to liberate the majority from the yoke of poverty. Palestinian children as young as kindergarten age are out in the street throwing rocks at the Israeli soldiers occupying Palestinian land. Forward-thinking whites and blacks in South Africa are uniting to usher in a new era of democratic change in a country where apartheid produced great wealth for a small minority, while some 50,000 black children starved to death every year.

The African continent—scene of today's worst hunger—has experienced more democratic transformations in the past two years than in the previous twenty. This sweeping transformation is due in large part to the organized pressure of grassroots organizations and their international allies.

In many parts of the world and in many different ways, people are showing that they can reach out across boundaries of race, class, nation, and gender to build a new world order that will provide for everyone.

Conclusion: What Is Our Responsibility?

A key point to remember is that the process of colonization is still going on. True, there are few formal colonies left. But if we define colonization as a process by which people are pushed around by outsiders, with their resources taken away for the benefit of others, then the ongoing nature of colonization is obvious. Where does the money from rainforest destruction end up? Where does the money from Appalachian coal mining end up?

One can even find the colonial process of dispossession continuing in one of the very first places Christopher Columbus set foot. The government of the Dominican Republic is building a colossal lighthouse monument in Santo Domingo to celebrate the 500th anniversary of Columbus's arrival in the Americas. In the process, it has forcibly removed some 500,000 slum dwellers who were in the way.

Another place we can see the continuing effects of the colonial economy is in the way populations that were enslaved for hundreds of years are still suffering great impoverishment today. For example, African Americans are 12.1 percent of the U.S. population, but they accounted for just 7.8 percent of personal income for Americans in 1990. A black man with a college degree can expect to earn just slightly more than a white man who didn't get past high school. While 15.9 percent of white children live below the official poverty line, 44.8 percent of black children live in poverty.[7]

Throughout the Americas—except in Cuba—black populations can be found concentrated at the lower strata of the class structure. They suffer from greater unemployment, shabbier housing, poorer health care, lower-quality education, and shorter life spans.

Like it or not, we are the inheritors of the colonial legacy. We should not bother feeling guilty about the benefits we reap from global inequality; it would be better to expend our energy changing the world.

And change it we must! The problem of global inequality was traditionally discussed in moral terms. Now we must also think in terms of the survival of our species and the planet.

Shared Interest

Fortunately, there are many shared interests between the toiling classes in northern industrial countries and workers and peasants in underdeveloped countries of the southern hemisphere. Contrary to what most Americans have been taught, we have much in common with the hungry of the world.

o Foreign aid—which comes from taxing the working classes of wealthy countries—is used by the rulers of first world countries to cement alliances with the business, politicial, and military leaders of Third World countries. Very little of official foreign assistance reaches the hands of the poor. The satirical definition is largely true: "Foreign aid is when you take money from the poor people of rich countries and give it to the rich people of poor countries." A more democratic reorientation of foreign aid policies could simultaneously save money for taxpayers of the North and strengthen the workers of the South in their struggles against their own ruling classes.

o The debt crisis afflicting most Third World countries is causing them to implement policies harmful to most people on the planet. Under the enforcing arm of international organizations, such as the World Bank and the International Monetary Fund, Third World debtor nations are exploiting their natural resources to the hilt in order to make payments to Western banks. For example, the destruction of tropical rainforests—the lungs of the planet—is in direct response to desperation by Third World governments to maintain their credit ratings and receive continued funding. The original loans did not benefit the poor majority, and the tax write-offs gained by Western banks for making stupid loans are ultimately paid by citizens of the developed countries.[8]

o The low wages paid in Third World countries undermine the standard of living of workers in developed countries. Massive unemployment is caused by runaway shops that leave industrialized countries, such as the United States, for Third World countries, primarily to take advantage of low wages and lack of trade unions. First world workers would directly benefit if Third World wages were raised to first world levels.

o Both Third World and first world majorities would benefit from a reorientation of agricultural practices. The chemical-dependent farming promoted throughout the Third World by the "green revolution" comes back to haunt first world consumers in the form of deadly pesticide residues in coffee, tea, cocoa, bananas, beef, and many other products.

In addition, the same U.S. agricultural policies that bankrupt family farmers here are also undermining family farming in Third World countries. The subsidies paid by the federal government to farmers of basic grains, such as corn, wheat, and soy, serve to hold down the market prices of these crops. These low prices benefit the big corporations that dominate the processing, wholesaling, and retailing of these products and their derivatives. And because low prices force farmers to push for greater yields per acre, the corporations producing farm inputs such as machinery, pesticides, and chemical fertilizers also benefit. But family farmers are squeezed between the low prices they receive for their output and the rising costs of land, machinery, and chemical inputs. The same subsidized, low prices that hurt small farmers here also undermine farmers in Third World countries. Large agribusiness firms are able to sell our "cheap" grain in Third World countries at prices lower than the local production costs in those countries. This knocks peasant farmers out of business and forces them to either take work on large plantations or drift into cities, where they swell the ranks of the homeless and unemployed.[9]

- The same sense of "other" that allowed western European capitalism to conquer many peoples around the world also allowed it to conquer nature. The consequent destruction of the natural resource base—whether in the form of soil erosion, water pollution, or ozone depletion—is steadily lessening our ability to sustain all the people of the planet.

In trying to convince fellow Americans that we share interests with the world's poor majority, we must be careful not to oversimplify the problem. We should not portray the world as if our problems are the same as those faced by people in the Third World. What we are trying to do is illustrate the connections—the ways in which challenging institutions that are operating to the detriment of the world's poor can also better our own lives.

Our Historic Role

The colonization process did unify the world into one global economy, albeit with extreme violence and resultant inequality. Now we are moving to a higher stage, in which that global connectedness is being infused with morality and human solidarity. The same fax machines and computer modems that are used by transnational corporations to exploit the Third World are also being used by grassroots activists to organize across national boundaries to combat exploitation.

When a group of us formed Global Exchange in 1988, we were guided by a deeply felt knowledge that there are many ways in which we can change the world that will simultaneously benefit us and people in the Third World. A basic tenet behind the grassroots internationalism we promote is that by linking people from different parts of the planet (preferably in a shared task), we can overcome the sense of "other" that allows us to ignore the hunger and related injustices that hurt so many people every day. It is this coming together across barriers of race, gender, class, nationality, language, and religion that helps us achieve a greater purpose in life. We become part of the human bouquet, rather than remaining isolated flowers.

Why should we struggle against injustice? Because it's there. My father used to tell me, "struggle builds character." He was right. The best people I have met are those who have learned how to struggle, while maintaining their dignity and humor. We should struggle because it makes sense for us, as well as for the oppressed.

And what if we fail to attain our goals of a more humane and peaceful world? The old maxim, "It is better to have tried and failed than to have failed to try," is true. It is better to die in the process of struggling for justice, than to die comfortably as a cynic: able to understand the problem but too cowardly to lift a finger to fix it. The cynic dies a profoundly lonely death. But a person struggling for justice dies in the company of all those people who have been uplifted by the struggle.

Notes

1. Carlo M. Cipolla, *Guns, Sails and Empires: Technological Innovation and the Early Phases of European Expansion* (New York: Minerva Press, 1965), 81.

2. The superiority of naval vessels mounted with cannons was demonstrated as early as October 1571, when a Christian fleet of 208 galleys took on a Turkish fleet of 230 galleys at Lepanto. During three hours of fierce combat, the Christians sunk 80 Turkish ships and captured 130, with just 40 escaping.

3. Christopher Columbus, *The Journals of the First Voyage*, edited and translated by B. W. Ife (Warminister, England: Aris & Phillips, 1990), October entry.

4. Alfred W. Crosby, Jr., "The Biological Consequences of 1492," *Report on the Americas, Vol. XXV*, no. 2 (September 1991), 12.

5. Alan Cowell, "Mobutu's Zaire: Magic and Decay," *New York Times Magazine*, 5 April 1992.

6. From Bartolomé de las Casas, *History of the Indies,* translated and edited by Andree Collard (New York: Harper & Row, 1971).

7. Andrew Hacker, *Two Nations: Black and White, Separate, Hostile, Unequal* (New York: Ballentine, 1992).

8. See Susan George, *The Debt Boomerang: How Third World Debt Hurts Us All* (Boulder, Colorado: Westview Press, 1992).

9. See Kevin Danaher, "US Food Power in the 1990s," *Race and Class,* January-March 1989.

CHAPTER 8

Indians, Land, and Poverty in Guatemala

Beatriz Manz

There are few countries in Latin America where the link between discrimination and the absence of political democracy and economic participation are as marked as in Guatemala. The policies determined by the elite since the time of the Spanish Conquest have, through the years, led to increasing hunger, landlessness, environmental degradation, migration, and misery for the majority of the population—the Maya.

The distribution of land in Guatemala is among the most skewed in Latin America, a region hardly noted for its equitable land-distribution policies. The United States Agency for International Development (AID) points out that Guatemala "is characterized by striking inequalities in the distribution of land," a situation that "is more serious than in most countries in Central America and most other Latin American countries."[1] Since access to land is pivotal to economic survival in an agrarian society, this skewed land distribution has contributed to a sharp decline in the standard of living during the last decades. The percentage of people living in poverty soared from an already high 63.5 percent in 1981 to 86.3 percent in 1985, leaving Guatemala the poorest country in Central America, despite its excellent agricultural resources and climate.[2]

These statistics translate into devastating human consequences, especially for the 45 percent of Guatemala's population under the age of fifteen. Only 27 percent of children between six months and five years of age, for example, exhibit normal physical development.[3] According to the World Bank, 30.5 percent of children under five years of age weigh below 75 percent of the standard weight for age, the highest percentage of any country in Latin America. Moreover, the infant mortality rate and quality of life indicators, such as percentage of deaths attributable to infective and parasitic diseases, are also among the highest in the hemisphere.[4]

The Guatemalan land and poverty situation coincides with a deep and pervasive pattern of racism. Correspondingly, the issues of race and hunger in Guatemala are inextricably linked with issues of land distribution and social dominance. Guatemala has the highest concentration of indigenous people in Central America, but racial stratification has resulted in a large and expanding percentage of impoverished Indians living on a shrinking and deteriorating land base. The economic well-being, as well as the cultural identity, of the Indian population has suffered in the wake of extreme inequalities, human rights abuses, and a closed political system. Poverty and hunger are legacies of past and present policies pertaining to land, the environment, and development, all of which have been influenced by a pervasive and centuries-old racism.

This chapter explores the relationship in Guatemala between deteriorating living conditions and land policies in recent years, focusing on the tense intersection of politics, resources, and race. I argue that, without structural reforms of the economy, specifically land tenure, Guatemalan development policies are unlikely to change the overall conditions of poverty that the overwhelming majority of Maya Guatemalans experience and, in fact, may further the existing racial and economic polarization. The end result of this polarization for the increasing number of those on the bottom is hunger and death.

Land Tenure in Guatemala

Since the earliest days of colonization, the Mayan people have experienced systematic disruption of their relationship with the land, but in this chapter we will be concerned only with recent history. Since the overthrow of Jacobo Arbenz in 1954, a succession of Guatemalan governments have sought to squelch what the Catholic Church has termed "the clamor for land" and instead have opted for economic and agricultural strategies that avoided structural change. Instead of promoting agrarian reform, Guatemalan governments, U.S. development agencies, international lending institutions, and Guatemala's landed elites have all colluded in the colonization of national lands, leading to an emphasis on export crops and light assembly for foreign markets. The Guatemalan Right has argued that these efforts are central to a development strategy that they maintain will satisfy "the clamor for a better life." While reform is sometimes debated, ruling elites and the military effectively preclude its serious consideration within the political process. As a result, deteriorating social conditions play themselves out in a society that has closed off democratic participation. The conflict, therefore, is not between competing development strategies, but rather between military domination and oligarchical control versus any real democratic process.

I begin by briefly examining current land distribution and the effects of the government's policies of colonizing the rain forest and promoting alternative export crops. Later, I explore two influential though diametrically opposed conceptions of the role of land reform in Guatemalan society, one advanced by the Catholic Church and the other proposed by *Amigos del País*, a private-sector organization.

Land Ownership and Social Crisis

Having been displaced from the more fertile regions, Guatemala's indigenous peasants are concentrated in the highlands. In the central and western highlands, mini plots of land cover steep volcanic slopes, placing a tremendous pressure on the habitat. Accelerated erosion is quite visible, as new fields are put under cultivation and trees are cut for firewood. The rate of deforestation is placed by some as high as 50 percent since 1950, while other sources claim that 33 percent of the forest has been destroyed in the past ten years alone.[5]

The large plantations are in the fertile Pacific coastal plain where the commercial crops—coffee, sugar cane, and cotton—are grown and where the large cattle ranches are located. Coffee also is grown in the southern piedmont. In these regions, there are an estimated 2 million acres of uncultivated fertile land.[6]

One of the difficulties in analyzing the agrarian situation in Guatemala is the existence of only three agricultural censuses, the last taken in 1979. Fortunately, however, some reliable studies on the land situation have been undertaken since then. The most frequently cited is *Land and Labor*, published by the United States Agency for International Development (AID). In Guatemala, the "green book" (as it became known because of its cover) caused a furor when the Spanish version was first presented to the Rios-Montt government on 1 October 1982. For the majority of the population, AID's authoritative analysis of the land situation raised expectations about finding solutions to the untenable land situation, but it sparked anger among large landowners, who feared a breakup of their holdings and a political shift toward distribution of idle private lands. The plantation owners had reason to be fearful: their lands frequently had been obtained under dubious circumstances, they produced inefficiently and mainly for export, and they failed to provide a reasonable standard of living for those they employed.[7]

The AID report estimated that 88 percent of the landholdings were subfamily[8] and over 300,000 peasants were landless in 1979.[9] Other social scientists, at that time, placed the estimated number of landless at 400,000, and, by all accounts, the rural population with insufficient land or without any land at all has grown even further.

The rich and poor have received quite different responses from the Guatemalan government in relation to their agricultural and land needs. The government has promoted the concentration of the best land in the hands of the wealthy, partly in hopes of increasing export earnings. One of the key vehicles used to channel support to the wealthy ladino class is credit policy. Small land-holdings of less than ten manzanas (representing 88 percent of the total holdings in the country) receive only 7 percent of the agricultural credit. A look at credit allocation by agricultural product indicates a similar bias. Coffee, cotton, and sugar—which are grown on the large plantations primarily for export—received 80 percent of the credit between 1956 and 1980; staple crops, such as corn, beans, rice, and wheat—often grown by Mayan peasants on small plots—obtained just 10 percent of the credit. Large agro-exports received credit equivalent to between 22 and 30 percent of their production value, while basic grains received only 13 percent of their production value.[10]

The Plight of the Mayan Peasant

In light of land policies, it is not surprising that the conditions of the rural poor have continued to deteriorate. The land per capita available in the highlands has dramatically declined. In Huehuetenango, for example, land per capita slid from .69 hectares to .32 hectares between 1950 and 1980. In El Quiché, the decline was from 1.04 to .56 during the same period.[11] Not surprisingly, according to a Guatemalan government study, the category of "peasant not self-sufficient" rose from 47 percent in 1950 to 60 percent in 1979, thus making "non-self-sufficient" the defining characteristic of peasantry in Guatemala.[12] What is more, this study was based on 1979 data, prior to the large forced displacement of an estimated 1 million peasants (one in four Maya peasants). No doubt, conditions for the peasants have worsened considerably since then.

In addition to the fragmentation of land-holdings, the deteriorating standard of living for the highland Mayan peasants is due to land erosion, a corresponding decrease in animal husbandry, a higher cost of living, less availability of communal lands and firewoods, and contraction of the market for artisan productions. This situation has meant a further dependence on wages, rural to urban migration, and out-migration, especially to the United States.

Because of their inability to sustain a livelihood on a deteriorating land base, many Mayan peasants have turned to wage labor. Seasonal migration of up to half a million persons seeking—many desperate for any income at all—has created an oversupply of labor in the coastal regions. The standard of living of landless peasants who have become permanent rural wage earners (in the south coast) is quite bleak. A Guatemalan government study concluded that "the poor peasant when he becomes an agricultural wage earner, is not able to improve his social and economic conditions, rather he tends to worsen them."[13]

What are the general social and political consequences of this economic state of affairs? Malnutrition, infant mortality rates, and general indicators of poverty have soared, especially among the Maya. Urban migration has ballooned, while virtually no attention is paid to housing, health, or jobs in the urban sector. In the rural areas, a sense of both desperation and despondency has set in.

Various Paths, No Fundamental Solution

After the overthrow of democratically elected Jacobo Arbenz by a CIA-funded and partially directed coup in 1954, two national dynamics were set in motion that have been of profound significance to the peasantry. First, after Arbenz's aborted land-reform efforts, the possibility of significant, open, public debate over agrarian reform has sharply narrowed. The second trend, reinforcing the first, pertains to the militarization of the country; the government, even when outwardly democratic, has been subject to heavy military influence, if not outright control.

With meaningful political dialogue rare, and with the government dancing to the tune of the military, policies to address rural poverty, to the extent it has been addressed at all, have been short-term, shortsighted, and patchwork. In place of land reform, the government has promoted rain forest colonization and new export crops, and it has opened the gates to a tidal wave of *maquilas* (foreign-owned light assembly factories) that now flow into the country. These approaches do not deal with deeper structural problems in the society because the political structure has placed this off-limits. Most significantly, the denial of political participation, and the excessive power of the military, has meant that no feedback enters into the equation. The voice and experience of the peasantry cannot act as correctives to development policies because they are systematically excluded. Likewise, developments initiated by the rural population that may lead to political challenge are quickly and ruthlessly crushed.

Colonization of the Rain Forest

To substitute for genuine land reform, the government has promoted the colonization of the rain forest. Leopoldo Sandoval, the Minister of Agriculture during General Efraín Ríos Montt's regime, admits the obvious: virtually all efforts since the 1954 coup have been toward colonization and distribution of national lands, leaving untouched the sprawling underused plantations and the agrarian structure of the society.[14] The history of the colonization of the Petén and Ixcán northern rain forest underscores the shortsightedness resulting from the convergence of politics, social history, and development policies.

The Guatemalan rainforests are unique habitats, particularly the Ixcán. As has been observed, "The Western Transversal region has one of the few remaining lowland tropical rain forests in Central America. There is a growing world-wide concern about elimination of tropical rain forests because they possess a genetic pool of potentially useful trees, crops, and drugs, and because they represent seed sources for reforesting areas when soils have become depleted after agricultural uses."[15] Despite the rain forests' inestimable value, the Guatemalan government has promoted policies that have resulted in their massive destruction.

The issue here is not one of placing "pristine environment" above people or vice versa, but of finding a sensible means of coexistence between humans and the environment. While few would disagree that "all development programs change the environment,"[16] the question is what practices are most conducive to long-term sustainable human livelihood. The answer lies in assuring land conservation practices in all rural development schemes.

The Guatemalan government, ignoring the consequences of heavily populating the area, both for the natural habitat and for people, made it "more accessible to exploitation by constructing roads and ports to serve the area." This encouraged developers and "accelerate[d] logging operations and open[ed] the area to colonization."[17] The construction of the main East/West road, with funds from AID, was followed by oil explorations and large cattle ranching.

Colonization of the rain forest has contributed to the dramatic deforestation of Guatemala. Between 1969 and 1982, in the department of El Petén, the forests decreased from 36,000 to 32,000 square kilometers, or an annual loss of five million cubic meters of wood, a decline directly attributable to colonization, according to one study.[18] The Petén contains about 80 percent of the hardwoods in the country.[19] A study conducted by Guatemala's Rafael Landivar University, under contract with AID, refers to the deforestation as "alarming." It identifies colonization as the second major cause of deforestation, the first being fuelwood consumption.[20] For the Petén area, the study cites an annual deforestation of 5 million cubic meters, "attributed only to colonization."[21]

In terms of agriculture in the newly colonized regions, there are serious concerns about its sustainability. The forest soils will not support continuous crop production because their fertility is rapidly depleted. New areas must then be cleared, necessitating additional forest destruction.[22] Like so many of the government's shortsighted policies, the attempt to convert the forest to agriculture results in considerable long-term damage to the environment.

The decision to colonize the rain forest was made for political, not ecological, reasons. The colonization provided an expedient safety valve to deal with the growing landlessness in the highlands. As a team of seasoned observers of the Ixcán have noted, the northern rain forest was "vacant" on national maps, and political leaders were "anxious to fill it up."[23] As the Texas Tech team observed, "Prosaically promoting colonization in areas where land is 'free' also reduces pressure for land reform in other more densely populated areas"[24] or pressure for land reform in fertile areas controlled by the traditional large planters, even though "half of the agricultural land held by the land-owning minority is almost unused."[25]

From the point of view of the landless Mayan peasant, however, colonization of the rain forest was generally positive—at least initially—given the alternatives or, perhaps more accurately, the lack of alternatives. Along with the colonization came the organization of cooperatives, which provided positive economic, social, and political benefits. The commercialization of cash crops—especially cardamom—through the cooperatives translated into high revenues and lower costs. The income generated was put to socially useful endeavors, such as education and health care, that benefitted the entire community. However, these economic benefits, coupled with an emerging political confidence that stemmed from common action, began to create problems with the established authorities. Given Guatemala's political and social structure, it was only a matter of time before the new benefits were siphoned away and the cooperative movements stemmed.

Consider cardamom. The peasant colonizers of the rain forest began to rely heavily on this lucrative spice, propelling Guatemala into the number one producer of cardamom in the world.[26] Introduced to Guatemala some forty years ago, this plant is ideally suited to the rain forest, because it requires subtropical zones with humidity, shade, constant rain, and protection. By the mid 1970s, cardamom was the main cash crop grown in the Ixcán cooperatives.

Originally, the cooperatives provided the product directly to exporters in Guatemala City and were able to bargain over price with some leverage. However, in the 1980s, these practices changed in the wake of military repression and the destruction of the cooperatives. Once it became evident that cardamom production could turn a considerable profit, large landowners entered and soon dominated the market. As a result, individual growers now must sell the cardamom to intermediaries, and the small producers have lost their leverage over price.

It is also questionnable whether nontraditional crops, which are promoted by the government as a means of development for the highland peasants, are economically viable in the long term. Let us continue to consider cardamom. Initially, cardamom production appeared to be an economic boon to the peasant. The Association of Cardamom Exporters reported that the export of cardamom had assumed an important role in the national economy, employing some 50,000 people and generating more than Q60 million in foreign earnings, mostly from Saudi Arabia and Kuwait.[27] But as more countries began to produce the fruit, the decline in price on the international market was dramatic.

Large landowners also are vulnerable to fluctuations in the world market, but the rural population is both subject to changes in the world market and at a disadvantage in relation to the plantation owners. The large owners cannot do much to affect a worldwide recession or reduction in markets or prices for their products, but they have the political power to do something about the local conditions. If need be, wages can be cut, labor forces reduced, working conditions intensified and labor unrest squelched. The coercive arm of the state is at their disposal. Repression, violence, murder, terror, and impunity have become accepted and seemingly permanent parts of the powerful's tool kit. The poor have none of these buffers, and for those four out of every five rural persons living in a situation of extreme poverty, day-to-day existence has become increasingly intolerable. The lives of the poor, the poignant suffering of the Maya, point to the failures of past and current economic policies.

The Results of Militarization

Given their untenable situation, it is not surprising that the peasants have occasionally revolted. Land invasions by peasants, often followed by violent evictions, and extensive sit-ins have become routine. Politically, the country has relied on military force to quell the social discontent as the most expedient way to deal with the social problems. Human rights violations have been notorious in Guatemala, particularly against the rural population, especially against the Mayan people, even when their demands have been quite moderate in nature.

The most extreme case of military violence against the people, particularly the Maya, came in 1982. Under the Rios-Montt government, the army conducted counterinsurgency sweeps that destroyed hundreds of entire communities and caused the displacement of almost the entire population of the frontier region by the Guatemala/Mexico border and various municipalities in the western highlands. Thousands of innocent people were killed in the rural areas. Once the resettlement occurred a year or so later, not only was it difficult if not impossible to erase the memories of the terror from the minds of the survivors, but there also was no recognition or admission of wrongdoing from the military or, even less, any punishment for the massacres perpetrated. Under these circumstances, campesinos legitimately feared resumption of these heinous tactics.

Suffering takes many forms. The pyschological impact of racism and tyranny has been severe. The poor are afraid to improvise or suggest new approaches if these involve any level of organization at the community level. The fear of further violence hinders, consciously or unconsciously, the peasants' long term vision or planning. Fearing further repression, the peasants often make economic decisions on the basis of short-term benefits, often to the detriment of the environment and the families. This is quite in contrast to the cultural heritage of the Maya, who traditionally lived in ecological balance with their environment.

The logging of precious wood, such as mahogany, illustrates the insecurity felt by peasant colonists that results in environmental degradation. Depression in cardamom prices made many peasants desperate for other sources of cash, and they turned, under pressure from lumber companies, to indiscriminate logging. The peasants know full well that the logging practices are unsustainable, but the short-term gain is more important. Another example is the near depletion of the palm used for roofing. Despite a critical shortage, no concerted effort is under way to replant the palm. When I have asked colonists about practices such as these, their response is predictable. For example, when asked why they did not replant the palm, one peasant stated, "It takes five years for the palm fronds to be large enough to serve as roofing material."[28] Clearly, a sense of insecurity about either their titles or their safety makes such long term planning and investment difficult to do, especially if other more immediate needs require their labor.

Insecurity and fear lead to practices that further degrade the environment, linking environmental degradation, poverty, and repression. Land management that conserves the natural environment is possible only when people have sufficient resources to sustain adequate living conditions and a sense of security about their property and their physical safety. With regard to living sustainably on the land, the Mayan people have a long and deep tradition that can be tapped fruitfully, but under the current exploitative conditions, they have lost access to that tradition.

The Social Crisis Continues

If current economic and development policies are failures, why have they not been abandoned? Research on the agrarian policies of the past decades—policies based on colonization of national lands, the development of new cash crops, and the expansion of light industry—show that these have had very different effects on different sectors in the society. For example, according to the Economic Commission for Latin America, while "Guatemala showed a slight economic growth in 1991 [this] was not felt by the majority of sectors."[29] The erosion of the standard of living of campesinos has been steady. As the prologue to the International Labor Organization's report grimly summarizes: "The extent, depth and permanence of poverty in the rural areas is one of the most complex socio-economic problems facing the Guatemalan government. Large segments of the rural families subsist in extremely precarious conditions, despite the process of expansion and growth that characterized the Guatemalan economy."

Current policies are not abandoned because they benefit some—the economic elite—even though the majority slip ever further into the abyss of hunger and poverty. Guatemala's income distribution reflects these realities. The bottom 10 percent of the population suffered a reduction in its share of total national income, from 2.4 percent in 1980 to just 0.9 percent in 1987. In contrast, the wealthiest one-tenth of Guatemala's families advanced its share of the national income from 40.8 percent in 1980 to 44 percent by 1987.[30]

Such wide disparities need social and political rationalization, and the prevailing racism in the country enables the extreme inequalities to be excused or justified as an extension of the appropriate life circumstances of the ladino and Mayan populations. The fact that a significant segment of the poor are ladino does not undermine the essentially racist underpinnings of the ideological system. The concept of race—*raza*—in Latin America is more social than biological in character,[31] and the poor ladino are largely subsumed under the Mayan category.

The Land-Reform Debate

The most notable political collision involving land in modern Guatemalan history was Jacobo Arbenz's land expropriation decree 900 in June of 1952,[32] an event whose enduring legacy is still vivid today. Since then, Guatemala has staggered from one land crisis to the next.[33] Clearly, land reform will need to be a central component of any meaningful restructuring of social, economic, and racial relations in Guatemala. Despite efforts to squelch the debate, it fortunately continues, and I turn now to an examination of two recent and critical publications in this debate: the Catholic Church's official proclamation, *El clamor por la tierra,*[34] and the prompt reaction by plantation owners in their *El clamor por una vida mejor* and *El mito del la reforma agraria.*[35]

The Mayan Ties to the Land

For many progressives in the country, such as the Catholic Church, the call for land reform has been a traditional rallying cry in response to the poverty devastating ever-larger numbers of people, especially the indigenous. For the church, agrarian reform was an obvious remedy: Indians were the possessors of all the land prior to the European arrival, they are the neediest, and their culture is closely tied to land. The situation of the Maya needs to be analyzed in terms of both economic exploitation and cultural disruption, and both stem from their severence from the land.

Starting with the title, *The Clamor for Land,* the language of the Catholic bishops is direct:

> The CLAMOR FOR LAND is, without doubt, the loudest, most dramatic, and most desperate cry heard in Guatemala today. It springs from the hearts of millions of Guatemalans who not only are anxious to posses land, but who also want to be possessed by the land.[36]

The document makes reference to the Indian campesinos as *hombres de maíz*—people of maize—whose identification with the land is profoundly cultural and specific; they identify with the "furrows, the sowing and the harvest," yet they have been dispossessed and "prevented from uniting themselves with its fertile furrows due to a situation of injustice and sin."[37]

The "inhuman poverty" suffered by Mayan campesinos is reflected in their appalling standard of living, as evidenced by their high levels of mortality, illiteracy, inadequate housing, unemployment, and malnutrition. But the root of all these problems is the injustice over land. "There are many problems which afflict our brothers and sisters in the countryside on their long Calvary of suffering," the bishops wrote, "but the lack of land should be viewed as the heart of all our national social problems."[38]

Should the Guatemalan oligarchy have forgotten the historical context of their fortunate condition, they are reminded that the campesinos are now "strangers in the land which has belonged to them for thousands of years and they are considered second-class citizens in the nation which their heroic ancestors forged."[39]

The church's appeal is reflective, deeply cultural, and also powerfully concrete in its denunciation. The language is poetic; its statistics straightforward. It appeals to the humanity of all Guatemalans and directs its plea in particular to Catholics, at a time when the Christian Democrats were governing the nation.

From the point of view of the church, its pronouncement was simply a continuation of a long and cherished prophetic tradition, in which the poor and marginalized call the powerful to account for injustice. But President Cerezo was not about to antagonize the plantation owners. He assured the landowners that "they had nothing to fear, that only government-owned, unused land would be involved (in the commercialization of land)—and he (President Cerezo) was checking with senior (military) officers to be sure they would not oppose it."[40]

The Conservative Response

Not surprisingly, the conservative response was swift. Clearly, the church's statement that "perhaps no other theme awakens such inflamed passions and provokes such radical and irreconcilable attitudes as the ownership of land" resonated among the landed elite. In their *The Clamor for a Better Life*, a title meant as a sarcastic play on the church's document, they acknowledge at the outset that "Guatemala is still a poor and backward country." This poverty is reflected in the lack of "security, health, education and housing" and the "inability to provide sufficient stable and well paid employment to its growing population."[41] The authors of the document acknowledge that there is an economic and social problem and a need to "continue" looking for solutions for a better future. In the document's early reference to population growth but lack of allusion to land ownership/distribution, it is clear where the authors place the blame for the malady. The problem, according to the privileged private sector, is that "incorrect diagnostics and false 'solutions' constitute the very essence of our up to now endemic conditions of underdevelopment."[42] The clearest example of false solutions, from their standpoint, is redistribution of land, a solution that would require as a "logical corollary the 'urgent need' to utilize the coercive power of the state to radically modify its structure." Blaming all social ills on the unequal distribution of land, so much "in vogue" in Guatemala, is not just espoused by Marxist-Leninists, according to *Amigos del País*, but by the United States and European advisors and religious organizations.

Quite clearly, the Right in Guatemala has taken notice of the shifting international currents. But what is most interesting and ironic about their document is the negative reference to the "coercive power of the state." They maintain that such power would be used illegitimately if put in the service of legislative reforms or social programs designed to alleviate the economic problems facing the majority of the population. However, for decades, if not centuries, the Right has used (and continues to use) the coercive power of the state to kill and "disappear" citizens and negate the most fundamental rights of the majority of the population, particularly those descended from the original inhabitants of the land.

The unequal land distribution is not a problem in need of correction, according to the Right. What is needed is "socio-economic modernization." As an example of the foresight of this counterproposal, they cite statistics from the United States demonstrating that in the 1920s, only 10 percent of the U.S. population was employed in agriculture and by 1981 that figure fell below two percent. Likewise, in terms of ownership of land, they point out that in the United States, 1 percent of the population owns about one-third of the land under cultivation, and of these, 5 percent owns half of that land. Despite this land concentration, however, there is no loud clamor for land reform in the United States. Thus, the authors conclude, the fundamental clamor of the Guatemalan peasants is for a better life, not for land. Indeed, a better life "will not necessarily be obtained in the fields for increasing segments of the populations."[43]

The reasoning contained in *The Clamor for a Better Life* is both predictable and subtly racist. The powerful elite in the agricultural sector of Guatemala traditionally have been intransigent to change. Their denunciation of the peasants' call for land distribution not only draws spurious parallels to the United States, but also ignores the cultural connection of the Maya to the land. For the Maya, a bond with the fertile and nurturant land is key to reducing both physical and spiritual hunger.

In March 1989, another publication appeared. *El Mito de la Reforma Agraria*—the myth of agrarian reform—was the "academic document" promised by the Right in *Amigos del País* to clarify the agrarian situation in

Guatemala.[44] The central question *The Myth* sets to address is whether from an "economic perspective" it is "convenient" to have an agrarian reform. The authors do not define convenient for whom or say if other than strictly the narrowest of economic perspectives should be used to approach social problems. They also preface their remarks by establishing that an agrarian reform is a "deliberate governmental intervention" in the "patterns of land tenancy already established."[45] How this pattern was established is not addressed, nor is why an intervention to change or modify land use is problematic this time, but the previous forced colonization was *a priori* either necessary or positive.

The study uses a series of tables showing the higher yields obtained from larger land-holdings. For example, the yields for maize in holdings of less than 0.7 hectares is 1.31 metric tons/hectare, compared to yields in fincas larger than 900 hectares of 1.57 metric tons/hectare. This large difference appears impressive until one realizes that it does not take into account the differences in quality of land, a decisive factor for this type of comparison. Most small holdings are located in the highlands, a region highly susceptible to soil erosion. In the western highlands, for example, the area with the highest rural population concentration, soil losses have been estimated to range from five to thirty-five tons per hectare annually.[46] Steep land-holdings, even in the fertile volcanic highlands, reduce the productivity of the land considerably. In addition, even if corn could be produced more efficiently in the large farms, this does not address the central questions pertaining to lack of employment alternatives for the rural population, the amount of input into each hectare of production, or the important cultural consideration of the Mayan population's ties to land production.

To the church, the explanation for the poverty of the indigenous people is rather clear, as when they state that "such a deplorable and dramatic situation does not just happen; rather, it is the result of a sinful structure, which impedes a radical solution to the problem."[47] For the church, the poverty of the Maya has both economic and cultural roots and can only be addressed through restoring their rightful relationship to the land.

Conclusion

The Maya of Guatemala are doubly oppressed. They suffer from both political-economic exploitation and sociocultural destruction. Both of these are rooted in their disrupted relationship to the land, and, as a result, they hunger for both bodily and spiritual nutrition. The clamor for a better life and the clamor for land are inextricably related in countries such as Guatemala. For the foreseeable future, meaningful economic alternatives to agriculture have been blocked by the lack of democratic process, the dismal social and material infrastructure, and the general neglect of the country's poor. Furthermore, only a sweeping land reform will enable the rich cultural heritage of the Mayan people to once again be a source of strength, endurance, wisdom, and power.

Rigoberta Menchú spoke of the rights of indigenous peoples at the ceremony honoring her with the 1992 Nobel Peace Prize. She said the Indians have been divided and fragmented over the past 500 years and have suffered genocide, repression, and discrimination. The Nobel Prize, she stated, is a signal of hope for the struggles of the indigenous people of the entire continent, and for Guatemala, a step toward finding peace and social justice.[48] Hopefully, Ms. Menchú's prize will signal the beginning of a change in attitudes toward the Maya of Guatemala, an end of terror, injustice, discrimination, and hunger, and the awakening of a new social and ecological consciousness.

Notes

1. United States Agency for International Development (AID), *Land and Labor in Guatemala: An Assessment,* Washington, D.C., 1982.

2. Asociación para el Avance de las Ciencias Sociales en Guatemala (AVANCSO), *La Políca de Desarrollo Del Estado Guatemalteco 1986-1987* (Guatemala, 1990), 14. James Painter, *Guatemala: False Hope, False Freedom* (London: Catholic Institute for International Relations, 1987), 3.

3. Jeffrey, H. Leonard, *Natural Resources and Economic Development in Central America* (New Brunswick: Transaction Books, 1987), 38; and, Marcus Colchester, "Guatemala: The Clamour for Land and the Fate of the Forests," *The Ecologist*, 21, 4 (July-August 1991): 182.

4. See Leonard, op. cit., 47-48; Kjell I. Enge and Pilar Martínez-Enge, "Land, Malnutrition, and Health: The Dilemmas of Development in Guatemala," in Scott Whiteford and Anne E. Ferguson (eds)., *Harvest of Want: Hunger and Food Security in Central America and Mexico* (Boulder: Westview Press, 1991), 75-101. World Bank, *Guatemala: Population, Nutrition, and Health Sector Review*, 1986.

5. See Institute of Ecology, *An Environmental Profile of Guatemala: Assessment of Environmental Problems and Short and Long Term Strategies for Problem Solution* (Athens, Georgia: University of Georgia, 1981), 17, 60. This report claims that 90 percent of the wood cut in Guatemala is used for firewood.

6. AID, op cit., 52.

7. For an analysis of agriculture and the resource base, see Leonard, op cit.

8. AID, op cit.

9. Ibid.

10. See Oficina Internacional del Trabajo (OIT/PREALC), *Guatemala: Pobreza Rural y Crédito Agrícola al Campesino* (Santiago, Chile: 1985).

11. AID, op cit., 73.

12. *Agricultura de Exportacion, Poblacion y Empleo en la Costa Sur.* (SEGEPLAN, 1984).

13. SEGEPLAN, op cit., 73.

14. Leopoldo Sandoval, *El probelma de la estructura agraria de Guatemala en la poyuntura de un nuevo regimen constitucional en 1986* (Guatemala: Asociación de Investigación y Estudios Sociales, 1986): 12.

15. Institute of Ecology, *An Environmental Profile of Guatemala,* National Park Service with U.S. Man and the Biosphere Secretariat, Department of State, Washington, D.C., May 1981, 62.

16. Institute of Ecology, op cit., 28.

17. Institute of Ecology, op cit., 20.

18. See *Environmental Profile of Guatemala* (Guatemala: Rafael Landivar University, Institute of Environmental Sciences and Agricultural Technology, 1984).

19. Institute of Ecology, op cit., 19.

20. See *Environmental Profile of Guatemala,* op cit., 11.

21. Ibid.

22. Institute for Ecology, op cit., 62.

23. Phillip A. Dennis, Garry S. Elbow, and Peter L. Heller, op cit., 71.

24. Ibid.

25. Colchester, op cit., 177.

26. Fernando González Davison, *Guatemala, La Agroexportación y Las Relaciones Internacionales* (Guatemala: Editorial Universitaria, Universidad de San Carlos de Guatemala, 1987).

27. Ibid., Appendix 2.

28. Interview in the Ixcán, August 1990.

29. Cited in *Central America Report,* Guatemala City, 7 February 1992.

30. "Inside Guatemala: The Tragedy Continues," *Resource Center Bulletin,* Summer 1992.

31. Julian Pitt-Rivers, "Race in Latin America: The Concept of 'Raza,'" *Archives Europeennes de Sociologie,* 14, 1 (1973): 3-31.

32. See Piero Gleijeses, *Shattered Hope: the Guatemalan Revolution and the United States, 1944-54* (Princeton, N.J.: Princeton University Press, 1991); Richard H. Immerman, *The CIA in Guatemala: The Foreign Policy of Intervention* (Austin: University of Texas Press, 1982); and Stephen Schelesinger and Stephen Kinzer, *Bitter Fruit: The Untold Story of the American Coup in Guatemala* (Garden City, N.Y.: Doubleday, 1982).

33. These events include the Panzós massacre of 1978; the Spanish Embassy massacre of 1980; and the massive south coast agricultural workers' strikes in 1980. It is interesting to note that, just prior to Ríos Montt's overthrow, it was feared that a new agrarian policy might be introduced; thus, between 4 August and 7 August 1983, the Guatemalan press carried seventeen articles about rumors of an agrarian reform, six paid announcements denouncing any changes in agrarian structure, and five articles on U.S. Secretary of Agriculture John Block, who announced at a meeting with Guatemalan plantation owners a $50 million aid package for 1984. A week after all that press activity, General Ríos Montt was overthrown in a military coup.

34. Episcopado Guatemalteco, Carta Pastoral Colectiva, *El Clamor por la Tierra*, Guatemala: Febrero 1988.

35. Lionel Toriello Najera, *El Clamor por Una Vida Mejor: Anáalisis de la Estrategia de Desarrollo que Debe Adoptar Guatemala, a la Luz de un Enfoque Sobre su Realidad Agraria* (Guatemala, C.A.: Asociación de Amigos del País [AAP], 1989); and Pablo R. Schneider, Hugo Maul y Luis Mauricio Membreno, *El Mito de la Reforma Agraria: 40 Años de Experimentación en Guatemala* (Guatemala, C.A.: Centro de Investigaciones Económicas Nacionales, 1989).

36. Episcopado, op cit., 1.

37. Ibid.

38. Ibid.

39. Ibid.

40. Stephen Kinzer, "Walking the Tightrope in Guatemala," *The New York Times Magazine*, 9 November 1986.

41. Toriello Najera, op cit., 9.

42. Ibid.

43. Ibid., 11-12.

44. Schneider, Maul y Membreno, op cit.

45. Ibid., 1.

46. Leonard, op cit., 130.

47. Episcopado, op cit., 1.

48. *Discurso de Rigoberta Menchú, en las Recepcion del Premio Nobel de la Paz 1992.*

CHAPTER 9

Sweetness and Death: The Legacy of Hunger in Northeast Brazil[1]

Nancy Scheper-Hughes

A people that entrusts its subsistence to one product alone commits suicide.
-José Martí, *Inside the Monster*, 1975

My study originates in the "600,000 square miles of suffering," as Josué de Castro (1969) described it, that constitutes the pockmarked face of the Brazilian Northeast. The *Nordeste* is a land of contrasts, of cloying fields of sugarcane amidst hunger and disease, of periodic droughts and deadly floods, of authoritarian landowners and primitive rebels, of ecstatic messianic movements and liberation theology coexisting with Afro-Brazilian spirit possession.

Despite numerous "developmental" projects launched to rescue the Northeast since the 1930s, its widespread affliction (still) justifies Brazilian intellectuals' wry description of their country as "Bel-India"—half (the

---

[1] This chapter is excerpted and revised from chapters 1, 4 and 5 of Nancy Scheper-Hughes, *Death Without Weeping: The Violence of Everyday Life in Brazil* (Berkeley: University of California Press, 1992). Used with permission of the publisher.

Southeast in particular) Belgium and half (the Northeast) India. At present, 58 percent of the population of 35 million people spread among the nine states that constitute the region remain illiterate. Among the rural poor, the life expectancy is forty years (Scheper-Hughes 1992:3). Ten of every twenty childhood deaths in Latin America are of Brazilians and five are *Nordestinos.*

Throughout the early 1980s, diseases once thought to be safely under control in Brazil—typhoid, dengue, malaria, Chagas, polio, tuberculosis, leprosy, and bubonic plague—resurfaced to claim new victims, many of them children, especially in the Northeast. By the early 1990s, AIDS and then cholera were added to the list of afflictions. Although we tend to think of these pestilences (with the exception of AIDS) as tropical diseases, arising from the more or less natural interactions of climate, geography, and human ecology, we might do better to think of them as poverty diseases or as diseases of disorderly development. The social relations that produce rural to urban migration, unemployment, *favelas,* illiteracy, and malnutrition are the primary pathogens behind these epidemics.

During the late 1960s and 1970s, Brazil's military dictatorship propelled the nation toward a rapid industrial growth that made it the Western world's eighth largest economy and one of its most enterprising nations. But this now-tarnished "Brazilian Economic Miracle" failed to filter down to the millions of workers and migrants of the *Nordeste,* for whom the only economic miracle was that they managed to stay alive at all. Galeano (1975:75) chose an unsettling metaphor in writing that the political economy of the *Nordeste* had turned that region into a "concentration camp for more than thirty million people." It is a metaphor to which I shall return in the following pages.

The social, political, agrarian, and health problems of the Northeast extend back to the earliest days of colonization, when land-holdings were consolidated into large plantations dominated by a single export crop (sugar, cotton, or coffee) at the expense of diversified and subsistence farming. The site of this study is the *zona da mata* of Pernambuco (the fertile strip of what was originally natural woodlands). It is a region I first visited more than twenty-five years ago and have visited frequently over the years. In the *zona da mata,* sugar is "king," as it has been since the arrival of the first Portuguese colonists in the sixteenth century.

Sugarcane is a particularly predatory crop that has dominated both the natural and the social landscape. In every generation, sugarcane preempts more and more land; it consumes the humus in the soil, annihilates competing food crops, and ultimately feeds on the human capital upon which its production is based. Not only have the peasants' subsistence gardens been eaten up by cane, so also has the once dense and luxurious vegetation that gave the region its name, so that the "forest zone" is today virtually without forest.

The plantation workers and cane cutters who now reside on the Alto do Cruzeiro, a shantytown outside Bom Jesus da Mata that became my home on numerous visits, complain bitterly that they must travel farther and farther to find the kindling wood they once used to cook their garden crops: beans, sweet manioc, yams, and corn. Now that both the subsistence gardens and kindling have disappeared, these recently proletarianized rural workers must purchase virtually everything they need to survive. A growing dependency on wages and the loss of their gardens brought these plantation workers to the Alto do Cruzeiro and to the market town of Bom Jesus da Mata in the 1950s and 1960s during a transformation of the sugar industry, which will be described later in the chapter.

But what are the links between hunger, race, drought, and sugar? For this, we must go back to the history of Portuguese colonization and to the origins of the social and cultural institutions that grew up around sugar production. The totality and globality of the "sugarocracy" defined almost every aspect of life for both slave and free person, wage laborer, sharecropper, and migrant worker from the seventeenth century through the present day. Evocative of this total world of the plantation is Freyre's metaphorical use of the term *bagaceira,* which, in its original meaning, referred to the shed where *bagaço* (the residue fiber spewed out by the crushing of the cane stalks) was stored in huge mounds. Freyre uses the same term to refer to the plantation culture likewise spewed out as a by-product and residue of sugar cultivation in the Brazilian Northeast.

What is most remarkable, perhaps, about the history of Northeast Brazilian sugar-plantation society is its remarkable resilience throughout nearly four centuries, despite radical changes in the value and fortunes of that bittersweet commodity, cane sugar. "The story of a lump of sugar is a whole lesson in political economy, politics and morality," wrote Auguste Cochin (cited by Fraginals 1976:45).

Illustrating this point, Sidney Mintz (1985) traces the world history of that "favored child of capitalism," sucrose, as it moved in trading vessels between western Europe, Africa, the Caribbean, and Brazil, marking the transition from one type of society (mercantile) to another (industrial capitalist). It is a history of the perversity of the capitalist relations of production and consumption, including the production of new tastes, especially for the products of the colonized tropics—sugar, tobacco, and rum. In the beginning, it was the cultivation of a taste for sugar among European aristocrats that propelled the slave trade and slave labor necessary to cultivate the damnable sweet in the sickening humidity of the coastal tropical plantations of the New World. But in a mere two centuries, Mintz points out, sugar passed from being an expensive luxury of the rich to being a cheap necessity of the poor, so that it was the deadly overconsumption of sugar by the English working classes that was to maintain the tropical "sugarocracies" up through the twentieth century.

Obviously, the case of sugar is key to understanding the links between field and factory, between rural and urban populations, both of whom consume an inordinate amount of sugar. Consumption is the flip side of production, as people learn to relish what is made available to them, whether it is lumps of *rapadura* (brown-sugar candy that has been a special treat in the Northeast since the beginnings of sugar cultivation there) or artificially sweetened soft drinks.

In short, sugar is a powerful metaphor, and its fatal attractions, its power and danger, must also be located in its deep-seated associations with sex and pleasure and with the dark-skinned people who, to this day, are primarily responsible for the brute labor required for its cultivation and milling. "Brazil is sugar, and sugar is the Negro," wrote Gilberto Freyre (1986:277), but how much suffering is concealed by those only partly conscious associations! Even the dry and arcane social scientist Roger Bastide waxed poetic on the fantasized sensuality and sexuality of the mulatto sugar-plantation culture of the Northeast, against which he contrasted the lean, "leathery," and ascetic culture of the dry *sertão*. Bastide falls into the "sticky web of sugared metaphor" (Taussig 1987:154) when he writes: "The baroqueness of funeral processions in the plantation zone is sweetened by contact with black mothers, mulatto lovers, humid vegetation, and the heavy odor of sugar."

Bastide's incidental juxtaposition of death and sugar is apropos of the thesis of this chapter, for the history of the *Nordestino* sugar plantation is a history of violence and destruction planted in the ruthless occupation of lands and bodies. Fortunes were made in sugar and in black bodies. Like Bastide, I can never smell the rotting fermentation of cut sugarcane without smelling death, an association further etched in memory by the *Nordestino* custom of covering the tiny, hungry bodies of dead babies with cloyingly sweet, tiny white flowers.

The Nordestino World of Masters and the Slaves

The Old World, gorged with gold, began to hunger after sugar; and sugar required a multitude of slaves.

-Claude Levi-Strauss, 1955

By the time that Duarte Coelho disembarked on the coast of Pernambuco in 1535 to claim the land granted him by the Portuguese crown, sugar was already worth, pound for pound, almost as much as gold on European markets. Soon after his arrival, Coelho founded two colonies, Olinda and Iguaraçu, and by subdividing his land grant into large parcels of virgin forest (never mind that these were already inhabited by the native Tabajara and Cates Indians) and awarding them to his companions, he was able to supervise the establishment of five sugar plantation-mills *(engenhos)* in the first fifteen years of colonization. These mills and their accompanying plantation lands multiplied rapidly along river banks and near the coast, extending both north and south, so that by 1630, there were 144 sugar plantations in Pernambuco. By 1575, Duarte Coelho's son was the richest man in the region.

The labor shortage for all the many tasks of sugar cultivation and production—clearing land, planting, weeding, harvesting, transporting, and crushing and boiling cane in the mills—was acute from the start. The original Portuguese colonists were an indolent and syphilitic lot with an aversion to manual labor. The indigenous Indians made very unsatisfactory plantation slaves. As traditional hunting and gathering peoples, they were unfamiliar with, and unaccustomed to, the discipline of agricultural and milling tasks. Those who failed to escape into the interior of Pernambuco and were impressed into forced labor routinely sickened and died, some by their own hands. Consequently, from the very beginnings of the Portuguese sugar colony in Pernambuco, African slaves were imported in large numbers, so that the average *engenho* during the eighteenth century had between 100 and 200 black slaves. Nevertheless, African and Indian slavery coexisted on these plantations (although in greatly disproportionate numbers) until Indian slavery was finally prohibited by law in 1831. It would take another fifty-seven years before the abolition of black slavery in 1888.

The colonial *engenho* was built around the master's *casa-grande* (big house), in which resided his large extended family. These early plantation masters were prodigious reproducers, and their power and authority were so absolute that they openly took up second wives and live-in slave concubines, sometimes recognizing the resulting illegitimate and mulatto children.

At some distance from the traditional big house stood the *senzala,* the row of connected one-room huts that served as semicommunal slave quarters. In addition, the colonial *engenho* generally had a small chapel, where the women and children of the extended family assisted at Mass and received the sacraments, the priest's blessing, and the benefits of his "sugar-coated" theology. Finally, there was the mill complex: the various buildings and lean-tos for crushing the cane, boiling and clarifying the juice, and purifying the sugar crystals. Surrounding the mill buildings and the *casa-grande* were the outlying fields of sugarcane.

Gilberto Freyre, Brazil's first native anthropologist and social historian, and until his death in 1987, one of its dominant intellectual voices, introduced a rather soft and almost nostalgic and sympathetic portrait of *Nordestino* plantation society from slavery to the present day, owing perhaps to his own origins within that same society. His is a deeply personal social history in which it was "... *our* Mammy who rocked *us* to sleep. Who suckled *us.* Who fed *us,* mashing *our* food with her own hands...(and) who initiated *us* into physical love and, to the creaking of a cot, gave *us* our first complete sensation of being a man" (1986:278).

Freyre comes close to defending Brazilian slavery as a more benign and humane institution than elsewhere in the New World. The main thrust of his argument is that the customary practice of miscegenation between master and slave, openly in the bedrooms of the *casa-grande* and more furtively in the *senzala,* reduced the social distance between the mansions and shanties of the sugar plantation. Under the law of the Free Womb (1871), all children born of slave-master relations were declared free.

The presence of these brown-skinned offspring, Freyre argued, mitigated against any extreme form of racism. First the Indian woman and then the black woman, followed by the *mulata,* the *cabrocha* (the dark-skinned mestiza), the *quadrona* (one-fourth black) and the *oitava* (one-eighth black), entered the Big House as domestics, concubines and then later as wives of their white masters. And so, Freyre argued, miscegenation acted powerfully toward social democratization in Brazil (Freyre 1986a xi, xiv, xvi, xix-xx). Thus was born the great myth of Brazil's racial democracy.

What Freyre neglected in his monumental analysis of the *casa-grande* was an accompanying sociological analysis of the *senzala.* The world that the Brazilian slave master fashioned consisted of more than the bedroom and the nursery; it also encompassed the sugar fields and the boiling house, where both Indian and African slaves (as well as wage-earning freemen) sickened and died in great numbers.

The abolition of slavery in 1888 (making Brazil the last Western nation to free its slaves) should have thrown the sugar plantation economy into crisis. That it did not, and that sugar production remained virtually unaffected in the years following abolition, requires some explanation. From the beginning of the nineteenth century on, slave labor came into competition with wage labor. Virtually every *engenho* had large numbers of poor squatters, impoverished freemen (acculturated Indians, *mulattoes, mestizos,* and free blacks) who, in exchange for the right to clear a small piece of land, build a hut, and cultivate a garden or orchard, worked certain days for the plantation master for free or for a nominal wage (de Andrade 1980:76; Galloway 1968:298-299). These indentured squatters represented a huge rural reserve labor force, and they turned out to be crucial in the transition from slave to wage labor.

On the eve of abolition in the late 1870s, free workers already outnumbered slaves in every municipality of the *zona da mata.* After abolition, the newly freed slaves simply became indentured squatters and sharecroppers, "replacing the discipline of slavery with the discipline of hunger," as Mintz (1985:70) described the emancipation of plantation slaves in the Caribbean. As squatters, the ex-slaves continued to live in the converted *senzalas* or, more commonly, in mud and straw huts in small clearings near the sugar fields. Their diet remained scanty and limited: manioc meal, dried meat, and whatever they managed to cultivate in their small gardens or to poach from the plantation property. Impoverished, illiterate, and dependent upon the whims of their landlords, who could have them removed at any time—such was the "racial democracy" enjoyed by the dark-skinned rural workers from emancipation through the present day.

The Rise of the Modern Sugar Factory

Just before the turn of the twentieth century, the first central mills were established with the help of government incentives and foreign investors and capital. The Brazilian government had hoped that these central mills, fully mechanized with the most up-to-date technology, would render the traditional *engenho* as a mixed agricultural and industrial institution obsolete. The separation of the *cultivation* of cane from the *production* of refined sugar was deemed essential to the modernization of the sugar industry.

The modern sugar factories, the *usinas,* first appeared along the railway system that crossed the southern part of Pernambuco. Here, they replaced the traditional *engenhos* and turned the feudal sugar barons into simple "suppliers" of sugarcane. While the new *usinas* fought to dominate the *zona da mata,* the traditional *engenhos* resisted the onslaught for nearly half a century more. Finally, however, the smaller mills were confined to the more remote and hilliest northern regions of the *zona da mata.* By the end of the 1950s, even these last holdouts disappeared from the landscape, leaving behind only the dilapidated *casas-grandes* and their abandoned mill buildings.

The transformation of the plantation economy, completed by the mid-twentieth century, had a disastrous effect on the traditional peasant class—the tenants, sharecroppers, and conditional squatters (see Forman 1975, chapter 3). The most numerous had been the conditional squatters, who had lived on the *engenho* and had kept cottages and garden plots in exchange for one or more days of conditional, or free, labor on the plantation. Evictions began in the 1950s, when many *usineiros* and cane suppliers began to eye even the smallest and least accessible subsistence-based garden plots as more land for sugar cultivation.

In addition to outright evictions, some peasants and sharecroppers were simply starved off their lands when their landlords increasingly awarded them only the most useless, inaccessible, or exhausted plots of land or assigned them very temporary fields that they were allowed to use only between sugar harvesting and recultivation. Landlords also began to increase the number of days that conditional squatters had to work on the plantation, leaving them little time for tending their own gardens. Finally, they forced many peasants to leave the land by restricting the kinds of crops they could cultivate and by forcing peasants to grow sugarcane to be sold to, or shared with, them.

It was during this period that many older residents of the Alto do Cruzeiro were forced to leave the surrounding countryside to try their luck in town. Bom Jesus da Mata, centrally located within commuting distance of five large *usinas* and many smaller plantations, was a magnet for evicted or otherwise displaced peasant-workers. Cut loose from paternalistic bonds to a particular landowner, plantation, or sugar mill, they became "free agents" who sold their labor for wages on a temporary basis. In effect, they formed a ready, reserve army of rural day laborers.

Female Workers in the Cane

The transformation of rural labor in the plantation zone of Pernambuco affected women as well as men. Although the women always had been hard workers—working side by side with their husbands and sons, tending their small gardens, fishing in the river, weaving baskets from rushes, and selling small bits of excess produce in the marketplace—women had not worked in sugar cultivation on *engenhos,* nor had they worked in the *usina* mills. That was "men's work," although women and children might have assisted by carrying lunch pails and water buckets back and forth the many miles between home and the fields. With the dislocations and disruptions caused by the modernization of the sugar industry and the proletarianization of labor, however, women and children have entered the rural industrial labor force in great numbers, especially in the past ten years.

Although it is the rare woman indeed who would be caught cutting sugarcane, the most proletarian and masculine of all rural labors, it is not uncommon today to come across large rural work crews comprised wholly of women and children clearing fields in preparation for planting or engaged in the endless task of weeding. On a normal workday, many Alto women leave their huts before dawn and begin their long trek to often very distant fields. The women of the Alto prefer to walk to their assigned fields, rather than suffer the vulgarities and sexual overtures of male workers during the communal truck rides provided by the *usina* or plantation.

Women are paid by the *quadro* (square) of land, and they often suspect the work-team boss of mismeasuring the legally determined lot size to the advantage of the plantation owner. In the "old days," a man or a strong woman could clear a *quadro* in a single day; today it takes workers (especially women) two and sometimes three days to finish the same task. Women are aware that their bosses are getting free labor out of many women's young sons, boys who should be in school, but they shrug their shoulders and say, "But at least it's a way of getting by, isn't it?"

The Madness of Hunger

When I am hungry I want to eat one politician,
hang another, and burn a third.

-Carolina Maria de Jesus, "Child of the Dark"

During the summer of the drought of 1965, I was drawn one day by curiosity to the jail cell of a young woman from an outlying rural area who had just been apprehended for the murder of her infant son and her year-old daughter. The infant had been smothered, while the little girl had been hacked with a machete. Rosa, the mother, became for a brief period a central attraction in Bom Jesus, as both rich and poor passed by her barred window that opened to a side street in order to rain down invectives on her head: "animal," she was called, "unnatural creature," "shameless woman." Face-to-face with the withdrawn and timid slip of a girl (she seemed barely a teenager), I made myself bold enough to ask the obvious: "Why did you do it?" She replied as she must have for the hundredth time, "To stop them from crying for milk." After a pause she added (to her own defense), "Little critters have no feelings."

When I related the story later that day to Nailza Arruda with whom I was then sharing a tiny, mud-walled hut on a steep cliff path on the Alto do Cruzeiro, Nailza shook her head and commented sadly: "It was the *delírio*"—the madness—"of hunger." She had seen many good people commit acts for which they would later repent when driven to the brink by hunger-madness. At the time, I considered her words another example of the *Nordestino* imagination—vivid, dramatic, extravagant. But I soon had to reconsider.

Early one afternoon, while Nailza, Zé Antônio, and I were still resting to escape the inferno of midday, there was an impertinent knock on the door, and thinking that it must be something quite serious, I pulled myself out of the hammock and opened the upper half of the split door that opened into the room where we had been sleeping. A small woman, whose expressionless face I did not immediately recognize, stood there with a small bundle in her arms that I knew, at once, to be a sick child. Before I could close the door with a stinging reprimand to come back at a more convenient hour, the woman had already unwrapped the clean sugar sacking to show a child of perhaps a year whose limbs were wasted, leaving what seemed a large head attached to sticks— a veritable, living stick figure. He was alive but very still, and he stared, I recall, intently and without blinking. He also had a full set of teeth, which was unexpected in one so malnourished.

Seeing that the child's condition was precarious, I rushed him to the local hospital of Bom Jesus. "It's too late for this one," Dr. Tito said, frowning in disapproval and leaving me with an untrained practical nurse. Together, the two of us tried to find a usable vein in which to insert an intravenous tube. The once passive child threw his remaining energy into a fight against the tube, a reasonable enough response in a terrified and sick-to-death child. But the fight was just the beginning of an hour-long "delirium," during which the child went rigid, seemed to buckle, and then, finally, became wild, growling and snapping at our ministering hands until, thankfully, he died. The cause of death penciled into the head nurse's copybook, the only record of hospitalized cases, read: "malnutrition, third degree; acute dehydration." I was tempted to add: "*delírio de fome*"—the "madness of hunger."

I had occasion to witness other deaths like these over the years of my involvement with the people of the Alto do Cruzeiro, and they are not very pretty. Sometimes, following death from hunger-madness, the face becomes fixed in a terrible grimace, the "*agonia da morte.*" The people of Bom Jesus refer to deaths from malnutrition (especially child deaths) with the very stigmatizing term, *doença de cão,* the "dog's disease." They are referring to the similarities with death from rabies, which the people call *raiva,* literally "rage, fury, madness." The madness—the *delírio*—of hunger, is, indeed, very much like rabies, and death from hunger is, indeed, a dog's death.

Hungry Bodies

When Josué de Castro first published his classic book, *The Geography of Hunger* (1952), he framed his discussion of worldwide patterns of starvation and undernutrition as the breaking of a long-standing and implicit scientific taboo. Hunger, he wrote, was a well-kept secret about modern human existence, so that of all the calamities "that have repeatedly devastated the world... it is hunger which is the least studied and discussed, least understood in its causes and effects" (1952:5). In short, hunger was a base and vulgar instinct from which science had averted its gaze. But even as the Brazilian nutritionist was writing these lines, they were already being negated by a flood of biomedical and clinical studies that appeared in the wake of World War II. These were fueled by an almost obsessive need to document in minute detail, to quantify, every physical and psychological horror suffered by those interned in German concentration camps, abandoned in the Warsaw ghetto, and victimized by the famine that struck Holland in 1945 (see Zimmer, Weill, and DuBois 1944; Nirenberski 1946; Dols and Van Arcken 1946).

What de Castro might have said, but what he failed to note, was that the attention of biomedical scientists to the subject of hunger had to wait until white Europeans began to suffer from the same conditions that had long afflicted black and brown peoples in many parts of the globe, including the southern part of the United States. The ravaged face of hunger was a shocking novelty to the Allied forces who liberated the Nazi camp of Bergen-Belsen on 12 April 1945, but it was a common reality during periods of drought and famine in the Brazilian Northeast, where there are, even today, many hunger victims, most of them very young, who die alone, unattended, and *desconhecido* (anonymously).

In the context of this discussion, the "madness" of hunger has various and sometimes ironic meanings, but its plainest one derives from the writings and folklore documenting the history of famine and drought in the Brazilian Northeast. References to the madness of hunger can be found as early as the sixteenth century, in the diaries and other records left by Portuguese, Dutch, and French navigators, who documented the raving madness caused by hunger aboard ship on the seemingly endless voyages to and from Brazil. *Histoire d'une voyage fait en la terre du Bresil,* written in 1558 by Jean de Lery, a French Huguenot shoemaker who made the voyage to Brazil in the 1540s, contained the following entry:

> The food ran out completely at the beginning of May and two sailors died of hunger madness....During such outright starvation the body becomes exhausted, nature swoons, and the senses are alienated, the

spirit fades away, and this not only makes people ferocious but provokes a kind of madness, justifying the common saying that someone is "going mad from hunger."

References to *delírio de fome* appear in the literature of the Brazilian Northeast: in the novels of Euclides da Cunha (1904) and José Americo Almeida (1937) and in the ethnographic writings of Roger Bastide (1964). Chico Bento, a character from the play *O Quinze* (The Drought in the Year 1915) describes his loss of moral scruples when, "delirious with hunger" and "with trembling hands, his throat dry, and his eyes blackened, he clubbed down whatever stray animal crossed his path as he fled the land" (de Castro 1969:60). These writers have captured a popular expression of the horror of hunger and hunger-madness. *Delírio de fome* may be taken to signify the unfettered, primary experience of hunger, hunger before it was understood in the medical academy as "protein-calorie" or "protein-energy" malnutrition. It may be taken to represent, then, the subjective voice, the immediate experience, of hunger. It is the voice that emerges in the biting words of Carolina Maria de Jesus (1960), quoted earlier, and it is the rage that provoked young Rosa to destroy her year-old daughter.

The hunger of the coastal sugarcane workers and their children is not the same as the periodic famines that afflict the people of the Pernambucan interior backcountry. The hunger of the plantation workers of the *zona da mata* is constant and chronic. It is the hunger of those who eat every day, but rarely enough, or of an inferior quality or an insufficient variety, so as to leave them dissatisfied and hungry. By contrast, the hunger of the drought-plagued interior, the backlands and the "badlands" of Pernambuco, is cyclical, acute, and explosive. It descends ruthlessly upon a people who are generally energetic, self-sufficient, and well-nourished.

The hunger of the Northeast is undoubtedly part of the popular folklore of the region, and it is a subject of modern Brazilian literature, even as it appears in realist and surrealist theater and film. But just how real is the hunger of the *Nordestino?* To what extent might the common and frequent references to a person "dying" or "falling down" from hunger be a cultural convention, an expression of frustrated desires and longings that are more metaphorical than material? In accepting, at face value, Alto informants' descriptions of their "dry stomachs" and "trembling limbs," might not the naive anthropologist too willingly accept a collective myth similar to the symbolic "famine" of the Melanesian Wamirans, studied by Miriam Kahn (1986)? Is Galeano's (1975:75) reference to the Brazilian Northeast as a "concentration camp for more than thirty million people," a vulgar metaphor, a vile misappropriation of a space and an experience that has no equal and no parallel elsewhere?

In 1965, when I first joined Nailza and Zé Antônio in their tiny wattle-

and-daub hut near the top of the Alto do Cruzeiro I was still capable of being shocked at the conditions of Alto life, but over the years, and with the help of my Alto friends, I learned to *conformar* (to adjust, to accept), so to be able to listen and observe in a relatively detached and dispassionate way. The scenes of sickness, hunger, and (especially) child death are now commonplace to me, and only rarely am I moved by a particularly poignant scene or image.

Perhaps it was the scene of Terezinha carefully dividing four small rolls of bread into halves, one for each household member, regardless of age, irrespective of size. What kind of blind justice was at work here, what radically egalitarian ethos? It was uncharacteristic behavior in a hungry Alto household and, therefore, disturbing. Ordinarily, the heads of the household would take a disproportionate share, so as to be able to work. But on this morning, Seu Manoel, the father, took his tiny share without comment, shoving it into the pocket of his baggy pants. He would eat his later, after a few hours of work cleaning out the clogged drains and recently flooded main street of Bom Jesus.

"Won't you be hungry?"

"*Brasileiro ja se acostumou a fome,*" he said. "Brazilians have long since gotten used to hunger."

Or perhaps it was the words of Terezinha's seven-year-old son, Edilson, that reminded me that I can still feel something in the face of death. Edilson, who more than once has been given up for dead, continues to surprise everyone with his persistence in holding on to life. Edilson has survived, but he has not thrived, and he exists in a liminal social space, midway between death and life. No one, especially not his mother, expects Edilson to survive his next crisis, his next uphill battle. He is very small and without strength. Terezinha shows me Edilson's latest affliction: a tumor-like growth on his neck that makes it all but impossible for the child to swallow.

"Now the little critter eats nothing at all," she says with pity. "He's not going to live long. Soon he will join the others" (i.e., his dead siblings).

"Don't talk like that in front of Edilson," I say to his mother, trying to protect the boy, forgetting that he has walked in a liminal space on the edge of death since his birth and he is *bem conformado* (well-adjusted) to his ghost-like social status. And, so, it is Edilson who now silences and corrects me in order to protect his mother. He tugs at her skirt, anxiously, to get her attention, and he says of his own death:

"Hush, *mãe,* hush. I'm not afraid; I'm ready to go there."

Or perhaps it was the lean-to of Maria José, the discredited "widow," and her three children, dirty and the youngest one naked, dancing a *frevo* to a handmade drum and whistle.

"Where is your mother?"

"She's out looking for work," replied the oldest child, a girl with the shaved head of one who had been recently infected with head lice. With her shorn head, spindly legs, and torn shift, the girl looked for all the world like a refugee from a prison camp. It was high noon and the children must have been hungry, but there was no sign of a fire.

"Have you eaten today?"

"*Não,* nothing," was the predictable reply.

Her younger brother scowled and turned his back on me. "You are nosey; go away," his back announced. But I persisted.

"Let me see what you have in the house."

The girl pointed to two small reed baskets hanging from a rope thrown over a roof beam. In one there was half a coconut and a few shriveled peppers. In the other basket were several small dried fish, ugly, and covered with tiny bugs. I was nauseated and quickly replaced the dirty cloth that had covered the basket.

"Tell me, is your *mãe* out begging?"

The girl looked down and nodded her head.

"Do you sometimes beg for your mother?"

"I used to, but not anymore."

"And why not?"

"I'm older now and I'm ashamed."

But now I was suddenly struck with shame. I left the girl with fifty cruzados. She happily accepted the bill and said: "With fifteen cruzados I will buy a roll for each of us for lunch, and I will give thirty-five cruzados to my mother when she comes home." Like most Alto children, Francisca cannot read, but she is quick with numbers, which she has not learned from school (she doesn't attend) but from "studying" precious cruzado notes.

"Shall I dance for you?" she asked.

Or perhaps, finally, it was the *casa de nanicos* (the house of the "dwarfs") on the *Rua da Cruz* that jolted me from my state of "conformity." Here was a grandmother, two adult daughters (one of them mother of a year-old baby), and six children, four of them *nanicos,* dwarfs. But these Brazilian "pygmies" (as the Brazilian nutritionist Nelson Chaves [1982] refers to such children) have been stunted by chronic hunger and not by genes. The boys, ranging in age from six years to fifteen and in height from two and a half to little over four feet, have been raised on *mingau* (manioc flour, water, salt), bean broth, and steamed cornmeal cakes. The youngest, eleven month-old Paulo Ricardo, weighs barely five kilos and seems likely, if he lives at all, to follow in the stunted footsteps of his little uncles. The adult women explain: "The boys in our house are all puny and weak; they don't like to eat much."

"The major cause of chronic undernutrition may be purely economic," wrote the authors of *The Biology of Human Starvation* (Keys et al., 1950:3), "but the primary cause of modern starvation is political strife, including war." I do not want to quibble over words, but what I have been seeing on the Alto do Cruzeiro for two and a half decades is more than malnutrition, and it is politically as well as economically caused, although in the absence of overt political strife or war. Adults, it is true, might be described as "chronically undernourished," in a weakened and debilitated state, prone to infections and to opportunistic diseases. But it is overt hunger and starvation that one sees in babies and small children, the victims of a famine that is endemic, relentless, and political-economic in origin.

Since 1964, and with little let up over the decade (1975-1985) of the great "Economic Miracle" of Brazil, I have seen Alto children of one and two years who cannot sit up unaided, who do not or who cannot speak, whose skin over the chest and upper part of the stomach is stretched so tightly that every curve of the breast bone and of the ribs stands out. The arms, legs, and buttocks of these children are stripped of flesh, so that the skin hangs in folds. The buttocks are discolored. The bones of the hungry child's face are fragile. The eyes are prominent, wide open, and often vacant; sometimes they have sunk back in the head. The hair is thin and wispy, often with patches of baldness, though the eyelashes can be exceptionally long. In some babies, there is an extraordinary pallor, a severe anemia, that lends the child an unnatural, waxen appearance that mothers see as a harbinger of death. My daughter Jennifer, who often accompanied me in household visits, fell upon an apt designation. She called them "snowball babies."

In addition to frequent stunting, older children and adults show other signs of chronic hunger. Vitamin deficiencies lead to changes in skin pigmentation, and one sees children who are speckled like Easter eggs, with patches of white or grey on normally brown skin. There is a great deal of edema—swellings of the abdomen, limbs, and sometimes the face. The hair and skin of older children and adults can be dry and brittle. Skin infections are endemic in bodies that have virtually no resistance to scabies, impetigo, fungal infections, and all kinds of skin ulcers, invariably badly infected. Adults can live for years on end with untreated and badly infected sores that squatters refer to as *pereba.* Seu Manoel and Terezinha, for example, both suffer from chronic skin infections on their feet and legs that have burrowed so deep that one avoids looking for fear of seeing bone. Alto residents not only learn to live with such painful and ugly afflictions, they learn to work with them as well, which for local washerwomen means soaking their infected legs or feet for many hours a day in the polluted waters of the local riverbed and for rural workers walking many miles through the brush in open sandals.

Fazendo Feira: Making Ends Meet

In 1987-88, the minimum wage purchased only half the groceries it did in 1982, and a family's *cesta básica* (basic marketing) cost one-and-a-half times minimum wages. This situation had not changed significantly in 1989. Just the daily purchase of a kilo of bread would cost a rural worker more than half of his minimum daily wage. And, unfortunately, most residents of the Alto do not even have the security of a single minimum wage, as many are unemployed from February through September, when there is no cane to be cut.

Consequently, Saturday mornings are a time of nervous agitation on the *Alto do Cruzeiro.* It is the time when the market baskets must be replenished. If there is a man in the household, marketing is generally his responsibility. He is expected to provide and purchase food for the family. The woman's responsibility is to economize and to make the food last, to make sure that the house is never completely without food, especially beans and a little bit of fresh meat. Within the hierarchy of consumption on the Alto do Cruzeiro, ideally food comes before other wants and needs. One can postpone paying the rent, one can go without gas and cook with charcoal or twigs, one can always light the home with a kerosene lamp, and one can do without new clothing. Hunger is immediate. You can't do without food is the rule of thumb. But this is a rule that is frequently bent, as one emergency after another—an urgent need for medications, work clothes, transportation, or school materials—eats away at the market money. Meanwhile, the market, it is said, *come tudo,* (eats everything). And the specter of hunger is always in the foreground.

Seu Manoel is paid about $32.00 per month, about two-thirds of a single minimum wage, as a municipal street cleaner. It is illegal, of course, for workers to be paid less than the minimum wage, but it is a customary practice all the same. His weekly paycheck cannot provide for the basic necessities. Consequently, Terezinha sells popsicles and penny candies from a small wooden stand in front of their house. Their eldest son, Severino, age fifteen, is employed in various odd jobs and in scavenging. Pooling their collective labor and resources, this family of eight came up with one and a half minimum salaries. The following list represents the normal Saturday *cesta básica* for this family:

1 kilo of *farinha* (manioc flower)
4 kilos of sugar
2 kilos of brown or black beans
1 (or 2) kilos of rice
3 (200 gram) packages of corn meal
1 package of inexpensive coffee
(sometimes 1 or 2 packages of *macarrão,* a substitute for rice)
cooking oil, salt, garlic, parsley for flavoring
(a chicken or 1/2-1 kilo of chicken parts, if possible)
1 small plastic sack of powdered milk for the 9-month-old baby
soap

The variation from week to week and month to month is small, with the exception of June through August, when corn replaces rice and *macarrïo* (noodles). Fruit enters the diet occasionally when Terezinha's mother sends some from her garden in the country.

Terezinha, for her part, tries to sell enough sweets from her makeshift stand to provide for the morning bread—one small roll per person. Otherwise, the family breakfasts on black coffee. The main meal, eaten midday, is a serving of brown beans covered with *farinha* and usually one other starch, sometimes rice but, more frequently, spaghetti prepared with oil and a bit of tomato, or more often than not, with *colorau,* a red food coloring. Dinner is steamed cornmeal cake made from *fubá* (dried corn meal), salt, and water. When there isn't enough food to *mata fome* (kill, finish off, the hunger), Manoel and the children ask for *garapa,* a glass of sugar water, and they will go to sleep on that. And, so, the four kilos of sugar, which might seem excessive, is, in fact, a staple in this hungry family's diet.

There have been some changes in the diet of the people of the Alto since the 1960s, when brown beans slowly cooked for many hours with large, thick slices of native squash, pumpkin, and onions was the staple meal. Whenever possible, a bit of sun-dried beef or beef jerky was added. On the *Alto do Cruzeiro* today, beans are generally cooked *simples,* with only salt and cumin for flavor. The loss of their garden plots has reduced the use of squash and other vegetables, while dried beef (as well as the much loved salted codfish) has become prohibitively expensive. What have taken their place are bins of tiny, salted fish caught locally from the river and dried in the street that runs through the *zona* (the red-light district), where the cars of the local bourgeoisie drive over them. Those who own cars will never eat these fish, while the people of the Alto themselves often express their revulsion at having to eat them.

Increasingly, even beans have become prohibitively expensive to the poorest Alto households, where *fubá* has now replaced beans as the staple food. In the *casa de nanicos* and in the lean-to of Maria José, the discredited widow, and in the home of Seu Chico who has just arrived with his wife and seven children, beans have become something of a *festa* food, a "party" food. "In these days," Seu Chico says, "we learn to eat our *quarenta* [a corn meal mush] and be content."

In the home of Antônio Campos everything is *parado* (dead). Unemployed for several months, Antônio is stretched out asleep on a plastic covered sofa with more springs exposed than covered. His wife stands at the doorway with a crying toddler in her arms and two other small children at her side. "Yes," she tells me, "the family is hungry a good deal of the time." After he wakes up, Antônio explains how he manages to put together his family's weekly market basket:

"I spend a lot of time in the house of my friends. They're out of work, too. We ask ourselves, 'What are we going to do? We can't be like this forever!' But when Saturday comes, I have to do something. The only thing to do is to look for a friend and say, 'Amigo, have you got about 200 *cruzados* so I can get the children some *farinha* and a little milk?' Or you try to find a shop that will sell you a little something on credit. If that doesn't work, my

God, I don't even want to think about it."

But when it is a single woman, alone with her children, the search can be even more frantic. If she is out of work a woman will exhaust every resource, even stooping so low, Biu said, as to beg from an old lover or even from the *safado* (bum) who had deserted her and the children. "Who can stand by and listen to a child crying that its stomach is aching from hunger? You will do anything," she said. But children want more than just black beans, Biu continued. "They want meat, and here is the real struggle." Although Biu can resist her older children's demands for "luxury foods," she breaks down, she says, when it is the baby, her little Mercea, who asks for meat. "'Two pieces, mãe,' she says, holding up her little fingers," and Biu will take away from an older child so that the stoic and melancholy little girl, who has never had the strength or "courage" to stand up or walk, can have her wish.

To see Biu, exhausted after a day's work in the cane fields, climb the treacherous back side of the Alto, balancing firewood on her shoulder and a basket on her head, while her two youngest children cheer from their perch outside their smoke-filled hut on the first sighting of their "victorious" *mãe,* reminds me of a passage from the diary of another strong shantytown woman. "I feel so sorry for my children," Carolina Maria de Jesus (1962:34) wrote in an entry dated 13 May 1958. "When they see the things to eat that I come home with they shout, '*Viva mamãe!*' Their outbursts please me. But I've lost the habit of smiling. Ten minutes later they want more food."

Empty Pockets and Full Bellies: Poverty and Food

Within the poor population of the Alto do Cruzeiro, the double stigma of hunger and sickness visibly stamp them as *pobre, preto,* and *marginal*—poor, black, and outlaws. Food and medicine are the idioms through which Alto people reflect on their social condition. Poverty is defined by food scarcity and by dependency upon medications. The poor are those who are always sick and always hungry. The self-respecting poor organize their lives around the constant struggle to feed themselves and their children, but they "get by" and still have the strength to work. The truly wretched are those who must beg to eat and who are too sick or too weak to work.

The poor of the Alto draw distinctions between real foods, "foods that satisfy," and "luxury foods," foods that tempt the palate but tease the belly. Beans remain the prototypical food, the food that satisfies and nourishes, so that to say that a house is without beans is to say that the house is really without food, that people are hungry. Rice alone or pasta alone cannot fill the "hole in the belly." But, ideally, a meal consists of an ample combination of starches: beans, rice, pasta, and, of course, *farinha* sprinkled liberally over the plate. In the poorest households, a mixture of beans and *farinha* is rolled between the thumb and index finger into thick balls, which are then eaten by hand. For a people with considerable anxiety about hunger, satisfaction (a word used in reference both to sex and eating) consists of a sensation of fullness, even heaviness, following a meal.

The people of the Alto do not like to eat in front of others. There is a great deal of shame associated with eating. To eat is almost as private an act as sex or defecation, probably because of its ability to reveal so much about the person. Eating in public gives one away; it shows the extent of one's desires, the seemingly bottomless pit of one's needs.

Although Biu often stopped by my house, and would gladly accept a cup of coffee, she preferred not to eat with me, but to take whatever food I offered home with her. Her little Mercea would eat, however, but only if I put her on the floor facing the wall, with a tin plate in her lap, and left the room so that she could eat with her fingers unobserved. Otherwise, she would sit quietly and soberly, adamantly refusing to touch anything that was offered.

While beans, rice, pasta, and other basic foods *mata fome* (kill hunger), other foods only *engano,* (fool hunger). *Garapa,* the sugar water given to quiet a hungry child at night, is the most common of these. During lean times, the main meal may consist of a few beans cooked in a great deal of water to produce a bean broth that is thickened with *farinha.* Here, manioc meal serves as a food substitute more than as a food extender.

Sucking sugarcane is also seen as an *engano,* a trick played on an empty stomach, and as one of the ways in which hungry workers are "fooled" by their bosses. Normally, cane cutters may suck cane whenever they wish, as long as they are not wasteful. But cane workers know that this "free cane" comes at a high price, and that it is used to extract energy and productivity from tired workers.

In addition to exploited workers, babies and toddlers are a common target of *engano,* as mothers substitute *papa de agua* (a watery gruel) for expensive powered milk. "Babies fed on water soon have blood that turns to water," commented a disapproving older woman with reference to the pale, listless babies of the Alto do Cruzeiro. Despite its deficiencies, *papa de agua* is filling, and Alto babies take it quite greedily and then are gratefully quiet for several hours. In this way, even small babies learn early to conform to the adult pattern of heavy feedings and long delays between meals. Meanwhile, those who show the least disposition to eat are often the hungry toddlers, of whom mothers often say that the poor little creatures never really had a "taste" for food—or for life.

The Color of Hunger in Northeast Brazil

Brazil has long claimed for itself a "racial democracy" (see esp., Freyre 1986), achieved by generations of intermarriage and the, at least numerical, predominance of a racially blended social type (the *mulatto* or the *moreno)* in the Brazilian population. However, this ideology is belied in the national census figures and other statistical surveys, which consistently show that the descendants of African slaves in Brazil are uniformly poorer, less educated, and die younger than whites. The myth of racial democracy is a social anesthetic meant to distract poor black Brazilians from the reality of their situation. The ideology of racial mixing and "hybridization" is so entrenched that in rural Northeast Brazil race and racial discrimination are socially unmentionable and therefore "invisible" categories of oppression. A strong taboo prevents both white and black, rich and poor Northeast Brazilians from "noticing" the role that color plays in the everyday violence of social life—from subtle discrimination applied to membership in private clubs and postgraduate university education on one end of the class spectrum, to racially motivated "death squad" neighborhood "cleanup" campaigns (see Scheper-Hughes 1992, chapter 6) at the other end.

The color of hunger in Northeast Brazil is most poignantly revealed in the disproprionate representation of black to white infant mortality: 62 percent versus 38 percent for the town of Bom Jesus da Mata (Scheper-Hughes 1992:302). Black Brazilians have been hungry for five centuries. They were hungry on the first slave ships bound for Recife from Angola and Mozambique. They were hungry on the colonial sugar planations and in the sugar mills of Pernambuco. They were hungry before, during, and after emancipation, when the tyranny of hunger replaced the tyranny of the lash. They are hungry today in the urban shantytowns and rural *macombos* of contemporary Northeast Brazil.

Camp Rations

The caloric intake of the rural worker in the *zona da mata* of Pernambuco has been the subject of more than fifty years of research. The first scientific nutritional survey was conducted in the 1930s by the physician, nutritionist, and humanist without equal, Josué de Castro. He reported that the average daily intake of the rural worker in the area of the sugarcane monoculture was approximately 1,700 calories (1952:80). These intial studies were followed up by Nelson Chaves and his colleagues. In the last book published before his death, Chaves (1982) reported that the conditions first noted by de Castro remained largely unchanged. Chaves attributed the low productivity of the Pernambucan cane cutter (half that of the cane cutters of São Paulo) to the chronic undernutrition of the *Nordestino* rural worker. "In Pernambuco the cane cutter's caloric intake is extremely low, *averaging less than 1500 calories per day*" (1982:73, italics in the original).

Chaves refers to the so-called tropical laziness and indolence of the rural workers as chronic fatigue, "nothing more than the natural defenses of an organism adapting to a hostile environment." He argues that the slaves on the original sugar plantations of Pernambuco were better fed than today's rural wage laborers, because the slave masters had a greater concern for the well-being of their tools of production. In contrast:

> the rural worker of today is primarily a carrier of worms, and his stature is diminishing considerably over time, so that it is actually approaching that of the African pygmy. The women of the region are also of low stature, their pelvic structures are reduced, and they suffer from mammary hydroplasia and sexual immaturity. They give birth to small, premature infants, and they are predisposed to both physical and mental fatigue.

Chaves' radical conclusions concerning the gradual "pygmitization" of the rural poor *Nordestino* population (based on his group's statistical surveys and anthropometric measures) were both controversial and contested. However, his measures have been verified in more recent nutritional, growth, and developmental studies, which indicate gross differences in size and maturation of poor and privileged children in Pernambuco. In a recent study of 900 children (ages seven to seventeen)—226 from poor and marginal rural migrant families living in new shantytowns of Recife and 674 from wealthy families living in the same city—the differences were striking. While the mean values for weight and height of privileged children fell close to the fiftieth percentile by United States and British standards, the mean for the poor children fell below the twenty-fifth percentile. The boys from poor homes were especially disadvantaged with respect to height measurements, which fell below the fifth percentile for all age groups (Linhares, Round and Jones 1986).

Another epidemiological survey (see Batista Filho, 1987) indicated that two-thirds of all rural children showed signs of considerable undernutrition and stunting and, of these, 40 percent could be classified as nutritionally dwarfed, as *nanicos*. These startling findings were published amidst much heated public discussion and commentary in the newspapers of Recife. However, they passed by unnoted by the the public health personnel working in the state health post of Bom Jesus, where two mornings a week, rural mothers and their children fill that oxymoron called the "well baby clinic" for immunizations. The babies and toddlers are routinely weighed and measured, and the obvious stunting and underdevelopment of two-to-four-year-old children is the rule rather than the exception. The functionary in charge reads out the height and weight statistics to the mother, but the implications of the child's often gross underdevelopment are never explained. As for the health post workers, when asked why they didn't do more for the malnourished children who appeared each morning, a common reply was: "What can we do? The health post can't prescribe food."

There are multiple medical, developmental, psychological, and social risks that accompany physical stunting resulting from malnutrition in early childhood. Not the least of these, with reference to Alto residents, is the high-risk spiral that turns malnourished children into small and undernourished women, who give birth to premature, sickly, and low birth weight infants who are at excessively high risk of mortality in the first weeks and months of life.

There is a striking contrast between the stature of the people of the Alto and the middle- and upper-class resident of Bom Jesus, a contrast that begins at birth. The average shantytown infant is born weighing under six pounds, while the average middle-class infant of Bom Jesus weighs seven and a half pounds at birth. Middle-class children reach puberty at an earlier age, and as teenagers and adults, they conform to our norms for an average, although not particularly tall, population.

These marked differences feed Alto peoples' profound sense of inferiority. They interpret their small size in racialist terms as evidence of the intrinsic weakness of their "breed" (their *raça).* It is their diminished size that physically separates and marks them from the rich, the white people, the "fine people" of Bom Jesus.

It might be useful to put the data on the average caloric intake in the *zona da mata* into a comparative context. The *Nordestino* rural worker, with his average caloric intake of 1,500-1,700 calories is considerably better nourished than were the Jews of the Warsaw ghetto of 1942 (see Apfelbaum-Kowalski et al. 1946). At the Nazi concentration camp of Buchenwald, however, an internee, who later became a member of the French Academy of Medicine, reported that the food allotment there in 1944 was usually around 1,750 calories per day, or somewhat more than the average intake of the *Nordestino* sugarcane cutter today (Richet 1945).

The closest approximation of the dietary allowance of the rural worker in the *zona da mata,* however, is to that of the Minnesota starvation experiment (Keys et al. 1950), in which the thirty-two volunteers were submitted to twenty-four weeks of semistarvation; their daily intake was gradually reduced to a limit of 1,570 calories. Keys and his colleagues had designed an experimental study to observe the physiological and psychological effects, not of malnutrition, but of starvation. Insofar as their work still stands as the classic scientific study of human starvation, we might begin to consider the situation of the *Nordestino* rural worker and his family for what it really is: the slow starvation of a population—trapped, as Galeano suggested, in a veritable concentration camp for more than 30 million people.

References

Almeida, José Americo. 1937. *Paraíba e Seus Problemas.* 2d ed. Porto Alegre: Livraria do Globo, Barcellos, e Bertaso.

Apfelbaum-Kowalski et al. 1946. "Recherches Cliniques sur la Patologie du Systeme Circulatoire dans la Cachexie du Famine." In *Malade de Famine,* ed. Apfelbaum-

Kowalski et al., 189-225. Warsaw: American Joint Distribution Committee.
Bastide, Roger. 1964. *Brasil, Terra de Contrastes.* São Paulo: Difusão Européia do Livro.
Batista Filho, Malaquias. 1987. *Nutrição, Alimentação e Agricultura no Nordeste Brasileiro.* Recife: Embraer.
Chaves, Nelson. 1982. *Fome, Criança e Vida.* Recife: Editora Massangana, Fundação Joaquím Nabuco.
Da Cunha, Euclides. 1944. *Rebellion in the Backlands.* Chicago: University of Chicago Press. (Translation of 1904. *Os Sertões.* Rio de Janeiro: Livraria Francisco Alves.)
De Andrade, Manoel Correia. 1980. *The Land and People of Northeast Brazil.* Albuquerque: University of New Mexico Press.
De Castro, Josué. 1952. *The Geography of Hunger.* Boston: Little, Brown.
————. 1969. *Death in the Northeast.* New York: Random House.
————. 1983. *Fome, a Tema Proibido: Ultimos Escritos de Josué de Castro,* ed. Anna Maria de Castro. Petrópolis: Vozes.
De Jesus, Carolina Maria. 1962. *Child of the Dark.* New York: Dutton. (Translation of 1960. *Quarto de Despejo.* Rio de Janeiro: Livraria Francisco Alves.)
Dols, M. J., and D. J. M. Van Arcken. 1946. "Food Supply and Nutrition in the Netherlands During and After World War II." *Milbank Memorial Fund Quarterly* 24:319-355.
Forman, Shepard. 1975. *The Brazilian Peasantry.* New York: Columbia University Press.
Fraginals, Manuel Moreno. 1976. *The Sugar Mill: The Socio-Economic Complex of Sugar in Cuba, 1879-1960.* New York: Monthly Review.
Freyre, Gilberto. 1986. *The Mansions and the Shanties: The Making of Modern Brazil.* Berkeley and Los Angeles: University of California Press. (Translation of 1936. *Sobrados e Macombos.* São Paulo: Companhia Editora Nacional.)
Galeano, Eduardo. 1975. *Open Veins of Latin America: Five Centuries of the Pillage of a Continent.* New York: Monthly Review.
Galloway, James H. 1968. "The Sugar Industry of Pernambuco During the Nineteenth Century." *Annals of the Association of American Geographers* 58 (3):285-303.
Kahn, Miriam. 1986. *Always Hungry, Never Greedy: Food and the Expression of Gender in a Melanesian Society.* Cambridge: Cambridge University Press.
Keys, Ancel, et al. 1950. *The Biology of Human Starvation.* 2 vols. Minneapolis: University of Minnesota Press.
Linhares, E. D. R., J. M. Round, and D. A. Jones. 1986. "Growth, Bone Maturation, and Biochemical Changes in Brazilian Children from Two Different Socioeconomic Groups," *American Journal of Clinical Nutrition* 44:552-558.
Mintz, Sidney. 1985. *Sweetness and Power: The Place of Sugar in Modern History.* New York: Penguin.
Nirenberski, Martin. 1946. "Psychological Investigations of a Group of Internees at Belsen Camp." *Journal of Mental Science* 92:60-74.

Richet, C. N. 1945. "Medicales sur de Camp de Buchenwald en 1944-1945." *Bulletin Acad. Med.* (Paris) 129:377-388.

Scheper-Hughes, Nancy. 1992. *Death Without Weeping: The Violence of Everyday Life in Brazil.* Berkeley, Los Angeles, and Oxford: University of California Press.

Taussig, Michael. 1987. "History as Commodity in Some Recent American (Anthropological) Literature." *Food and Foodways* 2:151-169.

Zimmer, Richard, Joseph Weill, and Marcel DuBois. 1944. "The Nutritional Situation in the Camps of the Unoccupied Zone of France in 1941 and 1942 and Its Consequences." *New England Journal of Medicine* 230:303-314.

CHAPTER 10

Hunger Amidst Plenty: A South African Perspective

Tshenuwani Simon Farisani

Thanks largely to the excellence with which the apartheid system was implemented by the Nationalist Party for so many decades, the new democratic government of South Africa, brought into being in the historic elections of April 1994, has a nearly insurmountable task in dealing with the pressing needs of the black communities of our nation. The long shadow of apartheid extends far into our future.

Among the pressing issues the new government needs to address is "hunger in the land of plenty," South Africa. Statistics tell a story. On average, somewhere between 82 and 136 black children die every day from hunger.[1] No white children perish with their stomachs empty in this land of plenty. Mortality rates for African and colored children are thirteen times higher than for white children.[2] South Africa was and remains perhaps the most poignant exemplar of a global phenomenon: colored hunger alongside white tables of abundance.

To understand black South African malnutrition and poverty, I have chosen to look at it in the context of previous government policies as they affected and continue to affect the South African community, especially the black majority, who have been detrimentally impacted geographically, educationally, socially, economically, religiously, and politically. Of course, these spheres are not watertight compartments of reality; rather they are related dimensions of the same complex story. Our interest lies precisely in the fact that they related, within the context of apartheid, in such a way that they impacted collectively and negatively on the ability of the oppressed to have access to any reasonable means of livelihood on any meaningful scale.

The Legacies of Apartheid

Apartheid was a merciless assassination plot that did more harm to the nonvoters in a subtle way than it did in dramatic, visible, public ways. But once the mechanisms of the "plot" are properly understood and exposed, and the different elements realistically related, the ugliness of the whole ideology, as measured by its consequences and impact on its victims, emerges for all to see. If at the end of my contribution, I have managed to demonstrate that "hunger in the land of plenty" has nothing to do with the "laziness of the Bantu" and the "economic realities" of another Third World country, but that in the South African context, hunger was conceived in the womb of apartheid and nourished as part of a mammoth plot to sentence as many black people as possible to a life pattern of starvation while simultaneously trying to feed—and overfeed—as many whites as possible, I will have succeeded in my aim. The unfolding of this plot has manifested itself in a multiplicity of strategies in a variety of ways over the years. To uncover the plot, we need to retell, however briefly and partially, the South African story.

Geographical Alienation

The Dutch East India Company first entered what is now called South Africa in 1652. The new white settlers soon began to take land from the various tribes in the region. In 1795, the British invaded and took control of the important food and fuel station at Cape Town. Over the decades and centuries, with the piecemeal conquest of both people and territory, the blacks lost both dignity and land—a means of livelihood and a possession of pride for the community—to the descendants of Dutch and English invaders. With the Land Acts of 1913 and 1936, the geographical alienation of blacks from their mother/fatherland neared completion. Finally, the establishment by the apartheid government of the black "independent homelands" (which were independent in name only) on the most barren 13 percent of South Africa's land hit the last nail in the coffin of black living possibilities.

How does hunger for land translate into hunger for food? The black communities made a living from agriculture and livestock farming. When their land was confiscated, they lost both their land and their jobs—and their earnings. Most were forced to work on the "white man's farm"—in many instances the farm was the very land that the community had "lost" to the white farmer or the government. Those uprooted and now unemployed persons, mostly men in the initial stages, were forced to work for the whites in the urban areas as laborers in industry, in mines, and as domestic servants. They all had one thing in common: they earned, in varying degrees, wages below the poverty datum line. In a land with no minimum wages and, at that time, no black trade unions, starvation wages became the rule, rather than the exception. As black lands continued to shrink into tribal homelands and influx control took its toll, more and more blacks could not find jobs. Those with jobs often retired without pensions, and the injured lost their jobs without compensation and were immediately shipped to the "dumping grounds" (a more accurate name for the homelands), which also served as labor pools by providing younger, cheap laborers, who would ultimately also become exhausted, unpensioned material fit for the dumping grounds. The vicious circles of death continued uninterrupted and continue to haunt the new government that inherited this legacy. This inheritance includes the so-called independent and self-governing homelands that together contribute a hungry 3-5 percent of South African gross national product.

Social Alienation

The apartheid system systematically weakened the social fabric of black society in many different ways. For example, the architects of apartheid deliberately undermined black cultural values and norms by disparaging them as uncivilized and un-Christian. They destabilized families by fostering migratory labor and dehumanizing accompanying conditions. They separated African families on ethnic grounds, including such hierarchical divisions of blacks into Bantu, Indian, and Colored, which were further divided into smaller components. In this way, previously economically viable units were split into human fragments that could not survive economically except through one form of dependence or another on the white community. This was one of the strategies that was used to reduce black people into a population of mere "boys" and "girls" who turned green or red at the master's call. This social breakdown and family fragmentation left women tilling whatever land remained while their husbands unearthed gold and diamonds miles away, the rewards for which barely managed to keep themselves and their families financially afloat. Food, shelter, and clothing, among basic needs, became luxuries that a most could ill afford. Is it surprising, under these conditions, that kwashiorkor and marasmus—malnutrition-related diseases—found very fertile ground among the socially destabilized and the economically vulnerable?

To aggravate an already disastrous situation, separate residential areas were created, so that the starving might enjoy their democratic right to be poor and the rich celebrate their God-given right to daily bread (complemented, of course, with abundant meat, vegetables, fruits, and dessert), each in their respective worlds. Like the rails of a train, the black, hungry Third World and the satisfied, white first world of South Africa were designed to converge on the work floor but never at the table. Indeed, even in cases where meals were (and are) prepared by blacks—as they were in most cases—there is evidence that these cooks and chefs still did not have access to adequate quantities of the nutritional foods that kept their masters in good health. This sobering reality still confronts the new government that was ushered in after the first democratic elections.

Educational Alienation

The damage that "engineered" malnutrition inflicted on the developing brain-capacity of our young is beyond measure. Those who survived this total onslaught ended up, with reduced brain capacities, in the ill-funded, poorly equipped, blacks-only schools. For these brain-molested children, university education was and remains an unachievable dream and the sky is simply not the limit for them.

Bantu education—introduced specifically to cultivate technological and academic inadequacy in the black community—certainly made no small contribution to the noncompetence (not to be confused with incompetence) of the black force in the skills labor market. Hunger has to do with the ability to earn a decent wage, and earning a decent wage has to do with one's capacity to compete fairly with the rest of the potential workforce on level ground. The cumulative results of the apartheid education policy were devastating to the black community, even after the abolition (at least in theory) of job-reservation laws. Those blacks who acquired skills against tremendous odds, some at home and others abroad (still just a trickle in the ocean), had to break through lots of racial barriers to secure jobs that gave them a "healthy" living. In many cases the regime preferred to import white skilled labor from abroad rather than either absorb local skilled labor or train local black potential. In this way, inadequate education in inadequate facilities by insufficiently qualified teachers in crowded classrooms was a very effective instrument in creating an appearance of "doing everything for the poor black creatures," while in reality doing almost nothing for them. In fact, part of the explanation for black hunger is that some people arrogated to themselves the sole right to do things "for" rather than "with" their so-called beneficiaries.

The crisis in education that the new democratic government has inherited from almost five decades of an ideologically handicapped system will probably be addressed properly only when the former victims begin to do things for themselves. These days, the people's cry is for "people's education." Only a democratically conceived form of education will begin to address effectively the absence of blacks among the pilots of South African Airways, among the locomotive engineers of the South African Railways, among the judges of the South African Appellate Division, and the near absence of the majority among the engineers, scientists, chief executive officers, boards of directors, and other crucial sectors of the economy and society as a whole. Education, or lack thereof, is a major cause of hunger in South Africa, and, in reverse, hunger born of induced poverty has, in a vicious circle, become a major factor in keeping many blacks from the centers of education. The educational wheel of apartheid gathered momentum across decades, and it will be difficult, but not impossible, for the new democratic government to stop the wheel from grinding to death all in its path.

Apartheid Politics

Can we borrow an idiom from Shakespeare and speculate that some are born hungry, some achieve hunger, and others have hunger thrust upon them? South Africa's neighbors, such as Mozambique and Angola, were surely neither born hungry nor did they achieve hunger. Clearly, their hungry status was thrust upon them. It was thrust upon them by South Africa's direct efforts at destabilizing these neighboring peoples as punishment for the crimes of independence and antiapartheid policies. Now, if the apartheid regime had the capacity to export hunger and misery, it should be obvious that they did not lack a political strategy to fertilize the field and then sow seeds of hunger among their own "Mozambiquans" and "Angolans."

All the policies that affected the oppressed majority negatively in the social, economic, educational, and even religious spheres, were, in the first place, political decisions. They were political decisions based on the color and the race of a person or a community. Preceding all these antihuman policies was the deliberate decision, made many decades ago by the Nationalist party, to purposefully, consistently, and thoroughly exclude the black majority from exercising a vote in the country of their birth. Furthermore, South African whites who dared to throw their lot in with the oppressed were dealt with mercilessly if they proved unrepentant. These were whites whose hunger for justice was not suppressed by the plenty and the privilege that surrounded them and promised to increase if they remained faithful to the volk and its tried and tested path.

In one foreboding series of power-hungry legislative decisions, the sons and daughters of the European invaders condemned the black community to a life of perpetual hunger and want by denying them the power of the vote; the same decisions lifted the Afrikaner from the economic doldrums to a life of sufficiency guaranteed by an unassailable political base. Since that fateful day, white stomachs have remained full of food while ours continued to be full of hunger. All attempts to break away from these shackles of starvation were met with ruthless brutality, ranging from imprisonment to torture to outright assassination. The aim of it all? To keep most blacks hungry, some of them on the verge of starvation, and a given quota always falling headlong from malnutrition into those numberless graves in the dumping grounds.

Some have suspected that this form of "assassination by natural means" was designed, in part, as a population control mechanism, compensating the government more than adequately for their bungled attempts at birth control among blacks. It was a brutal policy that played a counterpoint melody to the tune of white population explosion by both natural means and immigration. This double-pronged strategy, it was hoped, would narrow the population's numerical racial imbalances, so that should God one day "condemn South Africa" to a democratic vote, the outcome would be "change without change," what Jürgen Moltmann would call the "utopia of the status quo, which is the worst of all utopias." But it didn't work.

Apartheid Failed

Many black people died—that is to say, were killed—at the hands of apartheid. Whether by starvation in childhood, bullets in adolescence, or prison brutalities in adulthood, blacks flooded apartheid's black-only cemeteries as quickly as fans into our soccer stadiums. But that is not the end of the story. Apartheid has been tried and found guilty as a crime against humanity. Now the truth is evident to everyone; it stares all of us straight in the eye: Apartheid has failed. Discrimination has failed. Repressive legislation delayed but could not smothered the hunger for justice.

Jails. Robben Islands. Torture. Murder. Banning orders. Exile. All wounded the lions and lionesses of the struggle, but they remained determined. They became even hungrier for justice and the liberation that would bring food and dignity with it. If not by immediate harvests, our liberation ensures that the plowing and planting season has begun; no longer will we watch the rains and seasons come and pass while we work in others' fields, only to watch hungrily as they take the fruits of our labor and smile the whole way to the bank, while our children groan the whole way to the grave.

APARTHEID HAS FAILED. Those that lost battles in a prolonged war of attrition and conceded several rounds in a boxing debacle characterized by low blows and unethical methods did not succumb. They knew that the final round belonged to the justice-loving people of South Africa, to the new society that will be big enough to accommodate even those who have labored to abort its birth. Thus, no degree of hunger has been able to throttle the freedom fighter's faith in the struggle. "It is better to fail temporarily in a cause that will ultimately succeed, than succeed temporarily in a cause that will ultimately fail."

Up until now, I have pursued loose threads that may not appear to form a pattern in the tapestry of apartheid. But they are not as loose as they appear. Apartheid was a political ideology. It was the mother and father of geographical alienation; it was the architect of social separation; it was the springboard of economic exploitation; it was the wisdom of denying the majority the normal exercise of their mental capacities and faculties. Apartheid was all of these, but it was and is one thing. Apartheid was a stillborn child determined to take the living mother to the grave with it. In its desperation, it wanted to drag the whole of South Africa to the cemetery of doomed antihuman ideologies, where Hitler and Mussolini reside. Hopefully, the people of South Africa will not grant it its deathbed wish. My pastoral instinct suggests that even those who have comfortably ridden on this whites-only horse will recover from the drug of apartheid before the horse gallops down the precipice that is forever hungry to receive those who have thrust hunger upon so many.

The New South Africa

Perhaps the challenges that face those whose policies now aim at feeding the hungry and clothing the naked in a new South Africa need to be highlighted. The new government will do well to remember that justice delayed is justice denied. The forces of exploitation will probably spend some time licking their wounds after their loss at the hands of democracy. They may have suffered a sudden shock at losing their Shakespearian position as the "monarch of all they survey, their right nobody to dispute." For the first time they are discovering that they are no longer as "constant as the northern star." But as they wake up to discover democracy is more reality than nightmare, they will begin to charter new ways to keep the newly won liberation at the level of "flag independence," where people will shout "Amandla! Ngawethu!" Power! To the people!

It is thus appropriate for all justice- and peace-loving South Africans to investigate now the strengths and weaknesses of different forms of social, political, and economic justice theories and their relevance and utility, as well as their viability in addressing South Africa's very unique problems, among which hunger for justice and food seem to top the list. Clearly, utopias of the status quo will not work. However, dramatic movement forward will have to be informed by the successes and failures of other models, without adhering to the discredited philosophy of "reconstruction without experiments." A great deal of local initiative and creativity will be demanded of both the leadership and the community, to come up with new visions while willing to explore other models of justice that have attempted to address the needs of their people both singlehandedly or in combination.

It may be necessary to look at utilitarian, contractarian, entitlement, balance of power, and human dignity perspectives. In a society emerging from a devastating hunger-inflicting environment, it cannot be overemphasized that whatever models we consult with—socialist or capitalist or a mixed economy—will have to take into account Africa's own contribution, guided by a liberation motif that requires people's meaningful and central participation in all structures that pretend to address their hunger for food, for justice, and for peace. With a culture of cooperation among political groups and trade unions already in place in South Africa, this need not warrant the reinvention of the wheel. While we should be wary of the trappings of power, we must be equally wary of the fact that unless we find a model that addresses the sources and not just the symptoms of our people's hunger, those who have inflicted untold hunger on the people will turn around and point a pharisaic finger at the "inefficiency, immaturity, and corruption of the so-called liberation movement." We might even begin to hear about "black on black hunger."

Notes

1. The lower figure is drawn from A. Seewat, *Crippling a Nation: Health in Apartheid South Africa*, International Defense and Aid Fund for Southern Africa, London, 1984. The higher figure is taken from "The poverty of apartheid," *The Economist*, 2 June 1984, 73. Statistics are problematic because the government, since 1966, prohibited public agencies from publishing or collecting data on malnutrition among blacks (cf. Kevin Danaher, "South Africa: Hunger in a Land of Plenty," Institute for Food and Development Policy, San Francisco, undated.)

2. Cf. Ben Wisner, "Commodity Relations and Nutrition Under Apartheid: A Note on South Africa," *Social Science & Medicine*, vol. 28, no. 5 (1989): 441-446.

CHAPTER 11

Overcoming International Apartheid

Dessima Williams

Each moment in history has its own special character in terms of the unique challenges posed and the opportunities available as people confront the daunting problems of social existence. As we face the advent of the twenty-first century, an intense struggle rages over access to and control of resources, who is given intellectual legitimacy, and what kind of integrity and quality of life will be available to different populations. Nothing determines, a priori, that a progressive, internationalist constituency or community will be victorious. To borrow a saying from today's business advertising, one doesn't get what one deserves, one gets what one negotiates. If this is true, then what we negotiate, how we negotiate, and with whom we form our negotiation team, will largely determine whether we meet two goals—the one explicit, the other implicit.

The explicit goal is to end hunger in our community, be that a homeless community in the United States, a barrio of Haiti, a displaced community of Guatemala, or a *favela* of Brazil. Hunger, in all its tragic dimensions, is the ultimate symbol of material deprivation, and its elimination is essential to the building of a global community concerned with peace, justice, and a good and healthy life. Our implicit goal, in the words of a Caribbean historian turned politician, is to satisfy an "inward hunger": attain happiness, maintain community, and sustain freedom. The two hungers are clearly related and interdependent.

Struggling to end our hungers—material and spiritual—has always characterized human existence. This search is reenacted today, responding to today's specificities. Offering the recently dismantled status quo in South Africa—apartheid—as a metaphor for the continuing state of today's world, this chapter proposes the term "global apartheid" as a conceptual and political framework for understanding the presence and persistence of world hunger.

The following exercise suggests the dimensions of global maldistribution of wealth and power that generates hunger today: If there were but 100 people in the world, about 33 of them would be rich or of moderate income, and 67 would be poor. About 20 would be suffering from malnutrition and hunger; several would starve to death. Half would be homeless or living in substandard housing. Looking only at the two-thirds who are poor, 55 of the victims of this malfunctioning system would be female; just under 60 would be people of color. In contrast, the 20 people of European origin would concentrate among the upper income. This is the unacceptable status quo. It is a status quo that breeds hunger, material and spiritual. I call it a system of global apartheid.

Hunger in the world today is overwhelmingly the outcome of explicit policies pursued historically and continuing today. The post-World War II drive for modernization worldwide, and with it the drive for superprofits, is at the core of this problem. In the so-called Third World, modernization took the form of what is euphemistically called development. Development, as international policy, targeted the Southern hemisphere as a "backward," "undeveloped" place to be "developed," meaning to be more fully integrated into an exploitative, racist global agenda. But, by all accounts, development policies failed. In response to the collapse of this paradigm riddled by war, waste, growing disparities, and growing despair, some contend for a New World Order predicated on Western hegemony, with the constant reliance on U.S. threat and use of force. With regard to racism and hunger, this New World Order, if it is allowed to stabilize, will reenact the old proverb, "the more things change, the more they stay the same."

At this important point in history, a conjunction of forces and opportunities gives us a chance to focus on more creative and democratic paths and to push forward for a more meaningful set of options to global apartheid. In pursuit of these goals, antiapartheid communities are demonstrating more deliberate reliance on what some have characterized as "cultures of resistance" to the dominant models of cooptation, control, and even of destruction.[1]

Urgently needed is the construction and reconstruction of more humane and sustainable paradigms. Indeed, there is but one definitive approach to resolving hunger and its attendant violence: dismantle global apartheid and construct humane alternatives out of its wreckage. Each of us is challenged to take responsibility and work actively toward this daunting but attainable goal.

Global Apartheid: Structure and Manifestations

The past 500 years have been characterized by some of the grossest inequalities in human history. Worse still, complex systems have been put in place that function to maintain and amplify that inequality. Without doubt, the largest and most pervasive (and invasive) of these systems is modern capitalism/imperialism. This system controls power, wealth, and food—and strongly influences even our thoughts about these. Through capitalist ideology, we think that the maldistributions, or systemic asymmetries, are permanent, acceptable, almost natural conditions. The distinct color of capitalist ideology results from broad strokes of patriarchy and racism that are glossed over, paradoxically, with a thin veneer of pervasive individualism. The belief in individualism is tapped to explain the "success" of those on the top of the capitalist hierarchy, while race and gender form background explanations for massive poverty and hunger. In the international context, these dynamics are often subtle, but they parallel the more obvious dynamics of apartheid in the old South Africa.

In South Africa, the Afrikaners—a religious and demographic white minority and a social and economic elite—in cooperation with descendants of the English, commanded, until quite recently, the entire life of black, colored, and Indian populations. This was done through apartheid—the institutionalized belief in separate and unequal development of peoples of different histories, races, ethnicities, cultures, and aspirations. Through the exploitation of predominantly black South African labor (men in mines, women in domestic and commercial work), as well as a barrage of legal, paralegal, economic, and constitutional arrangements (combined with no small measure of military repression), apartheid produced (and its aftershocks continue to produce) untold suffering and hunger inside South Africa. The unwilling subjects of apartheid, indeed its victims, are ill-fed, ill-clothed, and ill at ease under apartheid's regime and legacy.

Afrikaners promoted the apartheid ideology, and the entire South African population was expected to fall under its hegemonic spell. While military and paramilitary force prevailed outwardly for most of the century, the effort at hegemonic control largely failed from the beginning. Historically, most South Africans fought—in overt or subtle ways—against apartheid. The exploitive exercise of power invariably creates resistant power.

The profile of international distributions of wealth and power and poverty and hunger, as presented previously, makes the concept of apartheid, as experienced in South Africa, applicable on a global plane. Bear in mind that to go from national apartheid, as it were, to global apartheid necessitates thinking of the international system as more or less parallel to a nation. That is, laws, armies, ideologies, politics, economics, and populations must behave similarly, in practice as well as analytically, as we shift from national to international. There is, however, no absolute correlation. The attempt here is to see how the structures, functions, and effects of apartheid in a nation are similar to those at the global level, and how conceiving an end to hunger necessitates conceiving an end to apartheid. With that, we turn to some features of global apartheid, to its generation, accumulation, and use/misuse of wealth and power.

Symptoms of Global Apartheid

The United Nations' Human Development Report (1992) documents that the richest one-fifth of the world's population own and control 83 percent of the world's wealth, while the poorest one-fifth own 1 percent. In this study, the world's wealth is looked at in terms of economic activity, such as savings and trade investment.[2] According to the same report, the 60 percent in the middle scramble for the remaining 16 percent. This ghastly division of wealth, and complementary ghastly division of power, is what is taken here to be both the structure and manifestation of apartheid at a global level. It is no coincidence, as pointed out in chapter 5, that wealth (and with it food) is concentrated in the hands of those of European descent, while poverty and misery spread among people of color.

This maldistribution has produced continued and rapid increases in hunger in almost every region of the globe, with only a few countries spared. Hunger is on the rise, in part because expenses are escalating and in part because families—large, extended, and hard working—are becoming more and more impoverished. And if one holds to an ethic that says community begins in the family, then one is now sharing a smaller and smaller personal economic pie with one's ever impoverished family.

This is an important point to note. As academics and social-change activists who may seem to be financially afloat, we are often encouraged to gaze down into the swelling sea of the poor, the homeless, and the hungry, as if they were "other"; but we may well see ourselves among them, no longer seeing "us" and "them" as separate. Unless we reside within the top 10 percent of the global population that is fattening itself at the expense of everyone else then, let us be clear, we, too, are experiencing the economic and political erosion of global apartheid.

Looked at in this way, it becomes clear that part of the work we must do in the remaining years of the 1990s is to understand that "we are the poor." More specifically, we are the spiritually and materially poor if we both accept and are hurt by this system. So as South Africans dismantle apartheid and its legacies to bring bread and roses to a needy population, so, too, at the global level, we must be among the many doing systemic assault on the way societies and governments construct and reproduce themselves to conduct apartheid's business.

Gender and Global Apartheid

Another dimension of global apartheid, like apartheid in South Africa, is that its disparities, violence, and disempowering characteristics tend to fall disproportionately on women and children.[3] Because societies everywhere hold to a variation of the theme that women are less valuable and significant than men, in every society women are more likely to be victims of systemic injustices. This has been borne out, beginning even in the cradle and before.

Recent studies reveal that between 60 and 100 million females are "missing" worldwide, and that "a resurgence of female infanticide," particularly in parts of Asia, may be responsible.[4] Adding to the early deaths of girls, female babies and young children often are not given as keen medical attention as that given male children, especially in places such as China and India.[5] Child prostitution is higher for girls than boys, especially among poor families in the Philippines, Thailand, India, Taiwan and Brazil.[6] More women and children suffer from hunger than men,[7] leading analysts to speak of the feminization of poverty.[8]

If a woman wanted to change the laws and structures that generate such a crushing and inhumane existence, she would start at a considerable disadvantage. In 1990, only 6 (less than 4 percent) of the United Nations' 159 member states were headed by women. On average, only 10 percent of parliamentarians are women (with scores of countries without one single woman in parliament).[9] Not a single woman has run a serious campaign for president in the history of the United States. Against this backdrop of Western, male-dominated power, resides the phenomena of global poverty. In general, global apartheid does to women and children of the world what apartheid does to the South African woman and her children: it seeks to reduce her to an economic and political, if not legal, ward of the sexist, racist, system.

Global Apartheid: Resistance and Counterresistance

Beginning in the mid-1980s, resistance to global apartheid spread in many quarters. We saw even the mainstream media referring to runaway greed, capitalism on the rampage. Perhaps one of the most interesting examples of resistance, however, came from the Dominican Republic. During 1985, twenty years after the United States' invasion of the Dominican Republic, massive "food riots" took place in the capital, Santo Domingo, as well as in other cities. These so-called food riots were political rebellions against a government and a state system that had been impoverishing and disempowering the average Dominicana/o. The immediate cause of the riots was that gasoline and cooking oil prices were doubled and in some cases tripled under the demands of the International Monetary Fund's (IMF's) structural adjustment program. And this immediate rebellion against further economic pressures on the poor touched a political nerve already agitated by years of debilitating poverty. On average, in 1985, wages were U.S. $.57 per day for women in Trade Zone corporations.[10] Meanwhile the government of the Dominican Republic spent anywhere from $50 to $120 million (depending on whose figures one accepts) to construct a monument to commemorate the 500th anniversary of Christopher Columbus' coming to the Americas![11] Tens of thousands of poor city residents were moved forcibly to erect this huge cross-shaped edifice. In sad poetic injustice, one of the world's nations most impoverished by the legacy of Columbus failed to satisfy the basic human needs of its population, directing its state revenues instead to grandiose pandering to colonialism.

In Sierra Leone in 1986, similar consumer riots broke out over increases in the price of rice. Here is a country, once self-sufficient in rice, having to import it at prices kept high by IMF price-monitors resident in the Ministry of Planning and in the Ministry of Economic Development. These popular rebellions took increasingly political overtones as consumers made a link between their impoverishment, their government's complicity, and international economic policies.

Unfortunately, resistance is by no means universal, nor is it always successful where it exists. The present system has been legitimized and perpetuated by millions of organizations, subsystems, and citizens who accept and support, to one extent or the other, this oppression. As a consequence, material and spiritual hunger persists and spreads.

Bear in mind that multinational for-profit corporations continue to play an ever dominant role in defining and servicing the world's food needs. Let's take one example. Coca-Cola reported an 11 percent increase in its sales in the last quarter of 1991, mainly from its increasing international sales.[12] Even as some countries, countries where profits were extracted, sunk further and further away from the ability to feed their populations, Coca Cola's foreign operating profits rose from 19 percent in 1990 to 42 percent for the same period of 1991.[13] Most likely, these kinds of trends will increase in the coming years as so-called Free Trade Agreements, such as the recently enacted North American Free Trade Agreement (NAFTA), will make the world one safehaven for the unimpeded operation of international corporations.

Global Apartheid in the Centers of Power

The Reagan revolution and the Thatcher revolution of the 1980s were intended not just to change the role of the state, to change the way government is positioned, but also to fundamentally change society. And they succeeded. As one example of the impact of these policies, the richest 1 percent of U.S. families got 70 percent of the increases in family income in the period 1977-1989. According to a Congressional Budget Office report, the richest 20 percent of the families in the United States took more than 100 percent of the growth in average family income! How is that possible? It is possible because the bottom 40 percent lost ground, and what they lost went to the top 20 percent, who also gobbled up all of the family income gain.[14]

It must be noted that the dismantling of the Soviet Union has also had its impact on increasing poverty and hunger and solidifying global apartheid. According to one report, 56 percent, or by another report, 30 percent, of the people of the former Soviet Union live in poverty, in need of daily adequate nutrition. In addition, whatever its faults may have been, the Soviet Union had international agreements with numerous revolutionary movements in developing countries around the world, and the aid that flowed from those agreements assisted those nations in feeding their populations. That is now gone. The collapse of one regime and the entrenchment of another combine to form massive disempowerment at the material level: political global apartheid.

The Ideology of Global Apartheid: Alive and Well

The various examples discussed in this chapter feature one aspect or another of global apartheid. That is, they all share an underlying ideology of supremacy, held together by political practices developed over centuries that encourage inequality; they are ideologies held together by cultures that denigrate anything but compliance to this dominant mode. The outcome of this ideology is not unlike what we saw in South Africa—segregation of wealth, segregation of power, segregation of legitimacy, segregation of hunger—all in favor of European people.

In chapter 5, we were told of U.S. President Roosevelt's use and reenactment of the idealogy of "The White Man's Burden" at the turn of the century.[15] It is important to realize that the ideological and political descendants of Mr. Roosevelt are quite alive, most obviously in the white supremacist movement in the United States, and, much more subtly, throughout the mainstream.

Derrick Jackson, a *Boston Globe* columnist, published a commentary during the Bush years supportive of a more humane policy toward Haitian refugees entering the United States. Mr. Jackson's article received a number of hostile letters from the New England public. One said: "Thank God there are men like President Bush who have the moral strength to take a stand on Haiti. Haitians are worthless, genetically-inferior scum. The elimination of the nigger with the AIDS virus is the greatest thing that has happened to the world. The U.S. navy should use the Haitian boats for target practice."[16] This may be an extreme example, but the same underlying thought patterns can be found in more subtle form, even within the dialogue of the political and intellectual elite.

In the same column, Mr. Jackson reported the views of a leading U.S. idealogue, then Republican presidential candidate Pat Buchanan, on U.S. immigration policy. Asked Mr. Buchanan of his audience as he campaigned for votes: "If we had to take in a million Zulus next year or a million

Englishmen and put them in Virginia, what group would be easier to assimilate?"[17]

All this is pretty nauseating and tragic from those who do not have responsibility for official policy. Far more tragic and alarming is the fact that some holding public office harbor similar views. It was not that long ago, for example, when Robert Gelbard, then Deputy Assistant Secretary for InterAmerican Affairs, was in Haiti seeking to have an agreement signed between then-deposed president Jean-Bertrand Aristide and the de facto Haitian military government that overthrew him in a military coup. The U.S. diplomat invited a number of Haitian senators to dinner and attempted to broker an agreement. The Haitian Senate itself had deep differences with the populist theologian-turned-political leader, President Aristide; yet they and Haitians of all strata remember the years of U.S. occupation (1915-1934), and they were very distrustful of the United States. Not being able to resolve quickly—over dinner—complex and deep-seated differences among the Haitian senators and win them over to U.S. positions, the U.S. envoy blurted out: "Haitians have one chromosome too few, the one for consensus and compromise, and one chromosome too many, the one for conflict and discord."[18]

Here, again, is apartheid's ideology alive and thriving. This time it surfaces as a secular-based belief that genetics, in this case the presumed inferior genetic make-up of Haitian blacks, provides the explanation for political differences! Genetics is pandered as the explanation for why Haitians are not prepared to go back to a regime of oppression, for which the U.S. foreign policy has been a principal ally since the 1930s. One need not speculate how such thinking influences U.S. policy toward Haiti, as the Haitians are accused of being the original carrier of the AIDS virus, unsuitable in other ways for political asylum in the United States, and generally considered "the basket-case nation" of the Western hemisphere.[19]

These pronouncements of a Massachusetts citizen, a presidential candidate, and a government bureaucrat, as well as U.S. policy toward Haiti, all point to the deep-seated racism that is fundamental to the practice of global apartheid. What we hear expressed in all of these statements is the basic raw materials that can and have justified exploitation, destruction, and death of one group at the hands of another. For the purpose of supplanting apartheid, it is important to focus on the fact that throughout history there always has been resistance to this, a resistance seeking physical, cultural, and spiritual survival and growth.

The question then becomes what can be done? What can we do at this historical juncture?

Grenada: Contribution to Apartheid Resistance

It is critical that, above all, citizens of goodwill and democratic vision do not give up. We must never forget that there is another way we can live besides the current devastating one; we must not take for granted that global apartheid is for all time.

One personal recollection may be instructive. I recall, while growing up in Grenada, Prime Minister Eric Gairy saying on national radio, "My government is very, very strong." In a myriad of ways, he repeated that message. The irony was that his boasting occurred precisely at that moment when he was in his greatest weakness. Similarly, I recall that when President Ronald Reagan insisted that "America is standing tall," it coincided with a decline in the internal strength and international prestige of the United States.

The lesson here is that having a critical disposition to power, to the possibility of change, is important. To know and never doubt that there is a history of resistance to wrong and injustice—and alternatives to global apartheid—is itself empowering. Part of what our challenge is, therefore, is to make popular resistance become the dominant system of our lives and in our times.

Let me offer one example from my own history. Grenada offered a model for undoing the ideology, economics and politics that sustain the hunger-inducing system of global apartheid. The period of people's power in Grenada, 1979-1983, was an attempt to undo and replace de facto apartheid in Grenada, to undo the system of exploitation, with its accompanying sense of inferiority and dependence and defeatist vulnerability and self-worthlessness, that has been part of the legacy of the post-colonial Caribbean.

Grenada is populated predominantly by people of African descent. After three centuries of colonial rule, when the government of Maurie Bishop took office on 13 March 1979, it inherited a population in desperation. Among the rural and urban poor, which make up the majority of the population, malnutrition and anemia affected small children, as well as young women of childbearing age. Unemployment was over 40 percent nationally and much higher for women. The average wage for the nation's agricultural workers was less than U.S. $3 per week.

In the face of a near national emergency in food, nutrition, and human suffering, the new government, the People's Revolutionary Government (PEG), initiated a series of state policies and programs to invert power relations, wealth, and income, and to return to a disenfranchised population their sense of identity and worth. This creative experiment replaced comatose and moribund liberalism with participatory or direct democracy; trickle down economics with a model of mixed economy;[20] a distant and dysfunctional parliament with people's power in mass organizations; and national apathy, distrust, and division with government accountability, community self-emulation and celebratory activities, and a cultural and spirited and contagious democratic renewal of the common people. In slightly under five years, the centuries-old gross imbalance of wealth, power, attitudes, and beliefs began to be overturned. Grenada's apartheid was on the wane, as new hope, a new politic, and a new society began to emerge.

In the literature on revolutionary Grenada, one group of writers has taken the position that there was very slight or no real change.[21] This ambivalence and or denial of positive change in Grenada for the mass of the population is not borne out by the facts. The first and most credible results came directly from the intended beneficiaries of this socioeconomic, sociopolitical, and cultural revolution. A collection of personal accounts of hope and transformation, *Is Freedom We Making* tells a story not too dissimilar from what ordinary Haitian citizens say of the brief period under the LAVALAS movement of President Aristide: "feeling happy," "working harder," "eating better," "ready to live," "wanting to build the country," "belonging."[22] A 1984 survey poll found: "47.1 percent of the people believed that the PEG's attempt at participatory democracy was successful," (19 percent disagreed and 22 percent could not assess); 50.9 percent believed conditions of living had improved, (26.1 percent said conditions remained the same and 17.8 percent found deterioration); 75.5 percent said women's conditions had improved, (8.2 percent saw no change and 5.0 percent saw deterioration); 89.4 percent agreed that the PEG had "very good support" for running the country.[23]

Undoing Global Apartheid

Our response to the crisis of material hunger and spiritual hunger needs to be multidimensional—moral, intellectual, political, cultural, and activist. The self is a viable place to start. One of our great lessons comes from the protest hunger fast of Catherine Graham—an African-American professional dancer in St. Louis, whose career was built on her understanding and incorporation of Haitian art forms. At the tender age of 82, she underwent a hunger fast as her way of bringing moral outrage to bear on her own (U.S.) government's policy of returning Haitians seeking refugee status here. Like others, she believed Haitians who said they were fleeing repression in Haiti, not to mention starvation, were in grave danger when forcibly returned.[24] Ms. Graham's actions show us how we can challenge the system with what we have in abundance—our own desire and need for community and food. She withdrew from eating so that Haitians could eat. Over time, meaningful challenges such as this, seemingly small, suggest that global apartheid can be made ungovernable. Catherine Graham calls forth celebration and emulation. That inward hunger for justice, sisterhood, and the solidarity of peoples can find satisfaction in large as well as in small ways, in making personal sacrifices.

I was faced with such a challenge at the conference where the ideas in this chapter were first presented. My accommodations were at a small guest house within walking distance of the conference site. The place was a very modest inn; it had a very small unfurnished eating area, no newspaper on the premises, and no central telephone system, which meant no phone service in the rooms. It was owned by a very pleasant Sri Lankan widow, who, with a few Asians and Latinas, operated the facility. The absence of a telephone in my room and the lack of adequate dining facilities were most inconvenient, as I had to go out to the street early in the morning or late at night to use the phone or get a meal. This routine was at best tedious and often quite problematic, and I considered requesting another place. But then another thought occurred to me. The revenue generated by my staying there was a source of income for the proprietress, and, she hoped, publicity. She looked forward to chatting with me as I came and went. She was thrilled I knew Daun Aung Suu Kyi (a Burmese democratic movement leader), and she reminded me of my mother, who runs a similar enterprise in Grenada. Soon it was clear: staying there was more beneficial to her than leaving was convenient for me. I worked around my inconveniences and stayed.

How, really, do we resuscitate a world that is decaying at the personal and political level? I believe the answer may be all too simple. Change comes by good people doing good things. Small, medium, and large acts of moral rebellion and political resistance, taken altogether, erode the power of wrong and delegitimize injustice. As intellectuals, as religious people, as students, as shop-keepers, as poets, as lovers, as social-change activists, it is important that we delegitimize systems that dehumanize. Equally critical is support for alternatives.

In my view, for example, it is very important to support Cuba in these times. Some of the frightening problems of institutionally supported racism, hunger and homelessness, prostitution and drug abuse, gross income inequalities, and community decay—have been diminished or eliminated in Cuba. Life expectancy, at 75, is higher than in the United States. Beyond the country itself, Cuba plays a pivotal role in humanitarian and military-political support for antiapartheid forces in Africa. There are tens of thousands of African youth studying in Cuba, and they will be the architects of a hunger-free, antiapartheid Southern Africa.

In this period of socialist-bashing, it is important to remember that there are regimes that have tried to fashion, often under the tyranny of a hostile international system, more just and democratic possibilities for their people. It is important to give support for the good Cuba has done, even as we push it to do better, free from a U.S. embargo.

When we oppose wars and support indigenous agricultural development in places such as El Salvador and Mozambique, we undermine the dominant systems that cause and entrench both racism and hunger. When we support people-to-people trade that reduces the racket of foreign aid, we help to reduce middle-level exploiters, and we begin to construct a more democratic and respectful relationship among global citizens, so people on both ends of the trade can feed themselves and sustain families with dignity. Examples such as these could be multiplied manifold. The point is to act on alternative visions, not just think about them.

Let us be clear on one thing. Innumerable popular reports and studies abound about what is wrong—there are many thoughtful and provocative analyses of race relations, hunger, poverty, education, gender, urban decline, environmental concerns, and so on. What is needed is to turn studies, reports, and findings into personal and national policy. If nothing else, disrupting our personal emotional state of affairs by becoming conscious of and unaccepting of apartheid, wherever it manifests itself, is quite powerful. Working together with others, it can be socially transforming.

Notes

1. The major model/method of cooptation and/or control is the capitalist system against which various efforts to minimize and or to resist its impact have been mounted. Currently, the term "cultures of resistance" is associated, in part, with efforts throughout the American hemisphere, and particularly among native peoples, to mount a cultural, intellectual, and political resistance to the destructive era of capitalist development that commenced with the coming of Christopher Columbus to the "New" World.

2. Mahub ul Haq, *World Human Development Report: 1992* (Oxford University Press for the United Nations, 1992).

3. By this statement, I do not mean to minimize the devastating problems faced by men, especially poor men of color. For example, I do not wish to ignore the millions of men killed in battle and the millions more who suffer the physical and psychological pain of poverty.

4. See "The Grim Mystery Of World's Missing Women," in *The Boston Globe*, 3 February 1992, 21.

5. Ibid.

6. United Nations Liaison Office, "NGO Action on Children," April-May 1992, 13-15.

7. See Brenda Ringel and David Shields, "African Women Farmers: Overworked and Undernourished," *Overseas Development Network Journal* (March 1990).

8. The phrase "feminization of poverty" was introduced by Diane Pearce in "The Feminization of Poverty: Women, Work and Welfare," *Urban and Social Change Review* 10 (1978): 28-36.

9. See *The World's Women: Trends and Statistics, 1970-1990,* The United Nations, 31-43.

10. See Carmen Deere's *In The Shadow of the Sun.*

11. The Dominican Republic is reportedly one of the first places Columbus set foot.

12. *Wall Street Journal,* 5 May 1991.

13. Ibid.

14. See *Harvard Business Review,* July/August 1992.

15. See chapter 5, this volume.

16. *The Boston Globe,* 6 May 1992, opinion editorial page.

17. Ibid.

18. *Los Angeles Times,* 1 May 1992, A31.

19. Haitians are successfully combating all these charges through their programs inside Haiti as well as active campaigns inside the United States.

20. By "mixed economy," I mean that the state sector, the cooperative sector, and the private sector worked in a loose alliance, sometimes through budget planning and implementing, sometimes through periodic consultation, to sustain and expand a viable economy for "people's power."

21. See Frederic L. Pryor, *Revolutionary Grenada: A Study in Political Economy* (New York: Praeger, 1986). In one of the most comprehensive economic reviews of its kind, Pryor claims that "Retail prices in Grenada did not appear to behave much differently from those of most other OECS countries... The PEG did succeed in reducing unemployment ... aggregate production stagnated ... the average standard of living fell ...[and] the distribution of income may have become slightly more equal..." (214). See also Jorge Heine, (ed.), *A Revolution Aborted: The Lessons of Grenada* (Pittsburgh, Penn: University of Pittsburgh Press, 1990).

22. See Merle Hodge and Chris Searles, *Is Freedom We Making: The New Democracy in Grenada* (Government of Grenada Printery, 1981).

23. One footnote to the Grenada casestudy: Under President Ronald Reagan, the U.S. invaded Grenada in October 1983, purportedly to rescue United States citizens and to return democracy to Grenada/the Caribbean. Since the advent of U.S. presence in Grenada, there has been a sharp rise in unemployment, hunger and malnutrition, drug addiction, and violent crimes, and a sharp division in wealth, income, and opportunity.

24. Ms. Graham withdrew her fast after a visit from Haiti's President Aristide, and she travelled to Boston to speak at the Third Annual Haitian Studies Association Conference.

Index

accentuation effect: 39
Africa: 8, 10, 25-32, 49, 50, 64, 65, 72, 75, 77-79, 93-95, 97, 98, 121, 158
African Americans: 3, 4, 5, 6, 18, 19, 20, 21, 40, 50, 54, 99
Agency for International Development: 60, 64, 103, 105
Aid to Families with Dependent Children (AFDC): 6
Alexis, Marcus: 5
Alliance for Progress: 60
Allport, Gordon: 43, 46
American Indians: 3, 5, 18, 93
Amin, Samir: 82
apartheid: 9, 75, 98, 142-47, 156, 151-64
Aristide, Jean-Bertrand: 160
Attali, Jacques: 82
attribution theory: 44
Australia: 9

Baker, James: 59
Bangladesh: 81
Bastide, Roger: 122
Belize: 9
Bello, Walden: 63
Blakemore, Bill: 78
Bolivia: 9
Boyer, Peter: 79, 80
Brazil: 119-40
Bread for the World: 11
Buchanan, Pat: 161
Buerk, Michael: 79
Bush, George: 17, 18, 159

Canada: 9
capitalism: 20, 21, 90-91, 121, 155, 157
Catholic Church: see "Christianity"
cattle ranching: 108
charity: 86
Chaves, Nelson: 137-38
children: 16, 127, 131, 132, 134
China: 62
Christianity: 92, 98, 112-13, 115
civil strife: see "war"
Civil Rights Movement: 19
Coca-Cola: 158
colonialism: 9, 11, 29, 54, 61, 89-99, 120, 123, 137, 158, 161
Columbus, Christopher: 75, 91-92, 98, 99, 158
credit policy: 106
Cree Indians: see "indigenous people"
Cuba: 57, 60, 99, 163
culture of altruism: 77-78
cultures of resistance: 157

de las Casas, Bartholomé: 92, 98
de Castro, Josué: 128, 137
debt: 32, 60, 62-64, 87, 100
deforestation: 105, 120
development assistance: 7, 53, 57-61, 69-77, 100
development policy: 53-57, 75-76, 154
disability benefits: 6
discrimination: 9, 40-45, 48, 50, 51, 103, 115, 136, 146
Dominican Republic: 157
Douglas, Mary: 6
dualism: 36-38

Ehrenreich, Barbara: 8
environmental destruction: 107-11
epistemology: 49
Ethiopia: 32, 78-80, 88, 89
export agriculture: 94, 120

famine: 2, 8, 25, 26, 29, 32, 50, 77-80, 87-89, 92, 93, 128-30
Fanon, Frantz: 72-73
farm workers: 3
food aid: 58-59
Food Research and Action Center: 15
food riots: 157, 158
food stamps: 5, 16, 18
foreign policy: 54-61
foreign aid: see "development assistance"
Free Trade Agreement, 158
Freire, Paulo: 74
Freyre, Gilberto: 121-24

Gelbard, Robert: 160
gender: see "sexism"
Global Exchange: 101
Glock, Charles: 40
Goulart, Joao: 60
Graham, Catherine: 162
green revolution: 100
Grenada: 160-62
Guatemala: 9, 85, 103-16

Hacker, Andrew: 4
Haiti: 159, 160, 162
Hall, Tony: 8
hierarchical dualism: 36
Hispanics: 3-6, 18
human rights: 2, 61
hunger: v, 1-11, 17, 20, 25, 26, 35, 36, 48-51, 53, 56, 59, 64, 69, 70, 71, 74, 78, 81, 85-89, 93, 96, 103, 104, 114-16, 119, 124, 126-39, 141, 142, 144-47, 153-56, 158, 161-63
hunger statistics: 1, 3, 9, 15, 139, 141
hunger strike: 8, 162

immigrants: 3
imperialism: 29, 155
income distribution: 17, 111, 154, 156, 158
indigenous people: 7, 9, 93, 103-16
industrialization: 94
infant mortality: 4, 137, 104

Institute for Food and Development Policy: 63
International Monetary Fund: 63, 97, 100, 103, 157, 158
Inuit Indians: see "indigenous people"

Jackson, Derrick: 159
Japan: 61

Kipling, Rudyard: 55

land distribution: 103-15, 125
land reform: see "land distribution"
Latin America: 60, 61, 64, 65, 70, 93, 98, 103, 111, 112, 119
Lauren, Gordon: 54
Leland, Mickey: 80
Levin, William: 45
life expectancy: 3, 4, 163
Los Angeles uprising: vi, 18, 20

Malcolm X: 20
Manifest Destiny: 75
Marshall Plan: 61
mass media: 76-81
Mayan Indians: 9, 103-16
media: see "mass media"
Memmi, Albert: 72-73
Menchú, Rigoberta: 115
Mexico: 9
militarism: 8, 91, 77-78, 107, 110-11
military aid: 60
Mintz, Sidney: 121
Miskito Indians: 9
multinational corporations: see "transnational corporations"

national interest: 55
Native Americans: see "American Indians"
neocolonialism: 9, 57
New International Economic Order: 63
Nicaragua: 9
Niemoller, Martin: 20
Nilson, Linda: 7
nongovernmental organizations: see "private voluntary organizations"
North American Free Trade Agreement: 158

Pacific Islanders: 4
Persian Gulf War: 81
Pettigrew, Thomas: 38, 41
Piaget, Jean: 39
poverty: 3-7, 15-20, 22, 41, 50, 56, 71, 73, 99, 103-04, 107, 110-13, 115, 120, 131, 135-36, 141-42, 154, 155, 157
poverty line: 16, 99, 142
prejudice: 7, 35-52
Presidential Commission on World Hunger: 3
private voluntary organizations: 25-32
pyramid principle: 48

race: v, 1-11, 31, 35, 50, 54, 57, 74, 81, 82, 87-88, 136, 145, 157, 166
racism: 2, 17, 22, 69, 71-74, 91-93, 99, 104, 110, 123
racism: implicit: 69, 71-74
Rather, Dan: 81
Reagan, Ronald: 17, 18, 19, 63, 80, 158, 161
Robinson, Randall: 8
Rostow, W. W.: 75
Ruggles, Patricia 16
Ryan, William: 41

Said, Edward: 83
scapegoating: 43
self-esteem: 44, 48
sexism: 2, 46, 50, 88, 125-26, 157
Shields, David: 36, 46, 48
Sierra Leone: 158
slavery: 90, 93-94, 122-24
social identity theory: 42
Social Darwinism: 55
Social Security: 6
solidarity: 86
Somalia: 72, 77
South Africa: 98, 141-52, 155
Soviet Union: 159
starvation experiment: 139
stereotypes: 26-32, 40, 50
Streeten, Paul: 63
Sudan: 25, 88
sugar: 105, 120-26
Summer, Larry: 76

Thatcher, Margaret: 158
Third Worldism: 62
transnational corporations: 95-96
Trueheart, Charles: 3

unilateral developmentalism: 53-57
United Nations: 70, 72, 73, 82, 156
United States: 3-8, 15-23, 25-32, 50, 53, 57-61, 77-80, 89, 99, 100

war: 10, 26, 88, 131
welfare: 4-6, 18, 22
welfare reform: 5
white supremacy: 57, 61-63
"White Man's Burden": 55, 159
Wilson, Brian: 65-66
Wineman, Steven: 4
women: see "sexism"
World Food Conference: 9
World Bank: 63, 71, 76, 97, 100, 103

Zaire: 32, 95, 97

About the Contributors

Nazir Ahmad is founder of Overseas Development Network, a national coalition of student organizations involved in grassroots development work. Nazir, who worked as a consultant to several international agencies, is currently chair of the Strategic Decision Group.

Kevin Danaher is cofounder of Global Exchange, San Francisco. Among Kevin's many publications are *In Whose's Interest: A Guide to U.S.-South Africa Relations*, *Help or Hindrance? United States Economic Aid in Central America* (with Phillip Berryman and Medea Benjamin), and *Beyond Safaris: A Guide to Building People-to-People Ties with Africa.*

Tshenuwani Simon Farisani is a member of the new democratic South African Parliament and dean of the Lutheran Church of South Africa. During the years of apartheid, he was imprisoned and tortured three times. He is the author of numerous articles and two books.

Percy Hintzen is an associate professor of Afro-American studies at the University of California at Berkeley, where he also teaches development studies.

Mutombo Mpanya is a professor at World College West, where he also serves as director of the International Environmental Studies Program. A native of Zaire, he served as director of the Menno Central Committee, as assistant director of the University of Notre Dame's African Institute, and as coordinator of the PVO Program at the Helen Kellogg Institute for International Studies. He also served as a consultant to various international development organizations, such as the World Bank, the United Nations, and InterAction.

Beatriz Manz is an associate professor of both geography and ethnic studies at the University of California at Berkeley. She is also the director of Berkeley's Center for Latin American Studies. A native of Chile, she spent a great deal of time in Guatemala working with Myrna Mack, an anthropologist who was slain as she sought to document the story of military repression against the indigenous people.

Nancy Scheper-Hughes is a professor of anthropology at the University of California at Berkeley. Her latest book, *Death Without Weeping: The Violence of Everyday Life in Brazil* has been labeled "astonishingly brilliant" and "the product of one of the most fertile, brave, and controversial anthropologists of her generation."

David L. L. Shields is a research associate with the Peace and Conflict Studies Program at the University of California at Berkeley. Formerly, he was director of the Economic Justice Program at Unitas Campus Ministry in Berkeley. He is the author of *Growing Beyond Prejudices,* and (with Brenda Bredemeier) *Character Development and Physical Activity,* and numerous articles on social justice issues.

Michele Tingling-Clemmons is the senior field organizer for the Food Research and Action Center in Washington, D.C. Ms. Tingling-Clemmons has spent over twenty years working for social justice in a variety of disciplines, including health care, housing, and occupational and environmental health. Among her publications is *Breakfast: Don't Start School Without It!,* a school breakfast organizing kit.

Dessima Williams is a fellow of the Bunting Institute at Radcliffe College. She teaches international relations, Caribbean studies, and women's studies at Williams College. A member of the revolutionary government of Grenada from 1979 to 1983, she served as ambassador to the United States, the United Nations, and the Organization of American States.